W9-CHZ-657

A Nuclear-Weapon-Free World

A Pugwash Monograph

A Nuclear-Weapon-Free World

Desirable? Feasible?

EDITED BY

Joseph Rotblat, Jack Steinberger, and Bhalchandra Udgaonkar

EXECUTIVE EDITOR

Frank Blackaby

Westview Press

BOULDER • SAN FRANCISCO • OXFORD

Copyright © 1993 by Westview Press, Inc.

Published in 1993 in the United States of America by Westview Press, Inc., 5500 Central Avenue, Boulder, Colorado 80301-2877, and in the United Kingdom by Westview Press, 36 Lonsdale Road, Summertown, Oxford OX2 7EW

Library of Congress Cataloging-in-Publication Data
A Nuclear-weapon-free world : desirable?, feasible? / edited by Joseph
   Rotblat, Jack Steinberger, and Bhalchandra Udgaonkar.
      p.   cm.
   Includes bibliographical references and index.
ISBN 0-8133-8718-3
   1. Nuclear disarmament.   2. Nuclear-weapon-free-zones.
3. Security, International.   I. Rotblat, Joseph, 1908–   .
II. Steinberger, J.   III. Udgaonkar, B. M.
JX1974.7.N847   1993
327.1'74—dc20   92-21168
                                                                       CIP

Printed and bound in the United States of America

The paper used in this publication meets the requirements
of the American National Standard for Permanence of Paper
for Printed Library Materials Z39.48-1984.

10   9   8   7   6   5   4   3

Contents

Preface

The elimination of nuclear weapons has been the declared objective of the United Nations from the very beginning of its existence; this has been affirmed ever since in many declarations and resolutions signed by member states, including the nuclear-weapon states. During the period of the Cold War these desires were disregarded. The titanic struggle between Communism and anti-Communism generated an unrestrained arms race that resulted in absurdly huge nuclear arsenals--reaching a peak of nearly 60,000 warheads--and threatened the very continuance of civilization.

The idea of a nuclear-weapon-free world was put back on the world agenda by Mikhail Gorbachev in 1986 and was nearly endorsed by President Reagan. The end of the Cold War, a few years later, has so transformed the political climate that this idea is no longer fanciful; it merits serious study. In 1990 the Council of the Pugwash Conferences on Science and World Affairs decided to set up such a study. This book is the result. Its main purpose is to initiate a debate on this issue, so that it can be given careful examination. The question is, with the number of nuclear warheads coming down from 60,000 to 6000, should plans now be made for an ultimate move to zero?

It is now widely accepted that nuclear warheads have no military utility as weapons of war. In the famous words of Reagan and Gorbachev: *"a nuclear war cannot be won and must never be fought."* The only possible function of nuclear weapons is to deter their use by another state, but that argument becomes invalid if satisfactory guarantees can be given that no state possesses them. Since the retention of nuclear weapons by any state is bound to be an incentive for other states to acquire them, a nuclear-weapon-free world would appear a more desirable alternative, provided that it is found possible to establish an effective verification system. Thus, the main issues considered in this book concern the desirability and feasibility of a nuclear-weapon-free world.

The book is divided into five parts. Part A, consisting of one chapter, looks at the past attempts to eliminate nuclear weapons, and sets out the reasons for thinking that current attempts are more likely to be successful.

In Part B, the two chapters question whether the five major nuclear powers add anything to their security by retaining nuclear weapons. The doctrine of nuclear deterrence is critically examined. The main threat to world security, it is argued, now comes from the horizontal proliferation of nuclear weapons, and in the long run the only way to stop this is--as with chemical weapons--by an agreement to ban them entirely. The conclusion is that a nuclear-weapon-free world is desirable.

The question of feasibility is discussed in Part C. In seven chapters, the measures are considered that would be needed to safeguard and enforce observance of a treaty which established a nuclear-weapon-free world. These measures include technological and societal systems of verification of compliance with the terms of such a treaty. Possible ways of violating the treaty by breakout, that is the clandestine development of nuclear weapons after the treaty has come into force, are examined. There is a discussion of the terms of a treaty for the elimination of nuclear weapons, on the means of its enforcement in the political climate of a world without nuclear weapons, and on the security requirements of such a world. Ways to make nuclear weapons illegal are also examined against the background of existing treaties in this area. The general trend of opinion in the papers in this section is that a nuclear-weapon-free world is feasible, though some aspects of it require further study.

Three chapters in Part D examine alternative routes to a nuclear-weapon-free world. The case for endowing the United Nations with a small nuclear cache is argued, both for and against. An idea is also put forward of a gradual approach to the objective by creating an appropriate political climate.

The final chapter, in Part E, discusses the successive steps that might lead to a world without nuclear weapons.

The substance of the chapters is summarized in the Executive Overview, written by the Executive Editor, Frank

Blackaby. This represents his epitome of the material and arguments put forward in the book. It is the outcome of discussion with the authors, whose comments have been taken into account.

Although the study was carried out under the auspices of the Pugwash Conferences on Science and World Affairs, all authors contributed in their personal capacity and the views expressed are their own. Similarly, any mention of the institutions with which they are or have been associated is merely for the purpose of identification.

The contributors, as the notes on them show, come from eleven countries and represent a wide range of scientific disciplines and analytical approaches. All of them were involved in debates on the relevant issues in Pugwash meetings or other forums. A number of other scholars have also been involved in the project, either attending meetings of authors or reviewing chapters of the book. In particular, we want to express our thanks to the following: Professor Jack Boag, Dr. Pal Dunay, Professor Lawrence Freedman, Professor Knut Ipsen, Sir Ronald Mason, Dr. Harald Müller, Professor Robert Neild, and Lord Zuckerman.

In the preparation of the book we received prodigious help from Tom Milne, who, in addition to producing the camera-ready copy and the index, has also done much of the editing of the material.

The project would not have got off the ground without financial assistance. For this we are indebted to the W. Alton Jones Foundation for a generous grant. The Director of its Secure Society Program, George Perkovich, took an active part in our discussions.

Joseph Rotblat
Jack Steinberger
Bhalchandra Udgaonkar

About the Contributors

Frank Blackaby (UK). Disarmament and Arms Control. Former Director, Stockholm International Peace Research Institute (SIPRI) and Deputy Director, National Institute for Economic and Social Research, London.

Maxwell Bruce (UK). International Law. Member, Planning Council, International Ocean Institute. Senior Associate, Foundation for International Law, King's College, London. Formerly, Special Fellow, United Nations Institute for Training and Research.

Francesco Calogero (Italy). Physics. Professor of Theoretical Physics (on leave), University of Rome *La Sapienza*. Secretary-General, Pugwash Conferences on Science and World Affairs. Former Member of Governing Board, Stockholm International Peace Research Institute (SIPRI).

Horst Fischer (Germany). International Law. Executive Director, Institute of International Peace-keeping Law and Humanitarian Law, University of Bochum. Formerly, Secretary-General, German Pugwash Group.

Shalheveth Freier (Israel). Physics. Senior Associate of the Weizmann Institute of Science, Rehovot. Former Head of Israeli Atomic Energy Commission, Director of Defence Research at the Ministry of Defence and Chairman, Presidential Panel for Science Policy.

Essam E. Galal (Egypt). Endocrinology. Medical practitioner. Former positions: Professor, Faculty of Medicine, Al Azhar University; Senior Adviser to Egyptian Academy of Science Research and Technology, and to Ministry of Health.

Richard L. Garwin (USA).   Physics. IBM Fellow and Science Advisor to the Director of Research, IBM Research Division, Yorktown Heights, New York.   Adjunct Professor of Physics, Columbia University. Consultant to the US government on military technology and arms control.   Member, USA National Academy of Sciences Committee on International Security and Arms Control.   Former Professor of Public Policy, Harvard University, and Member, President's Science Advisory Committee.

Vitalii I. Goldanskii (Russia).   Chemical Physics. Member, Academy of Sciences of Russia.   Director, N.N. Semenov Institute of Chemical Physics, Russian Academy of Sciences. Chairman, Russian Pugwash Group.   Former member of the Congress of People's Deputies of the USSR and of the Committee of the Supreme Soviet of the USSR for International Affairs.

Jozef Goldblat (Switzerland).   Political Science. Senior Lecturer and Research Fellow, Graduate Institute of International Studies, Geneva. Consultant to the UN Institute for Disarmament Research. Formerly, Director of Arms Control Studies, SIPRI.

Martin M. Kaplan (Switzerland).   Microbiology and Epidemiology. Consultant to World Health Organization. Former Secretary-General, Pugwash Conferences on Science and World Affairs and Director of Research Promotion and Development in the Office of the Director General at the World Health Organization.

Carl Kaysen (USA). Economics and Education. Emeritus Professor of Political Economy at the Massachusetts Institute of Technology. Member, Defense and Arms Control Program, MIT. Former Deputy Special Assistant for National Security Affairs to the President of the United States and Director, Institute for Advanced Study, Princeton, New Jersey.

James F. Leonard (USA). Diplomacy. Executive Director, Washington Council on Non Proliferation. Former US Ambassador with State Department Foreign Service, at the United Nations, the Middle East, Moscow.

Robert S. McNamara (USA). Politics. Former US Secretary of Defense and President, World Bank.

Thomas Mensah (Ghana). Law. Director of the Division of Legal Affairs and External Relations of the International Maritime Organization. Former Member of the National Advisory Council of Ghana.

Marvin Miller (USA). Arms Control. Senior Research Scientist, Faculty of Nuclear Engineering, Massachusetts Institute of Technology. Formerly with the US Arms Control and Disarmament Agency.

Mikhail Milstein (Russia) (died 19 August 1992). Military history. Lieutenant General of the army of the Soviet Union. Professor of History. Senior Research Fellow, Institute of USA and Canada Studies, Russian Academy of Sciences. Scientific Advisor to the Palme Commission.

C. Raja Mohan (India). Arms Control. Research Associate, Institute for Defence Studies and Analyses, New Delhi. Executive Secretary, Indian Pugwash Group.

George W. Rathjens (USA). Political Science. Professor and Director of the Department of Political Science, Massachusetts Institute of Technology. Former Director of Weapon System Evaluation, and Assistant Director of ACDA

Stanislav Rodionov (Russia). Physics. Senior Scientist, Institute of Space Research, Moscow. Member, Committee of Soviet Scientists for Global Security.

Joseph Rotblat (UK). Physics. Emeritus Professor at St. Bartholomew's Hospital, University of London. Worked on the atom bomb during World War II in Liverpool and Los Alamos. Signatory of the Russell-Einstein Manifesto. President of the Pugwash Conferences on Science and World Affairs.

Jack P. Ruina (USA). Electrical Engineering. Professor at the Massachusetts Institute of Technology. Former Director, Advanced Research Project Agency, US Department of Defense, President, Institute for Defense Analyses and Consultant, White House Office of Science and Technology.

Benjamin Sanders (USA). Arms Control. Executive Chairman, Programme for Promoting Nuclear Non-Proliferation. Formerly IAEA Safeguards Official and Director, UN Department for Disarmament Affairs.

Jack Steinberger (Switzerland). Physics.   Galilean Professor of Physics, Scuola Normale, Pisa. Nobel Laureate in Physics. Former Professor, Columbia University, New York and senior researcher at CERN.

Theodore B. Taylor (USA).   Physics. Independent consulting physicist.   President, Southern Tier Environmental Protection Society (STEPS). Former Staff Member, Los Alamos National Laboratory, Deputy Director for Technology, Defense Nuclear Agency and Chairman, International Research and Technology Corporation.

Maj Britt Theorin (Sweden).   Politics.   Member of Parliament. President, International Peace Bureau. Former Ambassador for Disarmament, and Chairperson of the UN Study on Nuclear Weapons.

Bhalchandra M. Udgaonkar (India). Physics. Emeritus Professor, Tata Institute of Fundamental Research. Former President, Indian Academy of Social Sciences and Special Adviser and Deputy Chairman, Planning Commission.

About the Book

The world total of some 50,000 nuclear warheads is beginning to fall off sharply. It should be well below 10,000 by the year 2000. Should the ultimate target be zero?

The idea of a nuclear-weapon-free world (NWFW) was put back on the world agenda by President Gorbachev in 1986. President Reagan also had a vision of a world without nuclear weapons. A number of politicians in the nuclear-weapon countries are beginning to see that such a world could be in their best interests. The disintegration of the Soviet Union and the collapse of the Communist regime have removed the main purpose of existing nuclear arsenals. The threat to world security now comes from nuclear-weapon proliferation, and the only effective way of stopping this is to have an enforceable worldwide ban.

The contributors—many of whom are experts with long experience in the field of nuclear weapons—seek to answer two key questions regarding the concept of a NWFW: Is it desirable? Is it feasible? They outline what they see as the essential provisions of a NWFW treaty and examine the inevitable problems of enforcement. All stocks of weapon-usable materials—civilian as well as military—would have to be closely monitored and guarded. Any technological or official efforts would have to be supported by "societal verification." That is, it would be the duty of all citizens to notify authorities of any suspected violations.

Despite the problems of creating such a treaty and enforcing it, the idea of a truly nuclear-weapon-free world is no longer fanciful. It deserves extensive discussion, and this book provides a solid, informed beginning of the debate.

A Nuclear-Weapon-Free World:

Executive Overview

Introduction

A nuclear weapon was dropped on Hiroshima on 6 August and another on Nagasaki on 9 August 1945. Many of the scientists who had been engaged on building the atom bomb, and the more prescient of the world's statesmen, realized the danger to world security from this thousand-fold increase in the lethal power of a single weapon. They foresaw what might happen if nuclear-weapon capabilities spread to more and more states. Further, some of the scientists believed that the hydrogen bomb was a possibility which could escalate the destructive power of a nuclear warhead from kilotons to megatons.

So, in the immediate aftermath of Hiroshima, a widespread belief emerged that a world with nuclear weapons would be very dangerous. In November 1945, the US President, together with the Prime Ministers of Great Britain and Canada, urged the United Nations to establish an Atomic Energy Commission, with the instruction that it should (together with other duties) develop proposals for eliminating atomic weapons from national armaments.

In its very first resolution, in January 1946, the UN General Assembly unanimously adopted this proposal. Phillip Noel-Baker, reporting on that period, said: "*Not a single voice was raised in any country against the proposal that atomic weapons should be eliminated*

Because of the frequent repetition of the phrase *nuclear-weapon-free world*, the acronym NWFW is used throughout this book.

from national armaments; the press of every shade of opinion was unanimous."

In June 1946 Bernard Baruch presented to the UN Commission the US proposal for an International Atomic Development Authority, which involved the renunciation of the atomic bomb as a weapon. This was followed by a Soviet proposal also calling for the outlawing of nuclear weapons. However, the USSR insisted on retaining its right of veto, and also wanted the abolition of nuclear weapons to precede the establishing of a control system. The USA differed on both these points.

Those early plans foundered. The prospect for international agreement disappeared in the emerging rivalry and military confrontation between the USA and USSR. The gap between the discussions and what was actually going on in the world grew year by year. By 1950, the USA had some 400 nuclear warheads. Seven years later the USSR was beginning its own substantial deployment, with around 100 warheads. The British government had decided that the possession of nuclear weapons was essential for great power status. France and China followed.

By the end of the nineteen-fifties, the debate about the elimination of nuclear weapons had become part of the discussion on general and complete disarmament. In September 1961, the two states issued a joint declaration of agreed principles as the basis for negotiations; this became known as the McCloy-Zorin Statement. The agreement envisaged the elimination of all weapons of mass destruction, and the USA and USSR later tabled separate treaties for putting the proposals into effect. But once more the negotiations foundered on the issue of control and inspection.

This failure marked the end of serious negotiations about eliminating nuclear weapons. For by then the number of nuclear warheads was doubling every few years. The armies and navies on both sides were acquiring tactical nuclear warheads, and the world stockpile of nuclear warheads was moving up into the tens of thousands. It is true that lip-service was still paid to the idea of eliminating nuclear weapons as some kind of distant ideal. The objective was still to be found in the various treaties concerning nuclear weapons which were negotiated in the next twenty years. But the idea of a NWFW had lost any political reality.

Some twenty-five years after the McCloy-Zorin Statement, the idea of a NWFW was brought back into the disarmament discussion by Mikhail Gorbachev. In a speech in January 1986, he outlined a programme for the complete elimination of nuclear weapons by the year 2000. He removed the main obstacle to progress with the McCloy-Zorin proposals, by accepting fully the principle of on-site inspection. Mikhail Gorbachev brought the proposal to Reykjavik. For a brief period it seemed possible that Reykjavik would produce a joint USA-USSR statement of intent; for President Reagan also had his vision of a world without nuclear weapons. To the consternation of his advisers, and also of his NATO allies, the US President indicated that he also was prepared to put all US nuclear weapons on the table for negotiation. However, a central part of the US proposal was the untrammeled development of a possible space-based anti-ballistic missile system, and this the Soviet side could not accept.

That chance was lost. But at least a genuine process of reduction in nuclear arms is now moving ahead. If present agreements and proposals hold, around the turn of the century the world stockpile of nuclear weapons should be reduced to nearly a tenth of its peak figure. That is still a long way from zero. But at least the Gorbachev proposal, the Reykjavik discussion, and the large reductions now in train, have put into play the idea of zero as the eventual goal, and this idea will not now go away.

A NWFW: Is It Desirable?

Many of those who find difficulty with the idea of a NWFW accept that it is desirable, but argue that it is not feasible. Increasingly, even advocates of the continued indefinite possession of nuclear weapons agree that their only possible function is to deter their use by another state: in other words, a policy of No-First-Use. This was clearly implied, for instance, by the joint declaration of Presidents Reagan and Gorbachev that "*a nuclear war cannot be won and must never be fought.*" If the sole function of nuclear weapons is to deter their use by another state, then there is clearly no need for them, once there is a firm and durable structure guaranteeing that no other state possesses them, or can quickly produce them.

Indeed already, with the disintegration of the Soviet Union and the collapse of the Communist regime, there is a certain unreality about the nuclear confrontation between the nuclear-weapon powers. The enemy image of the Soviet Union has not been transferred to Russia: Russia is not considered an expansionist power with a world-threatening ideology. It is considered a friendly state, not only by the USA but also by the other members of NATO. What is the function of nuclear weapons in relations between friendly states? Without some radical and retrogressive change in the regime in one or other of the nuclear-weapon states, it becomes very hard indeed to envisage circumstances in which any of them would use, or threaten to use, a nuclear weapon.

Those who advocate the retention of nuclear weapons are now saying that they are needed, not so much to deter the old enemies, but to deter other states which might acquire nuclear weapons in the future. Since a NWFW regime, with an enforceable Treaty, is potentially an effective and legitimate way in which such proliferation might be prevented, this risk of proliferation can better be used as an argument for getting rid of nuclear weapons rather than as an argument for retaining them. The idea of a NWFW may increasingly commend itself to the self-interest of the present nuclear-weapon powers.

There are still some strategists who argue that nuclear weapons should be retained to deter an attack with conventional weapons. For many years NATO took this view, on the grounds of the Warsaw Pact's 'overwhelming conventional superiority'. That reason, of course, no longer holds good (if it ever did). The argument is sometimes put in these terms: the abolition of nuclear weapons would make the world safe for conventional war. There are two difficulties with this argument. First, the existence of nuclear weapons has not deterred a number of states from a military confrontation with a nuclear power. North Vietnam was not deterred by the fact that the USA had nuclear weapons. Argentina was not deterred from invading the Falkland Islands. The second argument against this idea is that it clearly favours extensive nuclear-weapon proliferation. If the nuclear weapons held by both sides deterred conventional war in Europe, why should they not do so in the Middle East, or in the two Koreas, or in Burma and Bangladesh, or in Hungary and Romania, or Armenia and Azerbadjan? There are not many people prepared to accept the logical consequences of this argument. With this scale of proliferation, the chance of some aberrant launch of a nuclear weapon becomes a virtual certainty.

Minimum nuclear deterrence is the main intellectual competitor to the idea of a NWFW. The proponents of nuclear deterrence have in the past stressed that the structure of mutual nuclear deterrence between the Soviet Union and the Western powers was a very stable system--"*99.5 per cent stable*", according to one authority. They clearly envisaged that it could remain, presenting negligible danger of the actual use of a nuclear weapon, into the indefinite future.

The belief that the deterrent system was highly stable referred to 'crisis stability': the degree to which the nuclear weapons deployment of the antagonists in all their dimensions--numbers, technical characteristics, command and control, etc.--did not provide one or other or both with an incentive to make a pre-emptive first strike in a moment of crisis. In a broader sense, the system has never been stable. Stability should mean a set of nuclear weapon systems left basically unchanged. There has, on the contrary, been a frenzied competition to develop new launching platforms, new warheads, longer ranges, and greater accuracies. This kind of competition may not be consistent with crisis stability. For instance, the deployment of MIRVed warheads --with up to ten independently targetable warheads on one missile --meant that one missile could launch an attack on ten targets on the other side. That provided a theoretical temptation to first use. Also, given the short flight-time of ballistic missiles, there was always the danger of a move to 'launch-on-warning', where a malfunction of the warning systems could trigger a nuclear exchange. Further, there was the absurd multiplication of numbers, with the total of warheads on the two sides reaching nearly 60,000. As the number of warheads and the number of different launch platforms multiplied, so the risk of accidents rose as well.

The advocates of minimum nuclear deterrence had in their minds the picture of a small number of states securely holding a relatively small number of nuclear weapons, with that structure remaining unchanged into the indefinite future. This is not now possible. Other nations will observe that, in spite of their undertakings in various Treaty preambles, the USA, UK, Russia, France and China treat nuclear weapons as necessary for their security, and also consider that they confer some special

international status. Why should nuclear weapons be necessary for
US security, and not also for the security of Israel, or India, or
Pakistan? Indeed, the smaller states could argue that they have
greater need for the equalizing power of nuclear warheads. If the
present nuclear-weapon states persist in retaining their nuclear
weapons indefinitely, then sooner or later other states will seek to
join them as nuclear powers and will be successful.

With chemical weapons, the major powers which possess
them have accepted that the only way to prevent proliferation is
a total world-wide ban. In the long run this is true for nuclear
weapons as well.

There is no way in which a world structure can be maintained
indefinitely with a handful of nations possessing nuclear weapons,
and all other nations forbidden to acquire them. It would be
difficult, if not impossible, for the nuclear-weapon states to use
military force to impose non-nuclear-weapon status on other
states. (Iraq was a special case, because of its invasion of Kuwait).
The alternative to a NWFW is not 'things as they are now'. It is a
world in which a large number of states eventually have nuclear-
weapon capabilities. Then it becomes inevitable that sooner or later
deterrence will not work, and nuclear weapons will be used--for
instance, if they fall into the hands of some leader who is mentally
unbalanced.

Is It Feasible?

The objection to a NWFW is usually phrased in this way:
nuclear weapons cannot be disinvented. The usual metaphor is
that the genie cannot be got back into the bottle. By itself, this is
not a sufficient argument: chemical and biological weapons cannot
be disinvented either, and yet the major powers have accepted a
ban on biological weapons, and have recently agreed a treaty to
ban all chemical weapons. (It has been argued that the nuclear-
weapon powers have only accepted the idea of a chemical
weapons ban because they could, if necessary, respond with
nuclear weapons. However, they have in fact all given solemn
undertakings--with reservations that do not now apply--that they
would not use nuclear weapons on a non-nuclear-weapon state).

The difference between chemical and nuclear weapons,

according to the objectors, lies in the immense lethal capability of nuclear warheads. With a chemical weapons ban, it would not be necessary to be totally certain that every country was observing the ban. If some state, in violation of the Treaty, developed some small quantity of chemical weapons, this would not confer a wide margin of military superiority. With nuclear weapons, the scenario which objectors to a NWFW fear is this. Some nation, although a signatory to the Treaty, succeeds in developing a small armoury of nuclear weapons; or it might be a former nuclear-weapon state which conceals some of its warheads. In either case, that state could, by the threat of the use of those nuclear warheads, blackmail other states. The verification required for a NWFW would have to be much stricter than for the Chemical Weapons Convention.

There is, however, a general qualification to these tough verification requirements. The world in which a NWFW was possible would be a world which was already partially demilitarized. All the existing nuclear powers would have to have agreed that a NWFW was in their interest. They would by then have already reduced their nuclear forces to minimum deterrent status. It would be a world in which the idea of a war between any of the major industrial nations had diminished greatly; where of course there were still disagreements and tensions between those states, but where the idea of trying to settle them by military force appeared absurd. It is not fanciful to assume that this is the way in which things might develop. Already war between the members of the European Community has become unthinkable. That is surely also in the process of becoming true for a war between the USA and Russia.

If this is the way things go, then it will certainly make it much easier to negotiate a NWFW Treaty. Would such developments make a Treaty unnecessary? This seems doubtful. Even in a world of relatively peaceful relations between the major powers, there are likely to be some states whose behaviour is more suspect. In those circumstances the present nuclear powers, before dismantling all their nuclear weapons, would want the protection of a Treaty, with the stringent verification structure which it would provide.

There is one other development over the next decade which would make a NWFW more possible--a reduction in the number of authoritarian regimes, with their demands for total obedience to the state. In a democratic regime which had signed a NWFW Treaty, there would be watchdog organizations, and investigative journalists, who would be in a position to find out if their Government was trying to re-establish a nuclear-weapon capability. (This point is developed more fully below). Now all the major nuclear-weapon states, except China, have a high degree of freedom of publication and expression. Under Stalin, or indeed Brezhnev, the Western powers would have distrusted any Soviet promise that it would dismantle its nuclear weapons. Now there is much less distrust.

On the one hand, therefore, a NWFW would require a high degree of certainty that a nuclear-weapon state would not re-emerge. On the other hand, over the next ten years there could well be processes of demilitarization, democratization, confidence-building and cooperation between the existing nuclear-weapon powers which made the requirements of verification less stringent than they would otherwise be.

What Should Be Verified?

A verification regime would need to do three things. First, it would have to establish a structure of containment--a ring-fence around all weapons-usable material, plutonium and uranium-235. This would have to cover the material produced in civil nuclear reactors as well. Second, in nuclear-weapon states it would have to ensure that all installations specifically dedicated to the production of nuclear weapons were dismantled. In non-nuclear-weapon states, it would have to ensure that no such facilities were constructed. Third, it would have to establish, with a high degree of confidence, that no nuclear-weapon state had hidden nuclear weapons, or created a clandestine cache of weapons-usable material.

The first of these requirements would need, in the first instance, safeguarded stockpiles of all nuclear weapons, and--as dismantling proceeded--of all fissile material. There would therefore have to be a ring-fence around all installations where nuclear weapons were stored or where dismantling was in process, so that any fissile material leaving the site could be monitored and measured. Further, it would not just be a question of monitoring movements. It would also be a matter of providing sufficient military force to ensure that illicit transfers did not take place. Such a force could be either under national or international control: this would be a question for negotiation.

There would have to be a similar apparatus of control to cover all civil stocks of weapons-usable material. All civil nuclear power reactors and many research reactors would have to be fully safeguarded. (The total of civil stocks of plutonium, in various forms, exceeds by a factor of about three the total which has been embodied in the nuclear armoury of the nuclear-weapon powers).

The construction of a ring-fence around all installations where weapons-usable material existed would obviously be easier if civil nuclear power did not exist. However, at present civil nuclear power provides around one-fifth of the world's electricity output. It seems unlikely that it will be replaced as a source of energy in the forseeable future (though any further accidents such as Chernobyl would formidably strengthen the opposition). Even if it were replaced, large stocks of civil weapons-usable material would still remain.

The obvious international agency to undertake these new roles is the International Atomic Energy Agency. The objection has been raised that the Agency also has the duty of helping in the development of civil nuclear power. That is true: but that part of its mandate could be changed if at any time the international community decided that world dependence on nuclear power should be reduced.

In fact, the Agency sprang from President Eisenhower's 'Atoms for Peace' initiative in 1953. The idea of that initiative was to take fissile material from the military sector and use it in civil power programmes. So if the Agency is given these new duties, it would in fact be performing precisely those functions which were originally envisaged for it.

This joint duty of military and civil verification far exceeds anything that the International Atomic Energy Agency has so far undertaken. Of course the Agency would have to be given much greater powers than it possesses now. The techniques which the IAEA has developed could be strengthened, and the research staff in the old weapons laboratories could be given the new task of constructing a foolproof system.

How far could there be certainty that all weapons-usable material had been safeguarded? Rough estimates can be made of the total of such material which has been produced since the beginning of the era of nuclear weapons and nuclear power, and of course records can be inspected. However, there is a fairly substantial margin of error here. It would not be possible to derive certainty from a statistical calculation of this kind. The source of confidence has rather to be in the fact that the nuclear-weapon powers themselves had in good faith decided that a NWFW was in their interest, and in the support which societal verification would give to the more formal procedures.

It would clearly be better to find a way of disposing of this fissile material, rather than maintaining it indefinitely in a safeguarded stockpile. While there is civil nuclear power, then the uranium-235 can be mixed with less enriched uranium and used as feedstock in civil power reactors. There is rather more of a problem with the stocks of plutonium. Breeder reactors are not the answer. The multitude of ideas to deal with this problem includes the building of special reactors or particle accelerators in which plutonium would be fissioned or transmuted and its energy content utilized for power production. Immobilizing the plutonium in rocks in an underground nuclear explosion, or shooting it into the sun using modern missile technology, have also been suggested.

In addition to the safeguarding of all weapons-usable material, there will also have to be a verification system to ensure that military-dedicated nuclear installations in the nuclear-weapon powers are dismantled, and not reconstructed elsewhere, and that no non-nuclear-weapon state builds clandestine facilities to produce weapons-usable material. An 'anytime, anywhere' inspection system will be needed, and there can be no buildings which are off limits to this inspection.

Fortunately, the process of uranium enrichment still requires substantial installations and sophisticated technology--although scientific and engineering advances may change this situation. Today, most developing countries would require imports of large quantities of specialized materials or components. It should be possible to set up an intelligence system which gave warning of any attempt by a non-nuclear-weapon state to establish a nuclear-weapon capability. However, the Iraq example shows that a comprehensive and intrusive inspection system is needed--a great deal more than the occasional visit of a single inspector to pre-announced sites.

There is the third possibility, of a small number of hidden warheads, or a cache of undisclosed fissile material, in a state which had previously possessed nuclear weapons. Since a NWFW could only come into being with the agreement of all the major nuclear-weapon powers, such an act of concealment would involve a process of deception which it would be difficult to maintain in a democratic country. Protection against this third type of infringement of a NWFW would depend heavily on a process of societal verification.

Societal Verification

In a NWFW, where it is much more important than with other weapons to identify possible violations, the official verification system should be supplemented by societal verification. It should be not only the right but also the duty of all citizens to notify to the international verification authorities any suspected breach of the NWFW Treaty.

There are a number of reasons for thinking that societal verification would be effective. Nuclear weapons are a thing apart, and a great many people are strongly hostile to them--the evidence is in the large number of organizations opposed to nuclear weapons, in the Non-Proliferation Treaty, and in the existence of nuclear-weapon-free zones. It should be possible to produce a widespread agreement that the world is better without these weapons, and that it would be a tragedy if they were re-introduced. National legislation should make it clear that it would not be an act of disloyalty to notify any suspicions to the international authorities--it would be analogous to providing information about drug-running.

Within the democracies there should not be any acute conflict of loyalties in this matter. The State would have signed the NWFW Treaty, including the clauses which refer to societal verification, and this would be widely known. There would be much more of a problem in the authoritarian states which remain. However, even in those states there could well be information from defectors. Iraq provides a current example: defectors have given valuable information about Iraq's nuclear installations.

International scientific associations should be encouraged to join in the process of societal verification. Physical scientists, concerned as they are with natural laws which know no national boundaries, should not find any difficulty with the idea of loyalty to the international ideal of the total abolition of nuclear weapons. Further, they would be well placed to know if any substantial moves were being made to re-establish nuclear-weapon capabilities. Any such attempt would require significant resources of scientific manpower and large installations. It would not be at all easy to conceal such a venture from the international scientific community

A NWFW Regime

To bring in a nuclear-weapon-free world there would of course have to be a Treaty. In a number of respects such a Treaty would have to be more stringent in its requirements than the arms control treaties which have so far been negotiated.

The Treaty would have to make illegal not just the use but also the possession of any nuclear warhead. Most arms control treaties up to now have not ruled that possession of a particular weapon system was illegal. The Treaty would have to include all the declared nuclear-weapon powers, and indeed all the states which have been classed as near-nuclear-weapon states. It is reasonable to suppose that all the non-nuclear-weapon states which have signed the Non-Proliferation Treaty would be signatories: after all, the NWFW Treaty is removing the discrimination of which many of them have complained. The Treaty should contain provisions to deal with the problem of one or two recalcitrant states which refused to sign--with a provision that, once the Treaty had been brought into force, it would be considered a threat to world security if any state, signatory or not, attempted to develop a nuclear-weapon capability. The Security Council would be entitled to take appropriate action to remove that threat.

The Treaty would have to include the stringent verification procedures already discussed. It would need to specify in detail the international system of control which would impose containment on all sites where fissile material was stored. It would also have to specify the rules for regular inspection of all sites which had previously been concerned with the military nuclear weapons programme, including research institutions. There would have to be an 'anytime, anywhere' entitlement for inspection.

The Treaty should include special provisions for societal verification. There should be a section which said that it was the right and indeed the duty of any citizen to report to the international verification authorities any violations of the Treaty, and this should be written into the national laws of all signatories. There should further be provision--including, if necessary, the provision of asylum--for any person who feared national punishment as a consequence of reporting a substantiated violation.

The Treaty should specify that enforcement of the Treaty should be left to the Security Council. It should be the duty of the Security Council to take whatever action was necessary to ensure that any violations of the Treaty were treated as threats to world security, and were brought to an end.

There should be no provision for withdrawal from the Treaty.

There is the problem of the interim stage during which the nuclear-weapon powers are dismantling their nuclear weapons and installations dedicated to nuclear military purposes. Some suggest that during this period the control of the remaining nuclear weapons should be put under some form of international control. It would clearly be difficult to decide on the form of this international deployment. However, it is argued that it would be wrong, in this interim period, to leave the control of nuclear weapons in national hands. Putting them under international control, and so removing them from national armaments and from national decision, would eliminate an element of danger.

The counter-argument is that progress towards a NWFW will be made as nuclear-weapon states, and others, come to the realization that these weapons serve no useful purpose: they have no function. The idea of a NWFW will only be accepted when it is widely recognized that these weapons are useless. The whole process of transferring them to international control, with all the discussion of the nature of the weapons to be transferred, their location, their delivery platforms, and so on, and the exact form of their control, would serve to restore legitimacy to nuclear weapons. It would convey the message that they did have some possible use.

Enforcement

In general, arms control treaties have not included any provisions for enforcement. It is simply open to any state to withdraw from a treaty if it considers that violations by some other signatory threatens its security. A NWFW would have to include provisions for enforcement by the Security Council. The Security Council should deal with any suspected violation as a threat to world security, in the usual way. If, for example, a state refused to allow inspectors access to any installation, then sanctions could be applied to that state until it agreed to the inspection. If the installation were found by the inspectors to have as its purpose the creation of a nuclear-weapon capability, then the state would be instructed to destroy it. If it refused, then the Security Council would have to undertake the destruction itself. This would not require the use of nuclear weapons by the United Nations. Any enforcement process would be entirely with the use of conventional weapon systems, unless any state had first used nuclear weapons.

Steps Towards a NWFW

For a number of years, those who advocate minimum nuclear deterrence, and those in favour of a NWFW, can travel the same road. On present plans, it will take from now to the end of the century to dismantle the nuclear weapons made redundant by the series of agreements culminating in the Bush-Yeltsin agreement of June 1992.

There is likely to be agreement between advocates of minimum deterrence and those of a NWFW on many of the concomitant measures which should go with this process of disarmament. These include a comprehensive test ban, the universal adoption of a doctrine of No-First-Use, an agreement to stop the development of new delivery platforms or new warheads, and a provisional agreement for the strengthening of the Non-Proliferation Treaty, giving the IAEA more extensive powers of inspection. However, those in favour of an eventual move to a NWFW may be more enthusiastic for more nuclear-weapon-free zones, on the grounds that it would be a useful prelude to a NWFW to clear at least part of the world's surface of these weapons. They may put greater stress on the need to introduce, at an early stage, measures of international control to supervise the dismantling process. Finally, they may favour any measures which increase the necessary delay before nuclear weapons could be used by keeping the nuclear warheads separate and some distance away from the delivery vehicles.

The more public support there is for nuclear disarmament, the better. The advances already made have only become possible because Russia is no longer seen as the enemy, and there is a certain degree of trust between the Western powers and Russia. Any actions which further diminish the enemy image and improve that trust--and many types of action fall into that category--would make the eventual transition to a NWFW more possible.

Conclusion

In the nuclear-weapon field, the main threat to world security is now the possible spread of nuclear-weapon capabilities to other countries. It is legitimate to ask whether it will be possible to prevent this proliferation unless there is, eventually, a global ban on nuclear weapons. For this and other reasons, the idea of a NWFW should no longer be dismissed as fanciful. It is an idea which deserves serious study. It is time to divert a good part of the immense research effort which is still going into nuclear-weapon development to work on the problems of a nuclear-weapon-free world. The purpose of this book is to stimulate further study and debates in wide sectors of the community on the ways and means by which nuclear weapons might eventually be eliminated.

PART A

Historical Review

1

Past Attempts to Abolish Nuclear Weapons

Joseph Rotblat

Introduction

The destructive power of the atom bomb was demonstrated for the first time in the Alamagordo test of July 1945. Even before that, scientists on the Manhattan Project, who foresaw the dire consequences of a nuclear arms race, pleaded for the setting up of an international authority to control, and subsequently abolish, nuclear weapons. After the bombs on Hiroshima and Nagasaki, such pleas became universal. The strong desire to rid the world of the nuclear monster was expressed by the General Assembly of the United Nations in its first resolution, and repeated time and time again.

This chapter reviews the main attempts in international forums to abolish nuclear weapons. Three phases can be discerned in these attempts: initial serious proposals for full international control; much more modest steps of partial measures; a return to radical solutions.

At the beginning, specific plans towards the abolition of nuclear weapons were formulated and extensively debated. On several occasions it seemed that agreement was about to be reached, but each time it came to nothing. Looking at it with the wisdom of hindsight, it should have been clear that no agreement could have been expected on such a vital issue in a world polarized by an ideological divide, with each side believing that the other side is bent on its destruction, and bolstering this belief by policies of fear, mistrust and hatred. Only now--after the end of the Cold War followed by the collapse of one of the adversaries, and the creation of the climate necessary for international agreements--has the vision of a nuclear-weapon-free world a chance of becoming reality.

An important observation that emerges from this historical review is that in all declarations from the United Nations, and in all relevant treaties, the elimination of nuclear weapons is the avowed ultimate goal. Resolutions to this effect have been approved by the leaders of all nuclear-weapon states. The creation of a nuclear-weapon-free world (NWFW) has been from the beginning--and still is--the officially declared policy of all members of the United Nations.

Pre-Hiroshima Warnings (1944-45)

The Danish physicist, Niels Bohr, was one of the most distinguished scientists involved in the Manhattan Project. Earlier than any other person living at that time, he realized the tremendous social and political implications of the discovery of nuclear energy and the development of nuclear weapons. He saw these events as a portentous landmark in the history of mankind, after which the world would never be the same again. He was convinced that if mankind were to survive and continue in the aftermath of that discovery, entirely new approaches would be necessary to world problems. In particular, he predicted with prophetic vision the dire consequences of a race in nuclear arms between East and West. Among the radical measures which he felt were essential to prevent such an arms race, was the sharing of the secret of the atom bomb with the Soviet Union. His specific proposal was that the Soviet leaders be told about the atom bomb *before* it was used, and that the potentialities of the discovery of nuclear energy be explained to them, with an offer of sharing them, on condition that they would agree on a system of joint management and control of nuclear energy in all its aspects.

Bohr's ideas were conveyed to President Roosevelt who appeared to be greatly impressed by them. He advised Bohr to put his case to Winston Churchill. Bohr came to London in May 1944 for an interview with Churchill, but this interview ended in a fiasco, with Churchill completely rejecting Bohr's proposals.

Eight weeks before the atom bomb was dropped on Hiroshima, scientists of the Chicago branch of the Manhattan Project voiced their deep concern about the intended use of the weapon. This concern was expressed in the Franck Report [1] which analysed the long-term implications of the discovery of nuclear energy. The Report pointed out that other nations were certain to acquire nuclear weapons within a few years, and that the inevitably ensuing arms race would dominate and poison the world climate ever after. The release of nuclear energy was the strongest single argument for the establishment of a World Authority, but until such a supra-national body was set up, international control of nuclear weapons would be an essential preliminary step. In order to make such control feasible it might even be advisable to renounce temporarily the large-scale production of fissile materials for industrial purposes.

The Franck Report was submitted to the US government, but since nuclear energy was still an official secret, the Report became instantly a classified document and as such could not be used to canvass support among scientists in the other laboratories of the Manhattan Project. But when the war came to an end, and the discovery of nuclear energy became public knowledge, the scientists felt free to express their views. Their grave concerns and proposals to deal with the problem soon received backing from large groups of scientists. The ensuing vigorous debate eventually led to the Baruch Plan.

International Control: The Baruch Plan (1946-50)

The destruction of Hiroshima and Nagasaki took place *after* the United Nations Charter was signed in San Francisco, in June 1945, but before the first meeting of the UN General Assembly in London, in January 1946. Confronted with this awesome development, not foreseen in the Charter, and cognizant of the general abhorrence of the use of the atom bombs, the General Assembly determined to tackle this issue with the utmost vigour. Its very first resolution [1 (I)] [2] established an Atomic Energy Commission mandated "... *to deal with the problems raised by the discovery of atomic energy and other related matters*".

Its terms of reference called on it to

proceed with the utmost despatch and enquire into all phases of the problem, and ... make specific proposals: ... for the elimination from national armaments of atomic weapons and of all other major weapons adaptable to mass destruction.

At the first meeting of the Commission, on 14 June 1946, the United States representative, Bernard Baruch, presented the US proposals for international control. These became known as the Baruch plan.

The initiative for this plan, as well as for the major recommendations in it, go back to the above-mentioned discussions among scientists, mainly from the Manhattan Project. Dismayed by the use of the bomb on civilian populations, determined to prevent such use in the future, and inspired by the ideas of Niels Bohr and the Franck Report, the scientists set up working parties which considered specific proposals for the control of atomic energy, at the same time lobbying Congress to take action. Yielding to this pressure, the US Government set up a committee, chaired by Dean Acheson, then Under-Secretary of State. This Committee appointed a Board of Consultants, chaired by David Lilienthal, and including Robert Oppenheimer among its members.

The report issued by this committee, the Acheson-Lilienthal Report [3], contains specific proposals aimed at ensuring that nuclear energy would be used for peaceful purposes only. With this objective, the Report recommended the creation of an International Atomic Development Authority to which should be entrusted all phases of the development and use of nuclear energy, starting with the raw materials, and including managerial control or ownership of all activities potentially dangerous to world security, as well as power to control, inspect and licence all nuclear activities. The Authority, to be set up as a subsidiary of the United Nations, would be fully international in character, and its staff recruited on an international basis. Much stress was laid in the Report on developing a system of safeguarding against the military use of atomic energy.

The Baruch Plan [4] essentially incorporated the proposals of the Acheson-Lilienthal Report, but with some significant changes. The most important one was the insistence in the Baruch Plan on the provision of rapid and efficient sanctions against any violation of the agreement, without the right of veto by the permanent members of the Security Council. This turned out to be one of the main bones of contention.

The importance which the United States attached to the international control of nuclear energy is manifest in the apocalyptic phrases used by Baruch in introducing the Plan:

We are here to make a choice between the quick and the dead. That is our business.

Behind the black portent of the new atomic age lies a hope which, seized upon with faith, can work our salvation. If we fail, then we have damned every man to be the slave of Fear. Let us not deceive ourselves: We must elect World Peace or World Destruction.

After outlining the proposal for the creation of an International Atomic Development Authority, the statement goes on:

When an adequate system for control of atomic energy, including the renunciation of the bomb as a weapon, has been agreed upon and put into effective operation and condign punishments set up for violations of the rules of control which are to be stigmatized as international crimes, we propose that:
1. Manufacture of atomic bombs shall stop;
2. Existing bombs shall be disposed of pursuant to the terms of the treaty; and
3. the authority shall be in possession of full information as to the know-how for the production of atomic knowledge.

At the second session of the Atomic Energy Commission, a

few days later, Andrei Gromyko presented the Soviet counterpart to the Baruch Plan. This endorsed the need for international control, much along the lines of the Baruch Plan, but it differed in some significant aspects. The two main differences were: (a) the Soviet proposal called for the outlawing of nuclear weapons to come *before* setting up the control system, i.e. the reverse order from the Baruch Plan: (b) the right of veto must be maintained.

During the next few years, the two proposals were extensively discussed, and some changes were introduced, but the basic differences were not resolved. Although the General Assembly--where there is no right of veto--approved the Baruch Plan in 1948, no measures to implement it could be taken. The Soviet Government was clearly averse to an agreement that would have endorsed the American monopoly of nuclear weapons.

The last meeting of the Atomic Energy Commission was held on 29 July 1949. Exactly one month later the Soviet Union carried out its first nuclear test, and the nuclear arms race began.

General and Complete Disarmament: The McCloy-Zorin Statement (1959-62)

The US response to its loss of nuclear monopoly was to develop the hydrogen bomb, but in this too the Soviets followed suit quickly. With the development of ballistic missiles shortly afterwards, it became possible, for the first time, to destroy the largest city by remote control; the destruction of the whole civilization in a nuclear exchange became a realistic eventuality. The concern of people everywhere, aggravated by the intensive testing of nuclear weapons, found expression in mass movements and campaigns for nuclear disarmament. Echoing these concerns, the General Assembly of the United Nations, at its session in 1969, declared general and complete disarmament (GCD) to be its basic goal, and called for measures towards this goal to be taken in the shortest possible time.

Following a number of proposals from different countries, the Soviet Union and the United States issued a statement that an understanding had been reached between them to continue an exchange of views on disarmament issues. On 20 September 1961, a statement containing agreed principles as the basis for negotiations was issued jointly by the representatives of the two superpowers; it became known as the McCloy-Zorin Statement [5].

In tackling the problem of GCD, specific goals were enunciated about nuclear and other weapons of mass destruction, namely:

> *Elimination of all stockpiles of nuclear, chemical, bacteriological, and other weapons of mass destruction, and cessation of the production of such weapons;* [and] *Elimination of all means of delivery of weapons of mass destruction.*

Some months later, the Soviet Union and the United States supplemented these agreed principles with separate draft treaties for the implementation of the proposals.[6] These revealed significant differences about the stages towards the elimination of nuclear weapons.

Both drafts envisaged the achievement of GCD in a series of steps. In the original Soviet draft, the elimination of delivery vehicles was to be achieved in the first stage of 15 months (later extended to 2 years), and the elimination of nuclear weapons in the second stage, also of 15 months duration. In the US draft, the first two stages, of 3 years each, would see the end of production of fissile materials for weapons and a reduction of nuclear arsenals by agreed percentages; their total elimination was left to the third stage, which would not start until the first two stages had been completed.

The differences seem to amount to only a couple of years, but actually they conceal a fundamental difference in approach to the problem of control and inspection. The US plan called for a system of progressive zonal disarmament and inspection. The USSR strenuously rejected inspection of remaining stocks; inspection on its territories had always been regarded by the USSR as a means of spying on its defence system. This turned out to be an insurmountable obstacle, and eventually led to the abandonment of the GCD effort.

Partial Measures (1963-72)

The mounting anxiety among the public about the accelerating pace of the nuclear arms race, with its attendant threat to the health of the population from the testing of ever more and larger nuclear weapons, compelled governments to take partial measures to alleviate immediate worries. During the following decade a number of damage-limiting steps have been debated, and on some of them bilateral or multilateral treaties have been agreed and ratified. Although the pursuit of complete nuclear disarmament has been temporarily abandoned, it is important to note that many treaties on the nuclear issue contain statements that the elimination of nuclear weapons remained the ultimate goal. Only a few of the treaties are discussed here--particularly those containing such statements.

(a) Partial Test Ban Treaty (1963)

This treaty was agreed by the UK, USA, and USSR. It was a compromise with the United States, given its fierce opposition to a comprehensive test ban. By prohibiting tests in the three media (atmosphere, outer space and underwater) from where the radioactive debris could have reached and damaged the health of people everywhere, the immediate fears were abated. But the PTBT had little effect on the arms race, because testing continued underground (with the tacit assumption, since then seriously questioned, that these tests did not constitute a hazard to health). In the Preamble to the PTBT the signatories proclaim:

> as their principal aim the speediest possible achievement of an agreement on general and complete disarmament under strict international control .... and eliminate the incentive to the production and testing of all kinds of weapons, including nuclear weapons. [7]

Subsequently (1974), the treaty was supplemented by the Threshold Test Ban Treaty, limiting underground nuclear explosions to under 150 kilotons. The vigorous campaigns to bring about a complete test ban have failed so far, although a further moratorium on testing for one year was announced by Gorbachev in October 1991. France has also suspended tests until the end of 1992, and the United States too agreed on a nine-month moratorium from 1 October 1992.

(b) Tlatelolco Treaty (1967)

After the failure to achieve disarmament on a global scale, efforts were directed towards achieving it at least in specific areas, in the form of nuclear-free zones. The most important is the treaty for the prohibition of nuclear weapons in Latin America, known --from the venue in Mexico where it was signed--as the Tlatelolco Treaty.

In this treaty too [8], the Preamble recalls the UN resolution on *"the total prohibition of the use and manufacture of nuclear weapons"*. It further recalls *"that militarily denuclearized zones are not an end in themselves but rather a means for achieving general and complete disarmament at a later stage"*.

This treaty is still not fully in force because Argentina and Brazil insist on some amendments. Nevertheless, it served an important purpose, as a constraining factor against proliferation in that continent.

(c) Non-Proliferation Treaty (1968)

Another important partial measure is the Treaty on the Non-Proliferation of Nuclear Weapons. With vertical proliferation (the arms race between the superpowers) not amenable to control, the prevention of horizontal proliferation seemed an easier target. It was largely thanks to an early (1958) initiative and persistence of the Irish Government that the NPT was born.

Under its terms, the nations classified as 'non-nuclear-weapon states' agreed to give up the right to manufacture or acquire nuclear weapons, but on condition that the nuclear-weapon states would also eventually become non-nuclear-weapon states by taking steps towards disarmament. This is clearly stated in the Preamble [9]: *"Declaring their intention to achieve at the earliest possible date the cessation of the nuclear arms race and to undertake effective measures in the direction of nuclear disarmament"*, and in Article VI of the Treaty:

> *Each of the Parties to the Treaty undertakes to pursue negotiations in good faith on effective measures relating to cessation of the nuclear arms race at an early date and to*

nuclear disarmament, and on a treaty on general and complete
disarmament under strict and effective international control.

The future of the NPT will be decided in 1995. The length of
its extension will depend on the assessment by all its members of
the extent to which the nuclear-weapon states have fulfilled their
obligations.

(d) Anti-Ballistic Missile Treaty (1972)

Even the superpowers conceded that vertical proliferation--
with the associated danger of an inadvertent nuclear war--must be
restrained. A chief worry at that time was that the setting up of
defensive missile systems would bring about a large increase in the
number of offensive missiles, which are cheaper than anti-missiles.
This was the compelling reason for the American and Soviet
Governments to sign the Treaty on the Limitation of Anti-Ballistic
Missile Systems.

In the Preamble to the ABM Treaty [10] the two superpowers
are reminded *"of their obligations under Article VI of the Treaty on the*
Non-Proliferation of Nuclear Weapons", and that it is *"their intention to*
achieve at the earliest possible date the cessation of the nuclear arms race
and to take effective measures toward reductions in strategic arms, nuclear
disarmament, and general and complete disarmament".

UN Special Sessions on Disarmament (1978-88)

Notwithstanding the declarations in the cited excerpts, the
various treaties discussed above (as well as the Rarotonga Treaty
of 1985 establishing a nuclear-free-zone in the South Pacific) were
clearly intended as measures to mitigate the danger of a nuclear
war, rather than as steps towards the elimination of the weapons.
But even for this purpose they were not completely successful.
Nuclear tests continued underground; no further nuclear-free
zones have been established in inhabited areas; a number of
threshold states have refused to sign the NPT; and the ABM has
not stopped the increase in offensive weapons. On the contrary,
the development of MIRVs (multiple independently-targetable re-
entry vehicles) brought about a dramatic increase in the number

of warheads and a destabilization of the situation. Many states, particularly the non-aligned, became alarmed by these developments and resolved that the United Nations should again become directly involved in the process of nuclear disarmament. After much preliminary work, it was agreed that this should be tackled at a special session of the UN General Assembly.

The First United Nations Special Session on Disarmament (SSOD I) took place in May/June 1978. It was a notable event, the largest ever UN meeting entirely devoted to disarmament. It was attended by all member states, with many heads of state among the delegates. Another important feature was that NGOs were allotted time to make formal presentations.

After five weeks of debate, the Session culminated in a unanimously adopted Final Document [11]. This was a long (125 paragraphs) and impressive statement, with a much broader scope than anything previously adopted by the UN; it provided the elements for a comprehensive disarmament strategy.

Despite the dilution resulting from the effort to achieve a consensus, the Final Document included forthright utterances. Considering that it was approved by the superpowers, at that time engaged in enlarging their nuclear arsenals for security purposes, the Declaration (the second part of the four-section Document) contained powerful phrases:

Mankind today is confronted with an unprecedented threat of self-extinction arising from the massive and competitive accumulation of the most destructive weapons ever produced. Existing arsenals of nuclear weapons alone are more than sufficient to destroy all life on earth. Failure of efforts to halt and reverse the arms race, in particular the nuclear arms race, increases the danger of the proliferation of nuclear weapons. Yet the arms race continues... The increase in weapons, especially nuclear weapons, far from helping to strengthen international security, on the contrary weakens it... This situation both reflects and aggravates international tensions, sharpens conflicts in various regions of the world, hinders the process of détente, exacerbates the differences between opposing military alliances, jeopardizes the security of all States, heightens the sense of insecurity among all States, including the non-nuclear-weapon States, and increases the threat of nuclear war.

It then went on:

> *Removing the threat of a world war - a nuclear war - is the*
> *most acute and urgent task of the present day. Mankind is*
> *confronted with a choice: we must halt the arms race and*
> *proceed to disarmament or face annihilation.*

The third section, Programme of Action, which all states were urged to undertake as a matter of urgency, contained detailed specific measures towards disarmament. Nuclear disarmament was given in it top priority, because:

> *Nuclear weapons pose the greatest danger to mankind and to*
> *the survival of civilization. It is essential to halt and reverse*
> *the nuclear arms race in all its aspects in order to avert the*
> *danger of war involving nuclear weapons. The ultimate goal in*
> *this context is the complete elimination of nuclear weapons.*

> *The most effective guarantee against the danger of nuclear war*
> *and the use of nuclear weapons is nuclear disarmament and the*
> *complete elimination of nuclear weapons.*

Furthermore:

> *Real progress in the field of nuclear disarmament could create*
> *an atmosphere conducive to progress in conventional*
> *disarmament on a world-wide basis.*

The Document called for a Second Special Session of the General Assembly to be convened at a later date, in order to assess progress made. This (SSOD II) was held four years later, in June/July 1982, and was in a much lower key.

As it admitted in its report [12], *"developments since 1978 have not lived up to the hopes engendered"* by SSOD I. Indeed, with the advent of the Reagan Presidency, and his invective about 'the evil empire', and with the start of a rearmament programme, this was the wrong time to talk about disarmament agreements. Not surprisingly, the prepared document with a comprehensive programme of disarmament failed to be adopted.

The only positive achievement of SSOD II is probably the

setting up of the World Disarmament Campaign, to inform, educate and generate public understanding and support for the objectives of the United Nations in the disarmament field. The many publications which have emanated from the Campaign have indeed contributed materially to the wider understanding of the problem.

A Third Special Session was held in June 1988. It attracted even less attention, and ended without consensus on a final document.

The failure of the Special Sessions to give a real push to the nuclear disarmament programmes was largely due to the attitude of the United States--shared to a certain extent by the USSR-- which denied the United Nations a central role in the negotiations on nuclear arms control, and was determined to confine these to bilateral talks between the superpowers.

Breakthrough: The Gorbachev Era (1986-91)

On 15 January 1986, the then General Secretary of the Communist Party of the Soviet Union, Mikhail Gorbachev, made a historic speech in which he outlined a programme of nuclear disarmament: a step-by-step process to culminate in the complete elimination of nuclear weapons by the year 2000. The historical importance of this speech derives not so much from the actual proposal--essentially not much different from earlier Soviet proposals--but from the entirely new approach to the whole problem: a basic change in the concept of security, a new way of thinking.

Gorbachev enlarged on his thinking in his book *Perestroika* [13]:

> *The fundamental principle of the new political outlook is very simple: nuclear war cannot be a means of achieving political, economic, ideological or any other goals. This conclusion is truly revolutionary, for it means discarding the traditional notions of war and peace.... Nuclear war is senseless; it is irrational. There would be neither winners nor losers in a global nuclear conflict: world civilization would inevitably perish. It is a suicide, rather than a war in the conventional sense of the word.*

The new political outlook calls for the recognition of one more simple axiom: security is indivisible. It is either equal security for all or none at all. The only solid foundation for security is the recognition of the interests of all peoples and countries and of their equality in international affairs. The security of each nation should be coupled with the security for all members of the world community.... Consequently, there should be no striving for security for oneself at the expense of others.

This was not mere rhetoric. Gorbachev backed it up with the acceptance of on-site inspections as part of the disarmament process, one of the chief obstacles to agreements in the past:

I would like to call attention to the problem of verification, to which we attach special importance. We have declared more than once that the USSR is open to verification, that we have as much interest in it as anyone else. Comprehensive, very rigorous verification is perhaps the most important element in the disarmament process. The essence of the matter, as we see it, is as follows: Disarmament without verification is impossible, but verification without disarmament makes no sense. [14]

That this was not an empty gesture was proved shortly afterwards in the 1987 INF Treaty, by which the dismantling of intermediate range missiles was carried out without a hitch, under a strict verification regime. This success augurs well for the implementation of future disarmament measures.

The 15-year plan proposed by Gorbachev envisaged three stages, each of a five year duration, during which specified categories of nuclear weapons would be eliminated. It is worth noting that some of the steps (e.g. the elimination of tactical weapons) have already been adopted--by unilateral declarations--well within the Gorbachev timetable.

The plan was rejected by the United States as unrealistic--a view shared by some Soviet military and political analysts--but for a brief moment it was accepted by President Reagan at the Reykjavik Summit in October 1986. Indeed, even a shorter timetable--ten years for the whole process to go down to zero--was agreed by the two leaders, but this came to nothing because it was linked with the United States' SDI programme on which there was no agreement.

The need to adopt specific programmes was emphasized by other world leaders, notably by Rajiv Gandhi of India, in his Action Plan [15] which envisaged a slightly longer time, with the year 2010 as the target.

Naming a specific date for such a complex process is probably unwise. When important events occur at extremely rapid rates--as happened after the end of the Cold War--any project based on a fixed timetable is soon bound to be out-of-date. The main need is for the concept of a nuclear-weapon-free world to be accepted as a basic working principle by all nations, followed by the initiation of urgent measures towards its implementation. As stated in the Introduction, this seems now feasible.

In a certain sense the wheel has come full circle. Immediately after Hiroshima, it was clear to many people--including many politicians--that something had to be done to arrest the spread of nuclear weapons. Then the vision faded; the stocks of nuclear warheads grew; but the strategists assured us that the structure of mutual nuclear deterrence was stable. Now it has become clear that this structure was not stable at all, and the old ideas, of working towards total abolition under international control, are coming back; with the demise of the ideological struggle the prospects for their implementation are much more promising. Indeed, the onus of justification should now be not on those who want to eliminate nuclear weapons, but on those who want to retain them.

References

1. A Report to the Secretary of War, 11 June 1945; *Bulletin of the Atomic Scientists*, vol. 1, No.10, 1 May 1946, p.2.

2. "The United Nations and Disarmament 1945-1970", United Nations, 1970 p.11-12.

3. "A Report on the International Control of Atomic Energy"; US Department of State, March 1946, *Bulletin of the Atomic Scientists*, vol.1, No.8, 1 April 1946, pp.2-9.

4.   "International Control of Atomic Energy: Growth of a Policy"; US Department of State, June 1946, *Bulletin of the Atomic Scientists* vol.2, Nos 1&2, 1 July 1946 pp.3-5, 10.

5.   "The United Nations and Disarmament 1945-1970", United Nations, 1970 p.87.

6.   *ibid* pp.392-412 and 413-436.

7.   *ibid* p.450.

8.   *ibid* p.459.

9.   *ibid* p.474 and 477.

10. Arms Control and Disarmament Agreements ACDA, USA 1982.

11. UN document A/RES/S - 10/2.

12. UN document A/S - 12/31.

13. Mikhail Gorbachev, *Perestroika: New Thinking for our Country and the World*, pp140-142, Collins, London 1987.

14. Mikhail Gorbachev, Report to the 27th Congress of CPSU, 4 February 1986. Current Digest of the Soviet Press.

15. "Action Plan for ushering in a nuclear-weapon-free and non-violent world order", *United Nations Disarmament Yearbook*, 1988, pp.46-47 and 69.

Desirability of a NWFW

2

Nuclear Weapons After the Cold War

Carl Kaysen, Robert McNamara,
and George Rathjens

I

The Cold War had two chief features: continued confrontation on the border between the two Germanies that might, possibly without notice, have broken out into war; and an ideologically driven rivalry throughout the developing world.

Germany is now united within its 1945 boundaries, which have been recognized and accepted by all concerned; the Warsaw Pact has disappeared; so too has the Soviet Union; and Poland, Hungary and Czechoslovakia, no longer in thrall to it, are admiring petitioners to the West. Communism has lost almost all appeal outside the borders of the few remaining polities that officially adhere to it--China, North Korea, Vietnam, and Cuba-- and it is unlikely that it would survive even a modest easing of pervasive repressive central control in any of them.

While it will be many years, perhaps a generation, before it becomes clear whether the peoples of what was the Soviet empire have made a successful transition to stable democratic government, it is unlikely that even the resurgence of a new military-authoritarian regime, or regimes, would pose the same kind of ideologized threat to the West that the United States saw from

1945 to 1985. Thus, the great conflict that marked our lives for most of the twentieth century is over, and hardly more likely to be revived than the religious wars of the 16th and 17th centuries between Catholics and Protestants in Europe. With the end of the East-West rivalry reflecting that ideological conflict, it is hard to construct even a semi-plausible military threat to the United States or to Western Europe in the immediate future. As Colin Powell, chairman of the American Joint Chiefs of Staff, has noted, "*I'm running out of demons, I'm running out of villains. I'm down to Castro and Kim Il Sung*". [1] If this is so, it is reasonable to ask: 'What role will military force in general, and nuclear weapons in particular, play in the emerging world order?'

II

Efforts at answering this question must begin with a reminder of the extraordinary revolution in military technology in the last half-century. The development of nuclear weapons and the means of delivering them accurately at intercontinental ranges has opened a wide and increasing gap between what is technically feasible in the application of military power and what is politically usable.

In mid-1992, the world stockpile of nuclear weapons comprises some fifty thousand nuclear warheads. Ninety-seven per cent of them are in the hands of the United States, Russia, Ukraine, Kazakhstan and Belarus. The strategic weapons in the last four states are under centralized control from Moscow, and all tactical weapons have reportedly been removed to Russia. Beyond the three other states acknowledging the possession of nuclear weapons--China, France, and the United Kingdom--there are four or five states who either have some current nuclear capability or are on the threshold of achieving it.

The most striking fact about nuclear weapons is that, since their development and the demonstration of their feasibility in July 1945, only two have ever been used in war: those dropped on Hiroshima and Nagasaki in the first weeks of that August. As President Truman said in his last State of the Union message, after the first hydrogen bomb test:

*From now on, man moves into a new era of destructive power
.... We must realize that no advance we make is unattainable by
others, that no advantage ... can be more than temporary. The
war of the future would be one in which man could extinguish
millions of lives at one blow, demolish the great cities of the
world, wipe out the cultural achievements of the past - and
destroy the very structure of a civilization that has slowly and
painfully built up through hundreds of generations. Such a war
is not a possible policy for rational men.* [2]

Yet for thirty-eight years the United States has been building
ever larger arsenals to wage (or at least be prepared to wage) just
such a war.

The enormous build-up of nuclear weapons since 1945 was
primarily, but not entirely, the product of the Cold War. The
character of the military competition between the two
superpowers was shaped by the existence of strategic nuclear
weapons. Having hastily demobilized its armed forces at the end
of the Second World War, the United States by 1947 began to rely
heavily on nuclear weapons to counter the perceived threat to
Western Europe from the large Soviet army that had not been so
demobilized. The build-up of overseas US air bases on the
periphery of the Soviet Union, and the deployment to them of
nuclear-capable bombers, stimulated a corresponding, though at
first much slower, build-up of Soviet strategic forces.

The reciprocal fears aroused by the possibility of a devastating
bolt-from-the-blue nuclear attack intensified as the weapons and
their means of delivery continued to improve. Profound
ideological antipathy and demonization of the other side, the lag
between the decision to build new weapons and their deployment,
worst-case analyses, Soviet secrecy and successful Soviet bluffs
about the size and capability of their forces, and American belief
in the possibility of sustaining technological superiority, were all
factors in keeping the process going. In the tactical arena, similar
factors, and the belief that Soviet superiority in mobilized
manpower in Europe could not be overcome, led to the
nuclearization of first American and then NATO's ground and
tactical air forces in the 1950s and early 1960s.

For the United Kingdom, which had been a partner (with
Canada and Australia) in the US wartime effort, the decision to

acquire its own nuclear weapons was overwhelmingly political, without even an ostensible military rationale. It was the desire, in Harold Macmillan's words, to continue to *"eat at the top table"*, to participate in US military, particularly nuclear, decision-making as an equal.

France also invested in nuclear weapons for equally illusory political reasons, but with a difference. The French saw them as the symbol of independence, especially of the United States, but also of the United Kingdom, articulated in the absurd slogan 'defence à tous azimuts'--defence against attack from any quarter-- presumably including the United States.

China began its quest for nuclear weapons as early as 1955, as an ally and client of the Soviet Union. When the break between the two occurred (partly because of the Soviet refusal in 1959 to continue helping Beijing develop nuclear weapons), the Chinese pressed forward, as anxious about the potential nuclear threat from their neighbouring former ally as they had initially been about the threat from the distant United States. In 1964, they exploded their first test weapon, becoming the fifth avowed nuclear-weapon power.

India felt threatened by a powerful nuclear-armed neighbour, namely China, with whom it had an open political dispute, and at whose hands it had suffered a humiliating though limited military defeat. The Indians, however, declared their test a 'peaceful explosion', and denied that they had or wished to have weapons. Nevertheless, the major incentive for Pakistan's nuclear weapons programme has been the threat from India and India's nuclear weapons programme.

Israel does not acknowledge the nuclear capability it is widely believed to possess. With the exception of Egypt, heavily armed and deeply hostile neighbouring states do not recognize its legitimacy and have remained in a state of war with it since its founding. Until now, Israel has relied successfully on its conventional forces in four wars. However, its nuclear capability is the ultimate security guarantee. Evidence of it has spurred Iraqi and Libyan efforts to achieve nuclear capability.

It is noteworthy, however, that most states have not sought to acquire nuclear weapons. Some that clearly have the technical capability and resources to do so see no need or threat, or view the possible advantages as outweighed by the political costs.

These include professed neutrals such as Sweden, which started down the weapons path but then turned back (see Chapter 5), and potential adversaries, such as Argentina and Brazil, which have recently decided against continuing that path. Other states, such as Canada, Italy, the Netherlands, Denmark and Japan, have seen their security interests served best by alliance with the United States. Many countries, perhaps the majority, are simply too poor in both technical and economic resources to contemplate acquiring nuclear weapons.

III

What of threats to peace between 1945 and 1991? In Europe, there were many moments of crisis that in pre-nuclear times probably would have led to war: the repeated crises in divided Berlin, beginning with the Soviet blockade of West Berlin in 1948; the Soviet invasions to put down dissident governments in Hungary and Czechoslovakia; incursions by US military aircraft across Soviet borders, involving instances of shoot-downs of US planes; and American U-2 flights across the Soviet heartland. That war was not triggered by these incidents strongly suggests that deterrence worked, but it is by no means clear that possession of substantial nuclear armouries by both sides was a *necessary* condition for this. The memory of the enormous toll of death and destruction in Europe wrought by conventional weapons in World War II may have been daunting enough to both the European members of NATO and the Soviet Union to maintain the peace. And it is certainly relevant that from the early fifties to the early sixties, when the United States had clear strategic superiority, and even a near monopoly of effective nuclear capability, the Soviet Union was not deterred from using force, or the threat of it, to maintain suzerainty over its European domains.

Outside of Europe, the world changed continuously, beginning with the struggle for control of China. The former imperial powers of Europe retreated in Asia, Africa, and the Caribbean, in part voluntarily, in part under duress. New states were created, many with unstable regimes and shifting allegiances in the superpower competition. Many of the changes involved violence: colonial revolts and guerilla wars against the European powers, civil wars or less organized civil violence within new states, and conflicts among them as well.

In all these struggles, nuclear weapons played little, if any, part. The United States' near monopoly in deliverable nuclear weapons in no way deterred the Chinese Communists from their conquest of the Chinese mainland. North Korea was not deterred from invading South Korea in 1950, nor North Vietnam from its support of guerilla war in (and then its open invasion of) South Vietnam in the 1960s. Nor were Egypt and Syria deterred in 1973 from attacking Israel, which at the time had at least a 'screwdriver-away' nuclear capability; or Argentina from seizing the Falklands in 1982. Nor was Saddam Hussein deterred from seizing Kuwait in 1990, though he presumably knew that the United States, Britain and France would see such an attack, and its likely consequences for the control of Saudi oil, as a clear threat to their vital interests. Given that he apparently had developed only very limited capabilities to deliver chemical weapons, it is not even clear that nuclear weapons were a factor in his deciding against using chemical weapons in the war that followed.

From the start of the nuclear age in 1945, enormous expenditures of ingenuity and ink have been devoted to analyses and discussions of nuclear strategy within the military, in the higher reaches of civilian governments, in the specialized 'think tanks' that the Cold War spawned, in academies, and in the press. While most voluminous in the United States, such analyses have by no means been confined to it, and have spread over the entire world. Yet all this discussion has produced only one plausible scenario for the use of nuclear weapons in war: a situation where there is no prospect of retaliation, either against a non-nuclear state, or against one so weakly armed as to permit the user to have full confidence in his nuclear forces' capacity to achieve a totally disarming first strike against those of his opponent.

But even such circumstances have not, in fact, provided a sufficient basis for the use of nuclear weapons in war. Although American forces were in desperate straits twice during the Korean War, first, immediately following the North Korean attack in 1950 and then when the Chinese crossed the Yalu, the United States did not use nuclear weapons. At that time, North Korea and China had no nuclear capability, and the Soviet Union only a negligible one. Although President Truman's hasty response to a reporter's question at a press conference in November 1950 appeared to suggest that he was considering the use of nuclear weapons, political leaders recoiled from what they perceived to be the political costs. [3] Just the suggestion that the United States might use nuclear weapons provoked an immediate descent on Washington by Prime Minister Atlee, and a presidential assurance that no such action was contemplated.

Nearly four years later, when the besieged French in Dien Bien Phu were desperate, French and US military leaders considered the possibility of relieving the fortress by using US air strikes against the Vietnamese attackers. Within the US military, discussion favoured the use of low-yield nuclear weapons for that purpose. President Eisenhower later told his biographer that when these discussions were reported to him, he responded, "*You boys must be crazy. We can't use those awful things against Asians for a second time in less than ten years. My God*". [4] Self deterrence was as effective as mutual deterrence.

IV

The end of the Cold War clearly does not in itself mean the end of international conflict, but it need not mean a return to an earlier style of international relations based on the balance of power and shifting alliances, with its ultimate reliance on national military forces. The unlimited destructiveness of nuclear weapons and the increasingly devastating power of conventional weapons call into question the utility of war as a policy instrument. So does recognition that wars fail to settle the conflicts that lead to them e.g. the Arab-Israel conflict, or that between India and Pakistan.

What the end of the Cold War does mean is that whatever wars there may be are not likely to occur within the context of a bipolar world dominated by two great ideological opponents. What this era provides is new opportunity to strive for truly collective security and an international rule of law, in which self-help by the use of military force for resolving conflicts among nations loses its legitimacy. The United Nations Charter and the instruments available under it can gain increasing credibility through increasing use, and thus provide the framework and modalities for an evolving rule of law in which force is used only by collective decision.

The Iraqi invasion of Kuwait in 1990, and the international response to it, exemplify what can be done to delegitimize the unilateral resort to force, but also some of the problems in doing so. With the end of the Cold War, the United States was able to secure Soviet and Chinese acquiescence to its mobilizing the Security Council to go beyond merely condemning Iraqi aggression. The Council first approved a stringent economic blockade, and then sanctioned the use of force to expel the Iraqis from Kuwait. But it is by no means clear that using force, when and as it was used, was wise. We will never know whether economic sanctions alone might have accomplished as much at a lower cost; and, indeed, it will be some time before we have a clear picture of what those costs will have been. The great destruction inflicted on Iraq was neither clearly necessary for the eviction of Iraqi forces from Kuwait, nor sufficient for terminating Saddam Hussein's dictatorship or his nuclear weapons programme; another example, if one were needed, of how blunt an instrument is the use of military force and of the great importance of thorough, prior consideration of plausible consequences.

It is in our deepest interest, even in the short run, to continue on the path of delegitimizing war and the unilateral use of military force in relations among states, and to lead the way to world-wide acceptance of this view. This requires that we and others do better than we have done so far in the Middle East and elsewhere, not only in contesting overt inter-state aggression but in dealing with underlying causes of conflict. This is the aim which should inform our own military and diplomatic policies, and we must persuade others of its primacy. This should be the essence of the new international order that the end of the Cold War makes possible.

V

What of the role of nuclear weapons in this world? Against what kinds of threats might they be useful? What interests would the United States judge to be so vital that nuclear weapons would be critical and credible for their defence? What threat could even pose the possibility of their use for deterrence?

In our view, it is hard to see any near-term need at all for those of the United States, and it is hard to imagine any more serious threats for France or the other countries of Western Europe, including Britain as its North Sea oil is depleted, than that posed in the autumn of 1990 by Saddam Hussein, to which nuclear weapons were incredible as a deterrent, and therefore irrelevant. As for Russia and China, it is implausible that either could use such weapons effectively to deal with its internal problems, and by comparison with those problems, all other threats pale, including even that of one attacking the other.

But, so long as all these states retain nuclear weapons, each may see them as useful in the narrowest deterrent role: to make sure that no other nuclear-weapon state is tempted to attack them. In the changed world, however, the weight of international opinion, both official and public, against any use of nuclear weapons will be stronger than it has been, and the inhibitions on the use of nuclear weapons against states without nuclear arms will be stronger still.

But two states do face near or medium-term threats to their existences for which they might judge nuclear weapons credible deterrents or responses: Pakistan and Israel. The former is already seriously out-gunned by India with conventional weapons and the latter faces the near-certainty of being so some years hence by the Arab states, which together have many times Israel's population, much higher birth rates and oil wealth to boot. While nuclear weapons may not offer as great an advantage for 'war fighting', given the development of 'smart' technologies for delivery of conventional ordnance, nor be as credible as deterrents as they were believed to be some years ago, it is implausible that Israel will not insist on retaining them as weapons of last resort, absent a resolution of its fundamental security problem. This may be true for Pakistan as well. Its leaders are likely at least to want to keep open the option of acquiring nuclear capabilities quickly should India do so, or should hostilities with India seem close. In both of these cases probably only international action can resolve the underlying conflicts, or contain them below the level at which they might lead to war. Nuclear capability, actual or potential, cannot be relied on to keep the peace.

VI

But a nuclear-weapon-free world--desirable as it is as an ultimate objective--is at best a distant prospect. The five declared nuclear powers will each wish to keep some weapons as long as any of the others do. Further, all or most will claim the necessity for keeping some weapons as a hedge against the uncertainties of the status of 'threshold' states and the possibilities of 'breakout'-- open deployment of nuclear weapons by one or more of them. The current deployments, however, particularly of the United States and Russia, are absurdly large. All the purposes that these weapons can conceivably serve could be met by forces no more, and probably much less, than one-twentieth their current size.

To begin with, the more than 25,000 tactical warheads both powers together deployed can be entirely dismantled. Many of these weapons were developed, and deployed in Europe in response to the Soviet Union's achieving the capacity to deliver a devastating nuclear attack against the United States. This led to a growing belief in NATO that the USA could not and would not respond to an attack by Warsaw Treaty conventional forces against NATO Europe by immediately 'unleashing' its Strategic Air Command. Hence the birth of the concept of initiating nuclear action with the use of tactical or theatre nuclear weapons.

Although no responsible political or military figure ever came up with a truly convincing explanation of how nuclear weapons might be used in Europe without unacceptable risks of catastrophic escalation, the possibility could not be totally discounted.

Not surprisingly, NATO's deployment of theatre nuclear weapons came to mean all things to all men. To those fearful that a strategic nuclear exchange would destroy the United States, it offered the hope that war in Europe might be deterred by the prospect of Warsaw Treaty forces suffering unacceptable punishment, but without escalation to a strategic nuclear exchange. To those mainly concerned about the devastating consequences of any European war--mainly Europeans--the theatre weapons offered the prospect of coupling: making escalation from the use of conventional forces to the engagement of strategic forces of the superpowers sufficiently credible that Soviet leadership would be deterred from actions that might lead to conventional war. With these differences in beliefs and hopes about how nuclear weapons might be used, possible modifications in NATO force posture, whether as a result of Western initiative or in response to actions by the Soviet Union, inevitably had divisive effects within the Alliance. Hence the controversies about the 'neutron bomb', INF forces and American efforts to get the Europeans to increase their conventional forces and defence expenditures.

With the end of the threat of a devastating Warsaw Pact attack against NATO, the rationale for NATO's theatre nuclear weapons disappeared, and it became clear that all such weapons should be withdrawn from Europe. In fact, we see no case for their deployment or retention anywhere, much less for the development of new ones. Happily, radical movement in this direction has occurred, including notably decisions to eliminate ground-launched theatre nuclear weapons and to remove all tactical nuclear weapons from surface ships.

In shifting our attention from tactical to strategic nuclear weapons, we must recognize the particular interpretation of deterrence embodied in the structure and targeting doctrine of US strategic forces from almost the very beginning. The highest priority target has been the other side's strategic forces, both offensive and defensive, rather than the hundred-odd urban-industrial centres critical to the functioning of a modern society. Many military targets other than strategic forces further lengthen this target list. Our limited information about Soviet targeting--mostly statements of doctrine or inferences drawn from their force structure--suggests that the Soviets had a similar concept of deterrence. Despite our official doctrine of 'survivable second-strike deterrence', our forces have been structured and targeted as first-strike or war-fighting forces, and Soviet forces appear to have had the same character. The proponents of this force structure have seen it as essential to providing 'extended deterrence': deterrence of any Soviet military action against the West, not only a nuclear attack.

Notwithstanding the dissolution of the Soviet Union and the statement made by President Yeltsin that the strategic forces of the Commonwealth of Independent States would no longer be targeted against American cities or military installations, there has been great resistance within the American strategic policy community to changing its thinking about the utility and role of nuclear weapons in general and about strategic weapons in particular. The points are well illustrated in a 1991 National Academy of Sciences study [5] and by leaks of internal Pentagon studies [6].

The NAS study constructively suggests that "*the principal objective of U.S. nuclear policy should be to strengthen the emerging political consensus that nuclear weapons should serve no purpose beyond the deterrence of, and possible response to, nuclear attack by others.*" It then goes on to suggest that, in the immediate aftermath of the Strategic Arms Reduction Treaty (START), "*the United States and the Soviet Union should reduce the number of nuclear warheads in their strategic forces to 3000-4000 actual warheads*", numbers it is estimated would be required so that 1000-1600 aim points--industry and energy sources, conventional forces, naval and air bases, and strategic command and control centres--could be targeted. The study goes on to suggest that later, given progress in security cooperation, the number of targets might be reduced to 500-800 and the number of warheads to 1000-2000.

Why did the NAS study settle on numbers of weapons and targets that are so large? One clue is to be found in the text wherein it is noted that a purely counter-city targeting doctrine, which would presumably imply very much lower numbers of weapons and targets, might not be adequate for deterrence of anything "*short of a nuclear attack on US cities*". One is led to wonder whether the group really had convinced itself that nuclear weapons could not, and should not, be expected to serve the kind of 'extended deterrent' role asked of them during the 60s and 70s. Relatedly, W.K.H. Panofsky, who chaired the NAS study group and who defended its report before the Senate Foreign Relations Committee [7], noted that the group judged that the explicit targeting of cities would be neither credible nor morally acceptable, an argument that has also been advanced in other studies which rationalize the retention of thousands of strategic warheads.

We are inclined to dismiss the use of the moral argument as something approaching sophistry, given that the destruction of the kinds of targets called for in these studies would lead to economic and social chaos and would, according to Panofsky, result in tens of millions of people being killed, casualties comparable to those that would result with the delivery of many fewer weapons targeted on cities.

For this and other reasons, we believe such studies are seriously flawed, as are weapons acquisition and retention policies rationalized on them. Confronted with plausible crises, we do not believe American, or other, leaders would have made--or would, in the future, make--different decisions if either or both of two adversary nations had only what many have characterized as 'minimal' deterrent forces: forces of a size and structure that would permit the destruction of, say, a dozen or a few tens rather than hundreds or thousands of targets in a retaliatory attack. Thus, we do not see how commitment to forces capable of inflicting higher levels of destruction can offer American presidents, or other world leaders, politically exploitable military capabilities.

The acceptance of such 'requirements' has given too much influence on American policy to those committed to them, and to continued build-up and virtually unlimited modernization of strategic forces. These are points that clearly troubled both President Eisenhower and President Kennedy as they became aware of Air Force planning in 1960-61.

We earlier noted President Truman's statement that nuclear war could not be a possible policy for a rational man. A few years later, in 1954--the same year as his famous public 'massive retaliation' speech--Secretary of State John Foster Dulles observed within government councils that:

> *the increased destructiveness of nuclear weapons and the approach of effective atomic parity are creating a situation in which general war would threaten the destruction of Western civilization and of the Soviet regime, and in which national objectives could not be obtained through a general war even if a military victory were won.* [8]

These points have, or should have, troubled all succeeding presidents and secretaries of state. President Reagan expressed the same view when he said that a nuclear war could never be won and therefore must never be fought. Yet we continue to premise our war plans and procure our forces on the need for substantial counterforce capabilities. This has been a significant factor in keeping the Cold War alive, and has been excessively dangerous--a point driven home particularly in the last several years as we have come to understand better the extent of misperception and miscalculation that characterized various Soviet-American confrontations, particularly the Cuban missile crisis.

Continuing with such planning, and with force acquisition based on it, now seems totally absurd. With the Cold War over, it suggests that our strategic thinking remains chained to obsolete doctrines: that as a nation, we are incapable of reacting intelligently to changes in the world scene.

The most seriously discussed alternative to the kind of postures described in the NAS report has been the aforementioned concept of 'minimum deterrence'. There have been many efforts to define strategic force postures consistent with the concept, going back at least to the Eisenhower Administration when Donald Quarles, Secretary of the Air Force and then Deputy Secretary of Defense, asked the question 'How much is enough?' One of us (RM) suggested early in the 1960s, during the Kennedy Administration, that an ability to destroy in retaliation 20 to 25 per cent of Soviet population and 50 per cent of its industrial capacity, something achievable with the delivery of the order of 100 one-megaton weapons, was surely an upper bound. McGeorge Bundy --national security advisor to Presidents Kennedy and Johnson-- wrote in 1969 that much lower damage levels might suffice, that:

> *In the real world of real political leaders, a decision that would bring even one hydrogen bomb on one city of one's own country would be recognized in advance as a catastrophic blunder; ten bombs on ten cities would be a disaster beyond history; and a hundred bombs on a hundred cities are unthinkable.* [9]

Conceptually, force requirements for 'minimum deterrence' depend on the size of the other's nuclear forces and how vulnerable one's own forces are to adversary pre-emptive attack. This point too has been much discussed. In a recent paper, Herbert York, first director of the Lawrence Livermore Laboratory and the first Director of Defense Research and Engineering, has examined this question in the light of the inevitable uncertainty about the weight of pre-emptive attack. [10] He suggests that, assuming serious but feasible efforts to minimize the vulnerability of retaliatory forces, somewhere in the neighbourhood of 100 weapons might be about right.

Although we have no quarrel with York's estimate, nor with most of the other discussions of minimum deterrence in the last three decades, all have been premised on a need for deterrence of attack by the Soviet Union. With the end of the Cold War, attack by the successor states now seems among the least worrisome of imaginable threats to our society. If, as General Powell suggests, our only significant enemies are now North Korea and Cuba, we have *no* immediate military need for strategic nuclear forces for deterrence beyond that required for deterrence of nuclear attack by other nuclear powers. Looking ahead, moreover, we see no military need whatsoever for any modernization of our strategic forces for at least the remainder of this century.

Granting all this, the question we must address is how to proceed from here to our ultimate objective. Presidents Bush and Yeltsin have agreed on deep reductions beyond START, but it is clear that the objective of truly minimum deterrent levels will never be reached by the tedious and interminable-seeming process of negotiation on which we have relied so far. Reductions to levels of, say, 1000 warheads each for the United States and the Commonwealth of Independent States, could be achieved by a series of unilateral actions, what in a lost hopeful moment twenty years ago was called the process of 'mutual example'.

Notwithstanding recent demands that US strategic force levels must remain at least as large as those of the Commonwealth of Independent States and indeed as large as those of all other nuclear states combined [11], at these proposed levels of warhead numbers, effective strategic equivalence does *not* require equality or near equality in numbers of the opposing forces. It requires only that each of two adversaries recognize that the other can inflict unacceptable damage in a retaliatory strike. Equivalence is thus not a line, but a band of considerable width. From 1965 to 1980, although US strategic nuclear forces far outnumbered those of the Soviets, and were qualitatively superior in many ways, they were strategically equivalent. Gorbachev's understanding of the width of equivalence led him to accept the disproportionately large reductions in Soviet forces relative to those of the United States in the INF Treaty and the draft START Treaty. Thus the process of reciprocal unilateral reductions could go forward without risk of meaningful strategic imbalance. Realistically, at some point, perhaps in the neighbourhood of 1000 US and CIS warheads, France, the United Kingdom and China would have to be drawn into the reduction process if it is to continue.

Similarly, we can dispense with modernizing the remaining weapons. They are already efficacious enough to serve the residual function of deterrence of the use of nuclear weapons by any state against the USA or its allies, which is all that we can ask or expect of them. Moreover, for what it is worth--and we do not discount this--our simply getting on with reductions and foregoing modernization is likely to have a salutary effect in inducing emulation, not only by the Commonwealth of Independent States, but by the other nuclear powers. It is a better example than prolonged negotiations, which give the impression that the United States--which has had the most experience with them--continues to believe that nuclear forces offer such military and political advantage as to justify quibbling over the arcane details of force posture.

There are several reasons why it is desirable to reduce the number of nuclear weapons even further. Perhaps the most basic is the fundamental immorality of relying on the threat of death and destruction to civilians and the urban fabric of civilization on the scale that even a few tens of modern nuclear weapons would produce. Such a strike would put at risk not only the citizens of the nuclear powers involved, but, as Chernobyl made clear, millions of citizens of even distant non-belligerent states that might be affected by the fall-out of radiation. To be sure, the world has lived with a similar immorality ever since Germany, and then Britain and the United States, relied on air attack of cities as a major instrument of war; but the basic point remains, and at bottom reflects the deeper moral difficulty of relying on war as an instrument of state policy.

There are two, more pragmatic, reasons for seeking to continue the process of nuclear disarmament. First is the simple calculation that reducing the number and variety of weapons, and the geographic breadth of their deployment, will be likely to reduce the probability of their accidental or unauthorized use. At any level of effort devoted to ensuring the central control and security of deployed weapons, the fewer there are, the less the probability of failure.

Second is the influence of the size and growth of the weapons stockpiles of the nuclear-weapon states on the acceptance by the others of their non-nuclear status. Those states that have refused to sign the Non-Proliferation Treaty have always justified their refusal by the asymmetry of obligation between the recognized nuclear-weapon states and all others. The more the asymmetry is diminished the more likely it is that non-proliferation can achieve the status of an acceptable international regime. This too will require the involvement in the disarmament process of all the nuclear powers, not just the United States and the Commonwealth of Independent States.

If there is no need for most of our nuclear weapons, nor for the modernization of the modest number we retain, it seems obvious that there is not much of a case for continued nuclear weapons testing, or for the production of fissionable materials, or, even though it decays radioactively at 5.6 per cent per year, of tritium, a component of most modern weapons. The only remaining argument for continued testing--and it seems to us an argument of last resort--is that of safety. We have some weapons in our stockpile that are so susceptible to accidental detonation that some claim that further testing is required so that they can be replaced with new, safer weapons. With reductions on the scale we envisage, however, these more worrisome weapons can be eliminated without replacement.

Thus, we strongly advocate that the United States go along with the rest of the world--Washington and London are now the only clear hold-outs--to extend the proscription of the present Test-Ban Treaty to include underground testing as well. The vigorous underground test programmes of the United States and the Soviet Union under the present Treaty made it almost a sham as regards arms control--though useful as an environmental protection measure.

We urge consummation of a comprehensive test ban treaty in part because such action could have some direct effect on nuclear weapons proliferation. Parties to it could still develop simple fission weapons, but without testing such development would be somewhat more difficult, and for thermonuclear and other sophisticated weapons, probably impossible. But we argue for a comprehensive test ban treaty mainly because weapon testing has been so symbolic of the nuclear arms race: we might say symbolic of our commitment to nuclear madness. Perhaps more than any other single action, a comprehensive test-ban treaty would signal, both domestically and internationally, rejection of nuclear weaponry as a basis for security.

If the United States is prepared to do all this, why should it not lead, or at least join others, in a move for the abolition of all nuclear weapons? One of the standard arguments against this has been that notwithstanding undertakings to get rid of nuclear weapons, others might retain a few. The other is that even a world free of nuclear weapons would be intolerably unstable because in a crisis, or even at the hint of a crisis, the parties involved would be driven to develop, stockpile, and perhaps use, new weapons (see Chapter 5). The knowledge of how to make nuclear weapons is something from which we cannot escape. Both these points have merit, but focusing on them invites the search for a technical fix which will provide a way around them. There can be none. This is the more true in that technological developments, aside from those in nuclear weaponry, have meant that increases in our destructive abilities have so outpaced whatever increases there have been in the resilience of our social infrastructures that war with modern weapons has to be seen as an increasingly unacceptable means for dealing with differences. And so, we cannot emphasize too strongly the importance of seizing the moment--certainly, the best opportunity since World War II--to work on reducing motivations for the use of force to deal with the world's problems: to try to realize the promise of the UN charter and to establish an international rule of law.

We should view getting rid of nuclear weapons entirely as something that will be facilitated by that larger effort. To the extent we succeed in that approach, getting rid of nuclear weapons will be easier than if we concentrate our efforts narrowly and directly on their abolition, but getting rid of them will be of diminished importance.

References

1.   Jim Wolffe, "Powell: 'I'm running out of demons'" *Army Times*, 15 April 1991, p.4.

2. James B. Conant, *My Several Lives*. Harper & Row, New York, 1970, p.279.

3. McGeorge Bundy, *Danger and Survival*, Random House, New York, 1988, p.231.

4. Stephen E. Ambrose, *Eisenhower*, Simon & Schuster, New York, 1983, vol.2, p.184.

5. *The Future of the US-Soviet Nuclear Relationship*, Committee on International Security and Arms Control, National Academy of Sciences, National Academy Press, Washington, DC. 1991.

6. R. Jeffrey Smith, "US Urged to Cut 50% of A-Arms", *Washington Post*, 6 January 1992. Patrick E. Tyler, "US Strategy Plan Calls for Insuring No Rivals Develop", *New York Times*, 8 March 1992.

7. "Hearing on The Soviet Democratic Revolution: START and the Future of Arms Control", Committee on Foreign Relations, US Senate, 25 September 1991.

8. John Lewis Gaddis in *John Foster Dulles and the Diplomacy of the Cold War*, ed. Richard H. Immerman, Princeton, 1990, p.53.

9. McGeorge Bundy, "To Cap the Volcano", *Foreign Affairs*, October 1969, p.10.

10. Herbert York, "Remarks About Minimum Deterrence", a paper presented to a workshop on *The Role of Nuclear Weapons in the Year 2000*, held at Lawrence Livermore National laboratory, 22-24 October 1990.

11. See, for example, Thomas C. Reed and Michael O. Wheeler, "The Role of Nuclear Weapons in the New World Order", December 1991, p.28 (a report to the Director of the Joint Strategic Target Planning Staff, US Department of Defense).

3

A Nuclear-Weapon-Free World: Is It Desirable? Is It Necessary?

Jack Steinberger, Essam Galal, and Mikhail Milstein

The threat and fear of global nuclear destruction have been with us since Hiroshima. The first resolution of the United Nations, unanimously adopted by the General Assembly in January 1946, called for the elimination of nuclear weapons from national arsenals. [1] However the first attempts in this direction, the US Acheson-Lilienthal-Baruch plan [2], as well as the initiative of the Soviet Union of June 1946 to ban the production and use of nuclear weapons [3], were unsuccessful. The extreme dangers posed by nuclear weapons, and the ultimate goal of their complete elimination, were again clearly stated in the conclusions of the 1978 UN Special Session on Disarmament [4], which was signed by all member states, including the nuclear powers. Today, five countries openly stock nuclear weapons, three or four others are generally believed to possess them, and an unknown number of states are actively pursuing programmes to develop them. This proliferation cannot now be prevented legally, it can only be retarded by international conventions such as the nuclear Non-Proliferation Treaty, as well as by economic and technological sanctions. The yield of the most powerful weapons has increased a thousandfold since Hiroshima, and means of precise delivery anywhere on the globe have emerged. The people of the world have been threatened by nearly 60,000 nuclear warheads with a combined destructive power of the order of ten thousand megaton TNT equivalent, two tons for each member of the species.

In recent years the opinion that nuclear weapons are more threat than guarantor to their securities has been voiced by the heads of some of the major powers. Mikhail Gorbachev, in a speech of 15 January 1986, proposed a timetable for a nuclear-weapon-free world by the year 2000. [5] In the Reykjavik summit meeting of October 1986, Gorbachev and President Reagan proposed an even shorter timetable for the elimination of nuclear weapons. [6] There is definite progress in this direction. Since that time the INF Treaty, which programmed the elimination of one category of delivery, has been implemented. The START treaty which would have reduced deployed strategic nuclear warheads nominally by about 50 per cent, has been overtaken by the June 1992 Washington Summit of Presidents Bush and Yeltsin, where they agreed to reduce the numbers of strategic warheads to 3500 and 3000 each. The unilateral declarations of Presidents Bush [7] and Gorbachev [8] will, when implemented, go a long way towards removing the huge and dangerous arsenal of tactical nuclear weapons. These initiatives are of great significance, because they acknowledge the problem posed by the nuclear arsenals, and constitute a big step towards nuclear disarmament. Tactical nuclear weapons are particularly useless and threatening. The acknowledgement of this fact represents progress. But by themselves these reductions do not remove the nuclear threat. What will be left is still monstrously dangerous. Moreover, the reductions may in part be compensated by modernizations and technological improvements of the weapons.

Although the governments of the nuclear powers are shaken by the instabilities on the nuclear scene so vividly exhibited by the developments in the former USSR, and the United States and Russia are reducing their arsenals, the stated nuclear security strategies of the nuclear powers have not yet changed fundamentally. The full lesson has not yet sunk in. The basic strategy of the United States is still based on the power to destroy a large number of military and industrial targets after suffering a first strike, and the option of responding to a conventional force attack in Europe with nuclear weapons is still maintained by NATO, so that the USA is still not prepared to accept a no-first-use policy. Russia, although stating a preference for a non-nuclear defence position, and pledging no-first-use of nuclear weapons, deploys nuclear weapons in much the same way as the United States. France and Great Britain, each with about one tenth of the nuclear arsenals of the 'superpowers' (after the recently agreed reductions) believe their nuclear weapons buy them independence from the latter, and perhaps some advantage over their non-nuclear neighbours. China is a very large country with relatively modest forces. One of the more interesting nuclear situations is that of Israel, surrounded by hostile neighbours. Although Israel does not claim to have them, it is generally conceded that it has of the order of one hundred nuclear weapons, presumably serving as a deterrent. What will its situation be when a neighbouring state also possesses this weapon?

In the meantime the world has changed. The Warsaw Pact has dissolved and the Soviet Union is no longer. No one can claim that Europe or the United States face any military threat, unless that threat is nuclear. Equally important is the increased general acceptance of the 'common security' concept as the structural base of national security. It is now difficult to imagine any military use of nuclear weapons, unless it is to *deter* others from using their *nuclear* weapons. If a way could be found to eliminate all nuclear weapons convincingly, durably and globally, any plausible reasons for nuclear weapons in the hands of the big powers would have disappeared.

Proponents of the policy of nuclear deterrence habitually proclaim its inherent stability. One 'decision maker' even quantified the stability as "*99.95 per cent*". [9] But the recent political changes in the Soviet Union have brought the problem of long-term stability in the control of nuclear arsenals sharply into focus. Who will control the weapons stationed in the newly independent republics? This development demonstrates a fundamental flaw in present nuclear thinking: the premise that the world will forever be controllable by a small, static, group of powers. The world has not been, is not, and will not be static.

The changes in the East-West security relationship have not yet had a commensurate impact on the nuclear postures. Although one can perhaps believe the statements of the leaders of the Commonwealth of Independent States that they would welcome the mutual elimination of nuclear weapons, the position of the Western powers on the desirability and utility of nuclear weapons has not yet changed fundamentally. However, the historic arguments are no longer valid; the time is ripe for change; the opportunity is evident. In the next years new attitudes and nuclear postures must and will be found.

Those concerned with the threat posed by the world's huge nuclear arsenals can be divided into two main groups. On the one hand, the proponents of 'Minimal Nuclear Deterrence' believe that nuclear weapons will be with us for a long time, if not forever. The best we can hope for is to contain the damage and limit the number of weapons to a minimum, and somehow convince non-nuclear states either by reason, or by economic, political and military pressure, to stay that way. Below this minimum we cannot hope to go, either because we consider this minimum necessary for security reasons, or because it is a necessary hedge against cheating by others. The zero level is a Utopian, perhaps dangerous, dream.

On the other hand, the proponents of a nuclear-weapon-free world believe that minimum deterrence is still a nuclear posture inviting disaster. They believe that it will encourage proliferation and so contribute to the insecurity rather than the security of the present nuclear powers; that the thousands of remaining nuclear weapons represent an unacceptable threat to the world; and that, if the present nuclear powers really desire to liberate themselves from this yoke, adequate international institutions and verification methods can be created to guarantee effective compliance with a NWFW regime.

What is 'Minimum Deterrence'? What are the minimal levels of nuclear weapons which are proposed, and which countries should have them? There are no unique responses to these questions. The arguments in favour fall into two classes. There are those who believe that only the threat of nuclear disaster has prevented war in Europe since 1945, and that the military threat of nuclear response to nuclear or non-nuclear aggression is essential to security. This view is rarely expressed outside the NATO bloc. Recently a panel of the US National Academy of Sciences [10] has proposed a minimum level of 3000-4000 strategic nuclear warheads each for the USA and what was then the USSR, later going down to 1000-2000. It did not discuss the levels suitable for, say, France or China or Libya. The proposed number of weapons is based on the number of military and industrial installations that must be targeted to deter the would-be enemy.

This view of minimum deterrence supposes that to deter, it is necessary to be ready to fight a nuclear war.

For those proponents of minimum deterrence who subscribe to a no-first-use policy, the minimum level is lower. The perceived minimum level of weapons is then based on the need to deter nuclear blackmail and to confront possible evasion of the treaties limiting nuclear weapons. For this school, the number of necessary weapons is linked to the confidence in the verification scheme and the evolution of a response to possible violation of an agreement, and could decrease as the system improves. The Committee of Soviet Scientists for Peace and Against the Nuclear Threat has suggested the level of 600 warheads for each side (at a time when there were (arguably) two sides). [11]

These minimum deterrent levels are considerably lower than present levels. Such reductions would represent substantial progress. They will take some time to achieve, and for this period the abolitionists and the minimal deterrers can be fellow travellers. But, in general, when travelling a road, it is good to know where you want to go, so the differences in the visions are worth discussing even now.

We proceed to state here our concern about any minimum deterrent policy. Basically it is that minimum deterrence is still nuclear deterrence and therefore does not eliminate the nuclear threat.

Military Value of Nuclear Weapons

Do nuclear weapons have military value, apart from possible deterrence of other nuclear weapons? The affirmative answer was an essential element of NATO's nuclear policy during the Cold War period. It was argued that the threat of the use of nuclear weapons was necessary to deter the use of conventional forces claimed to be superior. This argument has now totally disappeared; NATO can no longer claim that superior non-nuclear forces exist anywhere. The old bipolar confrontation has been replaced by multipolar collaboration, and it is generally recognized that nuclear weapons add nothing to the stability of Europe, but rather constitute a serious security threat.

Deterrence Value of Nuclear Weapons

Nuclear weapons are often defended with the claim that they have prevented war in Europe. Those who believe that the NATO policies of 'extended deterrence' and 'flexible' nuclear response to a real or imagined Soviet conventional superiority have 'kept the peace' cannot prove this assertion. It can never be known if the threat of the use of nuclear force was ever credible. Which country would have signed its own death warrant? There is substantial ground for the belief that conventional forces constituted adequate deterrence. Who wanted a war anyway? When the Soviet Union invaded Hungary or Czechoslovakia, the West would have dearly wished to intervene; was it deterred by the nuclear threat, or was the conventional threat sufficient?

In the confrontations between the nuclear powers and non-nuclear states, nuclear weapons have been *irrelevant*. They were not used in Vietnam, although their *possible* use constituted a threat of world catastrophe. They played no role in the Gulf war. They did not deter the Argentine government from invading the Falklands.

It is sometimes argued that the abolition of nuclear weapons would make it less risky for a state to start a conventional war; but this argument presupposes that nuclear weapons deter the use of conventional weapons. The evidence does not support this. Twenty million lives have been lost in wars since the last World War.

Can the threat of retaliation be expected to deter terrorists or countries which feel they have nothing to loose?

Threat of World Catastrophe Inherent in the Deterrent Posture

Even minimum deterrent nuclear forces represent an unacceptable threat of global disaster. Sooner or later they will be used. If half a dozen countries were each left with 500 warheads, each with an average yield of 200 kilotons, this would represent a total destructive power twenty times greater than used in all previous wars combined. This large destructive power is an essential element of the concept of deterrence, minimum or other. It would still threaten the lives of hundreds of millions of human beings, the 'innocent' no less than the 'guilty'. We do not see how to defend this concept.

The deterrent forces would constitute a permanent threat of accidental nuclear war. Such an accident could be the result of miscalculation or misinformation at the highest level, as we now know we risked in the Cuban crisis of 1962, or the result of error in a computerized nuclear defence system, responding to the need for very quick decisions.

The deterrent concept rests on the assumption that leaders are rational. Is it reasonable to rely on this assumption, considering the disastrous consequences of an error?

Who Should Possess Deterrent Forces?

Those advocating nuclear deterrence usually couple this with an insistence on non-proliferation. But if nuclear weapons suit the present nuclear powers, why should not other countries follow their example? Developing countries, which for economic or technical reasons have not yet produced their own nuclear deterrence forces, may wish in the future to have their own minimum deterrent. And who would establish the relative strengths? Deterrence invites proliferation as well as escalation.

The Maintenance of Nuclear-Weapon Laboratories and Testing

As long as nuclear forces determine defence postures, nuclear-weapon research laboratories and nuclear testing will continue. This will provide ongoing stimulation and incentive for the development of novel, special purpose destructive devices which may pose new and unforeseen dangers.

Nuclear-weapon laboratories and nuclear tests also facilitate proliferation. As long as one nation tests, by what argument can one deny the right to test to others? Furthermore, the knowledge, as well as the scientists of the laboratories, may become a source of expertise for would-be nuclear nations.

Nuclear Weapons May Fall into Different Hands

This problem is illustrated dramatically by the political changes in the former Soviet Union.

Proliferation

By far the most dangerous aspect of a continued policy of deterrence, in our opinion, is the invitation to proliferation. No moral or legal argument can justify our possession of these weapons while denying this to others. And the existence of the weapons industry will facilitate the technology transfer.

The reduced levels in the arsenals of the big powers will make nuclearization more inviting to the small. One salient aspect of a future with many smaller countries in possession of nuclear arsenals is that, as we have seen in Vietnam and the Gulf, in the hands of the big powers these weapons cannot be used even to threaten, but in the hands of smaller powers, nuclear weapons may be an extraordinary threat to the big. Nuclear weapons are potential equalizers, interesting for small countries, but not for the big.

Whatever the merits of the arguments for nuclear deterrence may have been before the collapse of the Warsaw Pact, it is difficult to imagine them now, when all governments concerned are striving to strengthen common security in Europe, and the former Warsaw Pact countries are desperately trying to establish new identities and evolve new economies. The remaining security concern to the West is the problem of stability in the region, possible confrontation between these formerly united, now fragmented republics. But is there any possible way in which nuclear weapons can prevent or diminish these tensions and instabilities? Quite the reverse, the large number of strategic and tactical weapons left over from the inherited nuclear arms race constitutes one of the greatest security problems in the region. If there were a way to mutually and quickly eliminate all of the nuclear weapons, here and elsewhere, we would all feel more secure.

If nuclear weapons have no military value, and a deterrent posture does not deter, but does threaten catastrophe and invites proliferation, the only alternative is a policy seeking the elimination of nuclear weapons. Many consider this Utopian; we believe that it is the only sane policy. Its implementation presents great challenges, both technically and politically, but not greater than others humanity has met, including the invention of the nuclear weapon. Most important is the conviction that this is the only way, in the long-term, of avoiding nuclear disaster.

It seems hardly necessary to call attention to the economic benefits of a non-nuclear world. This would not only lighten the defence burden of the present nuclear powers, but, perhaps more important, it would help the economies and stability of developing countries (e.g. Pakistan), which would no longer be under pressure to spend vast sums of money and scientific resources for the design and construction of nuclear weapons.

One of the recurring statements of the sceptics is that the knowledge of nuclear weapons cannot be eliminated. This is of course true, but it does not follow that international institutions cannot be evolved which would give adequate assurance against breakout. In the same light, governments have agreed to eliminate germ warfare weapons and chemical weapons.

We will not devise adequate methods unless we work on the problem. In the next section of this volume an attempt is made to identify some of the questions. It should be viewed as the most important challenge for the nuclear powers to devise the technical and political means for getting rid of their arsenals safely and preventing their re-emergence anywhere. Although the nuclear-weapon establishment is globally supported at the level of perhaps $100 billion per year, we doubt that the level of governmental research on the technical and political means necessary to achieve and maintain a NWFW is at present more than one part in a hundred thousand of this sum.

The technical problems are substantial. Clearly all existing warheads must be identified and destroyed. Uranium-235 could be diluted with natural uranium for use in electric power reactors. The plutonium is a much more miserable problem. The tritium takes care of itself with a half-life of 12.3 years. Another difficult problem is that of guarding against cheating by hiding existing warheads. If we try to live in a NWFW while maintaining nuclear production of electric power, very strict global inspection institutions must be devised. All fissile material would have to be under international control. This would probably require an international institution with more power to interfere in national affairs than now exists.

The know-how for the reconstruction of nuclear weapons would still exist, at least in the countries which now have it. This asymmetry may be difficult to accept for those countries which have never had nuclear weapons. The verification system would need to be strict enough so that any new effort to reproduce nuclear weapons would be detected sufficiently early. The production of the necessary fissile material, starting from scratch, would take time--perhaps years to make a substantial number of weapons--time enough for the rest of the world to respond. But as time goes on, in a NWFW, the scientific and technical know-how will degrade with the disappearance of the nuclear-weapon laboratories. There may be little incentive for such a 'breakout'. If the argument is true today, that nuclear weapons are a negative security asset for the established powers, it is likely to be true tomorrow. And these are the countries in the best position to break out. This should be a sufficient assurance for the present nuclear powers.

The problem is not trivial. But the alternative of trying to live indefinitely with nuclear weapons can only lead to disaster, and therefore is not an alternative. One non-negligible favourable element is the fact that the production of weapon-grade fissile material with present technologies requires very large installations, which are not difficult to detect. Here the problem is considerably easier than is the case for chemical or germ warfare weapons.

The complete elimination of nuclear arms is a necessary goal, but will require a determined effort. One must admit that in the past the process has not received a great deal of support, not even from scientists. What is the reason for this? The reason may be found in the remark of Einstein, that nuclear weapons have changed everything save our way of thinking. But there has never existed a political situation so favourable for actual transfer to a nuclear-weapon-free world as the present. The threat of aggression in Europe and the possibility of war between East and West do not exist any more. The participants of former conflicting blocs have agreed a radical cut in their weapons. Unprecedented steps for verification and inspection have been taken. Olof Palme's notion of East-West 'common security' is now widely accepted, providing a new sense of security in the relationships between the nations.

How much time might the denuclearization process require? As long as the nuclear powers are not convinced of its necessity, it will take forever. If they should become convinced that it is in their interests, it need not take more than five to ten years. Where there is the will, there is the way (maybe). There is no other way. We need the will.

References

1.   "The United Nations and Disarmament 1945-1970",United Nations, 1970, p.11-12.

2.   *Bulletin of the Atomic Scientists,* vol.1, April 1, 1946 and vol.2, July 1, 1946.

3.   A. Gromyko, statement to UN Atomic Energy Commission, 19 July 1946, pp.8-10.

4.   UN document A/RES/S - 10/2.

5.   Statement by Mikhail Gorbachev, 15 January 1986, Novosti Press Agency.

6.   See eg. P.E. Haley "Lessons from Reykjavik", *Nuclear Strategy, Arms Control and the Future,* E. Haley and J. Meritt, eds., Westview Press 1988, pp.245-251.

7.   George Bush, Address to the Nation, 27 September 1991. Presidential Initiative on Nuclear Arms, White House, Office of the Press Secretary.

8.   Mikhail Gorbachev, 4 October 1991, reply to the Bush nuclear initiative.

9.   Scilla Elworthy, "Political Obstacles to a NWFW", *Towards a Secure World in the 21st Century: Annals of Pugwash 1990,* J. Rotblat and F. Blackaby Eds., Taylor and Francis, London 1991, pp.87-97.

10. "The Future of the US-Soviet Nuclear Relationship", Committee on International Security and Arms Control, National Academy of Sciences, Washington D.C. 1991.

11. A.A. Kokoshin, "A Soviet View on Radical Weapons Cuts", *Bulletin of the Atomic Scientists,* March 1988.

PART C

Feasibility of a NWFW

4

Technological Problems of Verification

Theodore Taylor

The focus of this chapter is on technical methods to verify compliance with the rules governing a nuclear-weapon-free world. These procedures are designed to verify the elimination of existing nuclear warheads and stocks of plutonium and highly enriched uranium (HEU) for nuclear explosives, and to reveal illicit nuclear explosives or undisclosed plutonium or HEU, or facilities for their covert production. I have not included verification of elimination of systems that could be used for delivery of nuclear explosives, since practically any vehicle one can think of might be used, under some conditions, to place nuclear explosives on target. Nor have I included non-nuclear components of nuclear explosives unless they could clearly have no purpose other than for making nuclear explosives (for example, assembled devices with all the components needed for a nuclear explosive except the needed special nuclear materials).

Along with many others, I have become convinced that effective technical means for *detecting* unlawful removal of objects or materials from *disclosed* facilities (including containers) exist or can be developed soon. Many of the methods for doing this with very high assurance are in place in national and international nuclear safeguards systems. One can think of very effective ways to fill gaps in this assurance.

I have, therefore, found that the greatest challenges are in the following questions:

*   How can unauthorized diversion of materials or devices from disclosed facilities be *prevented*, as opposed to *detected*, long enough to assure that the diversion does not present a substantial threat? This has to do not only with physical security against theft by non-national organizations, such as terrorists or other criminals, but also with a government that decides, for whatever reasons, to withdraw (perhaps suddenly) from international safeguarding agreements. It also relates to situations where there is a takeover of nuclear facilities by government factions, private enterprises, or revolutionary movements that do not abide by treaties.

*   How can a high assurance be achieved that no significant quantities of nuclear warheads or special nuclear materials have been secretly withheld or produced in undisclosed facilities?

*   What responses to detection of violations (including ones that have led to evident possession, or even actual use, of nuclear weapons) are possible that avoid rapid breakdown of the rest of a NWFW regime?

Technology can help provide answers to these questions. But non-technical actions may add further ways of deterring violations in a NWFW, and help prevent a breakdown of the principal infrastructure related to a NWFW in which significant violations have not yet happened. These are discussed in Chapter 6.

Definitions

Unambiguous definitions of what is forbidden (and, in some cases, what is allowed) in a NWFW are needed for specifying appropriate verification procedures. I have found the following definitions helpful for this purpose.

A *nuclear weapon* is a destructive system that incorporates one or more *nuclear explosives*. This definition excludes weapons that use non-explosive releases of nuclear energy, such as from a nuclear reactor or from radioactive materials, to cause damage.

A *nuclear explosive* is a device that, in less than 10 microseconds, can release at least as much nuclear energy as the chemical energy contained in a mass of chemical high explosive equal to the total weight of the device. This definition, which is somewhat arbitrary, is proposed to distinguish between pulses of nuclear energy that do not create shock waves, and nuclear explosions that create shock waves and release more energy per unit weight than chemical explosives. The definition of a nuclear explosive may be different in the context of a nuclear test ban, where even 'zero yield' (e.g. nuclear yield less than equivalent to one kilogramme of high explosive) nuclear explosions may be prohibited.

This definition excludes nuclear reactors that may release dangerous amounts of radiation following accidental or planned fast excursions, even though the heat energy released may be greater than the energy content of an equivalent mass of high explosive. Small nuclear reactors without shielding, and requiring less than one kilogramme of plutonium or HEU, could be pulsed to deliver high radiation doses out to several hundred metres or so, but I am not aware of their ever having been under serious development.

The total weight of a nuclear explosive is taken to include only those parts of it that are required for it to be armed, fused, detonated, and exploded. It would not, for example, include the weight of re-entry vehicles or guidance systems for missiles.

A *fission explosive* is a nuclear explosive that derives most of its energy from heavy nuclides that are capable of sustaining a fast neutron fission chain reaction. These *special nuclear materials* include uranium of which at least 6 per cent is U-235 or U-233; all isotopes of plutonium; and, possibly, any of several other transuranic nuclides. (Uranium enriched to less than 20 per cent in U-235 is now generally not called special nuclear material, but this rather arbitrary exclusion, I have argued, should be changed). This definition of fission explosives includes ones that are 'boosted' by the release of neutrons from contained mixtures of deuterium and tritium, whose *energy* release is small compared to the total.

The thermonuclear energy released in boosted fission weapons is equivalent to the fusion of the order of grammes of deuterium and tritium (equivalent to several dozen tons of high explosive).

A *thermonuclear explosive* is a nuclear explosive that derives a substantial fraction of its energy directly from thermonuclear reactions.

Although it may be theoretically possible to make nuclear explosives without using any special nuclear (fissionable) materials, this has apparently not yet been achieved. Serious efforts to develop pure fusion explosives light enough to qualify as deliverable explosive weapons have been underway since the late 1950s, but with no announced or strongly suspected successes so far. Inertial confinement approaches to fusion power would make use of very small thermonuclear explosions, but the total weight of the apparatus necessary to create the explosions still remains orders of magnitude greater than the mass of high explosive equivalent to the energy released by the explosions.

Some minimum quantity of special nuclear material is, therefore, required to make any kind of nuclear explosive. This minimum quantity is sometimes called a 'strategic quantity'. However, it is not well defined, on fundamental physical grounds, and it depends on the design and the practical accuracy of fabrication. The minimum actual quantities which have been successfully used are highly classified, and likely to remain so for the foreseeable future. These quantities are much smaller than the 20 kilogrammes of highly enriched uranium or 6 kilogrammes of plutonium that are often cited as needed for making fission explosives, and are approximately the critical masses of metal spheres of the materials at normal metallic density, if surrounded with good neutron reflectors. [1] The critical masses of special nuclear materials vary inversely with the square of their compression over normal density when rapidly assembled by a chemical implosion system. [2] Achievable compressions can be considerable, depending on the skills of the designers and fabricators. Note that the mass that needs to undergo fission to release 1 kiloton of energy is 60 grammes.

Guiding Principles for Technical Verification
of Compliance with Rules Established in a NWFW

Since special nuclear materials are required to make nuclear explosives, my main focus is on techniques to verify that no such materials are accessible for illegal incorporation into nuclear explosives. The non-nuclear components of nuclear explosives can vary considerably with their design, and many or all of them can be useful for other purposes and are widely accessible. I argue that the principal routes to making nuclear explosives inaccessible are the elimination of existing stockpiles and global control of all special nuclear materials and means for their production, to make them unavailable for unauthorized use.

Five steps are essential for these purposes:

1   Disclosure of existing stockpiles of nuclear explosives, military special nuclear materials, and facilities for their production.

2   Disclosure of existing non-military stockpiles of special nuclear materials, and facilities for producing them.

3   Application of the Principle of Containment to all disclosed nuclear explosives, special nuclear materials, and facilities that store or can produce them. According to this principle, all such materials and facilities (including shipping and storage containers) are contained within specified physical boundaries. These boundaries are monitored to assure that there is no undetected, unauthorized removal of materials or devices across them. The boundaries are also designed to inhibit strongly, by appropriate physical security systems, any unauthorized entry, or unauthorized removal of materials or devices. [3]

4   Dismantlement of all existing nuclear explosives (e.g. warheads), and safe and environmentally acceptable permanent disposal of all contained special nuclear materials and non-nuclear components.

5   Use of surveillance systems (including ones that are under national, as well as international control) designed to detect

undisclosed nuclear explosives, special nuclear materials, and facilities for producing them. Provisions would also be made for prompt on-site inspections of facilities suspected of use for such purposes.

Application of these technical principles cannot absolutely guarantee that undisclosed facilities, special nuclear materials, or nuclear explosives, have not been kept secret in violation of the rules of a NWFW. It will, therefore, also be necessary to rely on political and societal actions that not only deter cheating of any kind, but also stimulate people--who find out about cheating, whether within their own government or not--to reveal this to appropriate international authorities with minimum fears of reprisal. This broad category of safeguards, discussed in Chapter 6, should be an integral part of a global system of verification of compliance in a NWFW.

Each of the five technical aspects of such a system is explored in more detail in the following sections.

Disclosure of Existing Military Stockpiles and Facilities

Estimates Related to Military Uses

There are still about 50,000 nuclear explosives owned by the five announced nuclear-weapon states. More than 90 per cent are accounted for by the United States and the Commonwealth of Independent States (CIS). [4] Estimated total quantities of special nuclear materials in these explosives or associated production operations are: highly enriched uranium (HEU, at greater than 90 per cent enrichment in U-235), about 1500 tonnes; plutonium, about 260 tonnes. [5] Of these totals, the estimated quantities actually now in the warheads are: plutonium, 180 tonnes; HEU, 810 tonnes. [5] The considerable uncertainties in these estimates are discussed below.

Nuclear submarine reactors (mostly US) account for a total of about 50 tonnes of HEU. [5] Many submarines of other countries use only low enrichment uranium not suitable for high performance military nuclear explosives. (Actual enrichments and quantities are classified and therefore very uncertain.)

Perhaps several tonnes of HEU and plutonium are also under control of military establishments, for other purposes, such as CIS space power supplies, some low power military reactors, and for military R&D not directly connected with nuclear explosives. [5]

Perhaps several dozen tonnes each of plutonium and HEU are in scrap and other wastes accumulated from military production in the United States since the early 1940s. I have found no official tallies of totals of such US scrap and waste material, but have never been challenged for making this statement informally to a number of experts on the subject. Comparable quantities of similar scrap are probably also in CIS. The total of each in the other announced nuclear-weapon states may add up to a few hundred kilogrammes.

Besides disclosing quantities of nuclear explosives and accessible special nuclear materials, all existing facilities for producing or storing them would have to be disclosed, and verifiably dismantled, or made available for application of containment safeguards. Some military facilities for producing special nuclear materials not to be used in nuclear explosives might be allowed to operate, but only under containment safeguards. An example is uranium enrichment or fuel fabrication for ship propulsion reactors.

The number of physically separate facilities (i.e. buildings, bunkers) that have been or are now used for handling nuclear warheads, or military plutonium or HEU, probably exceeds 1000 (perhaps considerably) in the USA and CIS. At least several hundred more probably exist in the other announced nuclear-weapon states. I have been unable to find any systematic tallies of such facilities. Their locations are often still classified. All of them should be disclosed in a NWFW, and subject to detailed inspection and, where appropriate, containment safeguards. It is credible that data on the locations and status of all such facilities are widely dispersed among different agencies of each of the governments that have military nuclear programmes. I have found no tally of all such separate facilities (e.g. different process buildings, bunkers, missile silos, transport vehicles, etc. within which nuclear warheads or special nuclear materials might be hidden). But it seems clear that the global total number of facilities that should be subject to inspection and, in some cases, application of containment safeguards, must number in the thousands, at least.

Inherent Uncertainties in Military Stockpiles

The above estimates are not accurate disclosures by governments; they have been estimated from some government disclosures in the United States and from some other indicators of total production rates.

Even government people, with complete access to records accounting for nuclear explosives and special nuclear material flows associated with their manufacture, are faced with some *inherent* uncertainties in inventories of special nuclear materials in the warheads, in current process streams or storage, and in wastes. (I assume, I hope correctly, that all governments that have nuclear explosives know *exactly* how many of each type are deployed, in storage, or in transport).

There are no official published data on the accuracy of accounts of total present quantities of U-235 and plutonium (including its isotopic composition) now in the inventories (not including accumulated wastes) associated with military systems. It is credible that these are known in every country to within better than 1 per cent, perhaps much better. Note, however, that 1 per cent uncertainty in the present inventory of military special nuclear materials under US or Russian control corresponds to about 1000 kilogrammes of plutonium or 5000 kilogrammes of highly enriched uranium.

The uncertainties in the total, cumulative production of these materials, and the disposition of solid and liquid retrievable and unretrievable wastes, are much larger. Cumulative quantities of 'materials unaccounted for' (MUFs) in HEU and plutonium production, processing, and fabrication streams in the United States have been reported as several tens of tonnes of each. These estimates apply to imbalances in material accounting systems. The unaccounted for materials are presumed to be 'lost' in larger than measured production of wastes. Directly estimated cumulative, non-retrievable quantities of waste plutonium have been published by the US Department of Energy at about 7000 kilogrammes. This is the estimated quantity of waste plutonium earmarked for permanent disposal at the Waste Isolation Pilot Project (WIPP) site in southeastern New Mexico.

In short, official, actual uncertainties in the disposition of military special nuclear materials produced in the United States correspond to several tens of thousands of kilogrammes. Similar, or perhaps significantly larger absolute uncertainties probably apply in CIS, and proportionately, to the much smaller quantities in the United Kingdom, France, and China.

These inherent uncertainties could be directly used or manipulated to act as 'covers' for discrepancies in disclosed special nuclear material accounts that actually correspond to illegal diversion of substantial quantities.

Actual uncertainties in accessible existing quantities of special nuclear materials, as they would apply to verification authorities, could be much larger than the inherent uncertainties. One reason is that disclosures of past production and current stockpiles would be difficult to verify to better than perhaps 20 per cent without access to detailed records that are now secret. Disclosure of these records might be falsified.

Disclosure of Existing Non-Military Stockpiles of Special Nuclear Materials and Facilities for Their Production

By the end of 1992 some 425 nuclear power plants in 31 countries will have produced an estimated total of 880 tonnes of plutonium. [5] This is about three times more than the world's total of military plutonium. An estimated 670 tonnes of the non-military plutonium is in stored spent fuel awaiting ultimate disposition. Another 100 tonnes of plutonium are in the operating reactor cores, having not yet been removed in spent fuel.

An estimated total of 116 tonnes of plutonium have been chemically separated from power reactor spent fuel. Of this about 65 tonnes are estimated to be in storage, 37 tonnes in fast reactor fuel cycles, and 13 in thermal reactor fuel cycles of mixed oxides.[5]

Highly enriched uranium is much less abundant in non-military nuclear systems than plutonium. Most of this HEU is used in research and test reactors, or critical facilities that do not produce significant power. The estimated total quantity of HEU in the world's non-military inventories is around 35 tonnes. [5] Although much smaller than the amount of plutonium associated with civilian nuclear applications, this HEU remains very important to anyone concerned about its illicit use in nuclear weapons. Even the (estimated) 25 kilogrammes of HEU in fuel for Iraq's research reactors has caused enough concern to be at least part of the reason for bombing the largest of these reactors by Israel in 1981, and bombing of Iraqi nuclear facilities by the Allied Coalition during the Gulf War.

The nuclear fuel cycles that support present non-military uses of nuclear energy include uranium mines and uranium processing operations, uranium enrichment (mostly enrichment in U-235 to 3-4 per cent), fuel fabrication, reactors, and facilities for storage of fresh and spent fuel, mostly at the reactor sites.

The most critical of the fuel cycle facilities, up to the stage of exposure of the fuel to neutrons in the reactors, are the enrichment plants, which are potentially capable of producing highly enriched uranium. The technologies for this process have been proliferating since the early very large energy-consuming gaseous diffusion plants were built in the five announced nuclear-weapon states. Gas centrifuge enrichment plants are now the predominant technology of choice, but other methods continue to be under intensive development in several countries.

With few (but important) exceptions, the locations and many operating characteristics of non-military nuclear facilities are publicly disclosed, especially by the International Atomic Energy Agency (IAEA), Euratom, and various other energy agencies and nuclear energy trade organizations.

The inherent uncertainties in the quantities of plutonium produced in nuclear power plants are at least as great, in terms of percentages of totals, as the inherent uncertainties in military production. Since most of the non-military plutonium is in spent fuel, the quantities must be inferred from calculations and some spot checks using non-destructive and destructive analysis. The total uncertainty in the world's present inventory of non-military plutonium may correspond to more than 100,000 kilogrammes. This would correspond to about 10 per cent of the estimated total.

Application of the Principle
of Containment to Nuclear Facilities

The ultimate objectives of verification procedures in a NWFW will be to assure that no nuclear warheads, undisclosed nuclear materials (including uranium and plutonium of all isotopic compositions), or undisclosed facilities for their production exist, and that there is no unauthorized removal of materials or equipment from any disclosed facilities.

The principal function of containment-type safeguards is to achieve the last of these objectives. This function has two parts: prompt detection of any attempt to remove materials or objects from authorized locations or containers, and physical interference with such attempts. Safeguard systems with this function would be set up at all facilities for handling of nuclear materials for peaceful purposes (e.g. all components of civilian nuclear fuel cycles) or for authorized military purposes (such as all components of fuel cycles for naval nuclear propulsion systems).

Many of the specific technical requirements for such containment type safeguards for *detection* of violations can be met by procedures and equipment now used by the IAEA, but there is still much room for improvement. [6]

These types of safeguards, however, are not necessarily designed to interfere physically with theft by outsiders or covert removal of materials by facility employees or others authorized to be in the facilities. The IAEA does not have specific authority to provide physical security; this is left to authorities specified by the government that owns the safeguarded facilities. But detailed guidelines for physical security have been developed and published by the IAEA, to help governments in setting up their own nuclear security systems. [6]

Governments that have nuclear weapons have developed and put in place physical security systems that go considerably beyond those recommended by the IAEA. Detailed information regarding these systems tends to be classified, however, to make it harder for the systems to be defeated. This makes it virtually impossible for people without access to this information to assess the physical security systems now in place.

The number of places that would be subject to containment type safeguards, and the costs and effectiveness of those safeguards, will obviously depend on how rapidly military nuclear systems (including not only nuclear weapons, but other military applications) are phased out, or which will remain when a NWFW is achieved, and on the future of non-military uses of nuclear energy. The range of possible future numbers of such places is huge--from practically none if all military uses of nuclear energy are banned and nuclear power is rapidly displaced by renewable energy sources, to many thousands if nuclear power grows as rapidly as some predict. One possibility is that nuclear power is phased out in several decades, but some other applications of nuclear energy, such as for medical applications or for exploration in deep space, will flourish.

Elimination of Nuclear Warheads

How would nuclear warheads be disposed of? (The INF and START Treaties do not call for destruction of warheads; they are to be returned to the owner countries without restriction).

Verified elimination of nuclear warheads under future treaties or bilateral arrangements short of formal treaties has been a subject of several studies. One that was carried out as part of a joint project of the Federation of American Scientists and the Soviet Committee of Scientists for Peace concluded that nuclear warheads can be verifiably destroyed after they have been identified and made available for destruction, without revealing secret information about their design. [7] The process for doing this is an application of the Principle of Containment. All steps in the process are carried out within specified boundaries that are monitored to ensure detection of any unauthorized removal of warheads or their components, especially highly enriched uranium or plutonium, from these boundaries. Any plutonium or uranium removed from the dismantlement facility through authorized channels is immediately placed under full International Atomic Energy Agency safeguards until ultimate permanent disposal of the materials or their residue after cycling through nuclear power systems.

This process is summarized here. The first step is the tagging and sealing of warheads, or containers into which they have been placed, at deployment or storage sites, in the presence of inspectors. The tags, which cannot be changed without revealing tampering, serve as unique identifiers of each warhead or container. The function of seals is to reveal if warheads or their containers have been opened, for substitution of fake warheads or other objects for the original contents, before they are placed in contained storage at a warhead dismantlement facility in the owner country. Batches of specified numbers of containers for several different types of warheads are first examined externally by inspectors to ensure that tags and seals have not been tampered with. Containers for each type of warhead are also 'fingerprinted' by inspectors, without opening the containers. This is done by external active or passive radiation probes that will ensure that the contents of containers of warheads of a particular type are the same, but without revealing any secret information about the warheads. This ensures that any substitution of fake for real warheads, before they are tagged and sealed, would have to be made for *all* the warheads of a particular type.

All the warheads in each batch of mixed containers are then dismantled by nationals of the owner country, inside an enclosure that is subject to the containment principle, but not to inspection during the dismantlement process. The non-nuclear components are destroyed by nationals of the owner country, inside an adjoining enclosure.

The contained fissile materials (highly enriched uranium and plutonium) in the entire batch are separately mixed, without inspectors present, and made available for accurate measurements, by inspectors, of their total mass. This will not reveal the quantities of these materials in any particular type of warhead. These measurements provide the initial basis for detailed accounting for the plutonium and highly enriched uranium as they flow through subsequent steps. Depending on treaty specifications, any contained tritium is either returned to the owner country (to be used to replenish decayed tritium in other warheads not yet subject to elimination, or for use in future fusion reactors) or stored in a contained area until most of it has decayed with its 12.3 year half-life. In either case, measurements by inspectors of the quantities of tritium removed from the warheads would not be required, since tritium quantities associated even with a batch of several types of warheads may remain secret.

All objects and bulk materials removed from the dismantlement facility are probed with external neutron sources to assure that they contain no fissile materials. Any residues from the destruction of the non-nuclear components of the warheads that are shipped from the dismantlement site for ultimate disposal are also inspected with external probes.

The highly enriched uranium removed from the warheads can

be rendered incapable of sustaining an explosive chain reaction by diluting it with natural or depleted uranium. This diluted material, at an enrichment of about 3 per cent, could then be used as feed material for fuel for nuclear power plants. This material would be kept under IAEA safeguards until ultimate disposal of spent fuel from the reactors in which it is used. The approximately 1500 tonnes of HEU associated with the world's present nuclear warheads could provide fuel for the world's present power reactors for about 5 years. The is derived as follows: installed world nuclear electric power is about 400,000 MW(e), most of which uses low enrichment uranium. Fueling rates are typically about 25 tonnes of heavy metal per year per 1000 MW(e), at an average enrichment of about 3 per cent. This corresponds to about 10,000 tonnes of low enrichment uranium per year, containing about 300 tonnes of uranium-235. It would, therefore, take about 5 years for the world's nuclear power plants to consume all the uranium-235 associated with the world's nuclear warheads. This could save around $15 billion in future nuclear fuel costs, if rates of production of nuclear power continue at least at present levels for at least a few years. The real value of low enrichment uranium reflects the cost of mining new uranium feedstock for uranium enrichment plants, the cost of enrichment, and the character of the world market for uranium fuel. All of these are uncertain, especially for a future time, when excess uranium feedstock or uranium enrichment capacity may exist, suppressing the price that might be paid for uranium enriched by adding HEU extracted from warheads.

If, for whatever reasons, world nuclear power production declines sharply during or soon after a period of deep reductions in numbers of nuclear warheads, the highly enriched uranium could be diluted with depleted uranium, to bring its enrichment down close to that of natural uranium, for safe disposal in a geological formation, or, perhaps, for rapid dilution in the ocean. 1500 tonnes of HEU is enough to double the uranium-235 concentration of about 200,000 tonnes of natural uranium. Reported seawater concentrations of uranium vary by at least an order of magnitude, from a high of several parts per billion. [8] Thus, dilution of the HEU from the world's nuclear warheads to a concentration of uranium-235 comparable to that in the ocean would require of the order of a million cubic kilometres of seawater, roughly 1/1000 the volume of the world's oceans. It is not obvious that ocean dumping of the diluted HEU would not cause significant ecological effects.

The plutonium extracted from nuclear warheads cannot be isotopically diluted to render it incapable of sustaining a fast chain reaction, since all plutonium isotopes can do so. The critical masses of metallic spheres of any of the isotopes of plutonium are finite, unlike the situation for uranium isotopes. For Pu-240, for example, the critical mass of a bare sphere is about 50 kilogrammes, nearly the same as for HEU. [9] If used to supplement uranium-235 in nuclear power plant fuel, it would, therefore, remain usable in nuclear warheads if extracted from any *chemical* dilutants. This would also require widescale and expensive modification of fuel fabrication facilities now used for making uranium fuel. These facilities, and the transport links between them, would then be exposed to possible diversion or outright theft of plutonium that is relatively easy to extract for use in nuclear explosives, compared with isotope enrichment of natural or other low enrichment uranium to produce weapons-grade uranium-235, or extraction of plutonium from spent fuel that is extremely radioactive.

An alternative would be to dispose of the plutonium directly, without using it as fuel. Since no satisfactory method for ultimate disposal of the transuranic elements and fission products in spent fuel has yet been proven, the plutonium from warheads would have to be stored, probably in facilities that are under international authority, and subject to the containment principle and high levels of physical security, until such a method has been developed and is in routine use. Before placement in storage, however, the plutonium should be mixed with appropriate materials to assure that the mixture cannot, in any large quantity, sustain any type of fission chain reaction. These materials should have sufficient concentrations of non-fissioning nuclei that absorb neutrons at all energies emitted at fission, or at very low energies after slowing down in the mixture or any surrounding materials. Candidates are strong thermal neutron absorbers, such as cadmium or boron, along with other nuclei, such as tungsten, that have neutron capture cross sections, at several MeV, that are of the same order as the fission cross section of plutonium-239. The types and concentrations of the added materials should be such that neutron capture is sufficiently more likely than fission for an infinite mass of the mixture to remain sub-critical. Preliminary estimates indicate that the added materials needed to meet this criterion could have roughly the same total mass as the plutonium.

Possibilities for ultimate disposal of the plutonium include use as reactor fuel (which produces fission products and other actinides that would have to be safely disposed of). Warhead plutonium could be used for making mixed oxide fuel for light water reactors, or for plutonium fast breeder fuels. It could also be used in specially designed 'plutonium burner' reactors not containing any fertile material (e.g. U-238 or Th-232). Deep geological burial after considerable dilution has been the preferred method for disposal of nuclear wastes by both government and industrial nuclear establishments, but continues to meet considerable public resistance worldwide. Another method is fission and then transmutation of fission products to stable radionuclides, using excess neutrons from breeder reactors or from multiplying systems driven by neutrons from high energy particle accelerators. [10] A final suggestion is fail-safe disposal in space, perhaps into the sun, of the plutonium and any associated other radioactive wastes in packages that are indestructible under any conceivable accident conditions. [11]

All nuclear material products of the warhead dismantlement process would have to be kept under stringent international safeguards, such as extensions of those now set up and maintained by IAEA, until the uranium and plutonium have been permanently disposed of by methods that would make retrieval very difficult. Facilities for storage of warheads awaiting dismantlement, or plutonium awaiting final disposal would also need to be securely guarded against theft or forces trying to take over control of the facilities. This function might be appropriate for a UN security force with much greater related authority than is now given to the IAEA, which plays no direct role in maintaining physical security of nuclear materials under its safeguards. These are designed to *detect*, rather than *prevent* diversion of the materials to destructive purposes.

Verifying an International Ban on Production of Fissile Materials and Tritium for Nuclear Weapons

Actual demonstration of the above or similar procedures

would not necessarily require a treaty calling for the elimination of large numbers of nuclear warheads. But such a treaty, if it calls for elimination of the contained fissile materials for warheads, would only make sense if a ban on further production of fissile materials for warheads were also in force. Verifying such a treaty between acknowledged nuclear-weapon states has been extensively studied. [12] The conclusions are that such verification can be achieved with high assurance, provided that all the existing military plutonium production reactors are disclosed and shut down, and existing uranium enrichment plants that produce high enrichment materials suitable for nuclear warheads are either shut down or placed under bilateral, multilateral, or international safeguards to assure they do not produce material for nuclear warheads. Production of limited quantities of highly enriched uranium might be allowed, for some specified time, to supply fuel for nuclear propulsion of military surface ships or submarines. Verifying that this material is not secretly diverted to use in nuclear explosives is problematical, however. Although shipments of highly enriched uranium from enrichment plants to submarine fuel fabrication plants might be in tagged and sealed containers subject to inspection, diversion safeguards applied to the plants themselves, or to the submarines requiring refueling, would be difficult without revealing information that is now secret.

A ban on production of fissile materials for nuclear explosives might extend to a ban on production of tritium for weapons. Since the half-life of tritium is 12.3 years, tritium in warhead stockpiles would decay at a rate of about 5.6 per cent per year. If agreements were made to eliminate nuclear warheads at a rate greater than 5.6 per cent per year, and extracted tritium were returned to the owner country, remaining warheads not slated for elimination could, on the average, be replenished with tritium as needed. [13]

Verifying a cut-off in production of fissile materials for nuclear weapons focuses on the intended end use of the materials. All present announced nuclear-weapon states have nuclear power plants, some of which are dual-purpose plants for producing electric power as well as plutonium for weapons. The objective of IAEA safeguards, applied to civilian nuclear reactor, uranium enrichment plants, and other parts of nuclear fuel cycles, is to detect diversion of plutonium or uranium from peaceful to military use. They do not prevent stockpiling of these materials, such as plutonium separated from spent fuel for recycling, or plutonium contained in stored spent fuel. But they are designed to keep the materials under safeguards until their final, irretrievable disposal.

Thus, in effect, verification of a cut-off in production of fissile materials for nuclear warheads would require disclosure of all facilities capable of producing them, and placement of all these facilities under diversion safeguards until any contained fissile materials are not practically retrievable.

Verification of a cut-off in tritium production by disclosed nuclear reactors or particle accelerators would require development of new techniques, since present diversion safeguards apply only to uranium and plutonium.

The Problem of Secret Stockpiles of Nuclear Explosives or Special Nuclear Materials, or Facilities for Producing Them

There are various possibilities for secret accumulation of nuclear explosives or the key materials needed to make them, in direct violation of rules related to a NWFW. Among these are:

Secret storage of some of the items produced or otherwise acquired before a NWFW regime is in force or during the initial disclosure stages of the new regime. These might include complete nuclear explosives; fabricated special nuclear materials suitable for insertion into the non-nuclear parts of nuclear explosives; nuclear explosive assemblies without contained special nuclear materials; or bulk stockpiles of special nuclear materials.

Lack of disclosure of some existing facilities for producing and fabricating special nuclear materials or complete assemblies, in the initial stages of implementing a NWFW regime.

Secret construction and operation of undisclosed facilities for making nuclear explosives, including the needed special nuclear material, after a NWFW regime is in force.

Secret transfers of complete nuclear explosives, complete

assemblies of their non-nuclear components, or bulk special nuclear materials, from a country or non-national organization that has violated or has not been a party to a NWFW regime.

It is conceivable that such actions might be taken within a country without the knowledge of the government in power at the time when the terms for a NWFW are negotiated. The actions might have been taken by a previous government or faction, keeping them secret from subsequent governments but not from government factions or other groups without government authority after an NWFW regime is in force. They might also proceed during a NWFW regime, but without the knowledge of the government.

Detection of such violations by technical means cannot be absolutely guaranteed by any conceivable verification system. Global surveillance, including techniques now used for national intelligence activities, along with guaranteed rights of on-site inspection of suspected hiding places can help. The effectiveness of such measures could be enhanced by global encouragement of whistle-blowers, in a world in which a global taboo against any violations of the NWFW rules are widely and frequently articulated.

A possible framework for all verification of compliance with the rules in a NWFW is global abolition of any nuclear secrecy, perhaps eventually extended to abolition of any secrecy related to military matters. Essentially by definition, secrecy would be required to violate rules for disclosure of nuclear warheads and materials in a NWFW. Preventing such secrecy would appear easier to accomplish in a world in which the secrecy itself is forbidden than one in which secret nuclear activities are allowed.[14]

References

1. See, for example, H.C. Paxton, "Los Alamos Critical Mass Data", LAMS 3067, Los Alamos National Laboratory, May 1964.

2. See, for example, Robert Serber and Richard Rhodes, *The Los Alamos Primer*, University of California Press, 1992, p.27.

3.   Mason Willrich and Theodore B. Taylor, *Nuclear Theft: Risks and Safeguards*, Ballinger, 1974, pp.159-162.

4.   Robert B. Norris and William M. Arkin, "Nuclear Notebook", *Bulletin of the Atomic Scientists*, July/August 1991.

5.   David Albright, Frank Berkhout, and William Walker, *World Inventory of Plutonium and Highly Enriched Uranium*, (to be published).

6.   Lawrence Scheinman, "The International Atomic Energy Agency and World Nuclear Order", *Resources for the Future*, Washington D.C., 1988, Chapters 5 and 8.

7.   Theodore B. Taylor, "Verified Elimination of Nuclear Warheads", *Science and Global Security*, Vol.1, Nos. 1-2, Gordon and Breach 1989, pp.1-26; and Theodore B. Taylor and Lev. P. Feoktistov, "Verified Elimination of Nuclear Materials and Disposition of Contained Nuclear Materials" in *Verification: Monitoring Disarmament*, F. Calogero, M.L. Goldberger, S. Kapitza, eds., a Pugwash Monograph, Westview Press, 1991.

8.   Handbook of Chemistry and Physics, 1981-82, p. F-166.

9.   J. Carson Mark, private communication.

10.   G.P. Lawrence, R.A. Jameson, S.O. Schriber, "Accelerator Technology for Los Alamos Nuclear-Waste Transmutation and Energy-Production Concept", *Los Alamos National Laboratory LA-UR-91-2797*.

11.   Theodore Taylor (work in progress, to be published).

12.   See, for example, Lawrence Scheinman and Irakli Gverdziteli, "Verifying a Production Cutoff for Nuclear Explosive Material: Strategies for Verification and the Role of the IAEA", Chapter 6 of Pugwash Monograph (ref.7)

13.   See, for example, J. Carson Mark et al., "The Tritium Factor as a Forcing Function in Nuclear Arms Reduction Talks", *Science*, Vol.241, 2 September 1988, pp.1166-1169.

14.   For extensive analysis of the risks and pervasiveness of secrecy see Sissela Bok, *Lying*, Pantheon Books, 1978, and *Secrets*, Pantheon Books, 1983.

5

The Breakout Problem

Marvin Miller and Jack Ruina

Introduction

A key factor in assessing the stability and therefore the feasibility of a NWFW is the concern about 'breakout': the prospect that one or more nations openly or clandestinely develop a nuclear-weapon capability after having accepted a non-nuclear-weapon status.

In a world of sovereign nation-states, concern about breakout would lead to many nations maintaining a state of readiness that, in turn, would add to anxiety about the breakout potential of others. Unless we reach and have confidence in the continuation of an unprecedented state of tranquillity among nations, with very strict controls on *all* weaponry, breakout fears might well lead to much greater instability than we now have and the very purpose of having a NWFW would be negated. That is, if hostile relationships develop in a NWFW, a nuclear arms race might develop that would be both more intensive and more likely to lead to nuclear use than if nuclear stockpiles were maintained at minimum levels.

We have experienced concern about breakout in the past; it was particularly evident during the negotiations of the Limited Test Ban Treaty of 1963. To get internal acceptance of the Treaty,

President Kennedy had to agree to maintain a US state of readiness to resume atmospheric testing on very short notice. The military significance of one party or the other having a headstart in the resumption of testing when both the USA and the Soviet Union already had hundreds of tests seemed very small; nevertheless, the USA spent hundreds of millions of dollars for many years to maintain its readiness to resume testing.

A technical assessment of the breakout problem depends critically on assumptions about the restrictions imposed and accepted on national activities in a NWFW, the adequacy of verification of such restricted activities, and, of course, on the technological capability of the potential breakout state.

These issues apply differently to different nations. In this regard it is important to distinguish between different categories of nations, such as the current declared nuclear-weapon states (USA, Russia, UK, France, China), the undeclared weapon states (Israel, India and Pakistan), the advanced industrial non-nuclear states (e.g., Germany, Sweden, and Japan); and the less industrialized non-nuclear states, such as Iraq, Iran and North Korea which seem to have been pursuing nuclear weapons technology to some degree.

The technical problem of breakout will be considered in two parts: (1) designing and producing nuclear weapons assuming weapons-usable fissionable material is in hand, and (2) producing weapons-usable fissionable material.

Developing Nuclear Weapons

For industrial states, designing and fabricating nuclear weapons at this point in time would be far less challenging and less costly than it was for the existing nuclear powers when they developed their nuclear weapons more than thirty years ago. Any nation can now take advantage of the vast amount of open technical literature relevant to nuclear weaponry and can purchase materials, instruments, precision tools and computers that are beyond what was painstakingly acquired by the early developers of nuclear weapons. In addition, there are now many people worldwide whose services can be purchased, and who are trained and experienced in various aspects of nuclear science and technology.

We are not concerned here with the fabrication of a crude nuclear 'device' intended as a terror weapon. Such a device would probably be unsafe to handle and have a low and unpredictable yield. If a sufficient amount of fissile material is available, producing a terrorist weapon is obviously a much simpler task than generating a real weapons programme. We are concerned here about programmes to produce weapons in such quantity and quality as to be considered militarily useful in combat.

Simple Fission Weapons

In this category we include weapons similar to the designs of the first US weapons: the gun type that was dropped on Hiroshima without ever having been tested, and the implosion type dropped on Nagasaki that had been tested earlier in New Mexico.

A gun device is based on the principle that a supercritical amount of fissile material can be assembled by joining two subcritical masses. However, only enriched uranium can be used to fabricate this type of weapon, since the neutron emission from plutonium would inevitably cause 'pre-initiation' in this design.

A gun device has one major advantage: it is relatively simple and one can have a high degree of confidence of it working without testing, as did the USA in the design of the Hiroshima bomb. Its major disadvantage is that it is relatively inefficient in its use of uranium. Probably very few, if any, nuclear weapons of this design remain in the stockpiles of the nuclear powers.

An implosion device is based on the principle that the critical mass of fissile material varies inversely with the square of the density of the material, so that by applying sufficient compression a subcritical mass of fissile material can be made supercritical. In its simplest form, a solid sphere of a sufficient amount of fissile material is compressed by the 'implosion' of a surrounding chemical high explosive thereby increasing its density by perhaps a factor of two or more to bring it to a supercritical state. In this configuration the rate at which the assembly goes critical can be made much more rapid than in a gun device so that plutonium, as well as enriched uranium, can be used as the fissile material. This design can be made much more efficient in its use of fissile material, and there is much greater potential to increase substantially the yield-to-weight ratio of the total assembly.

The first US bombs were designed at Los Alamos in the period 1943-45. It took two years and the efforts of about one thousand scientists and engineers. In addition, there were Herculean efforts involving hundreds of scientists and engineers and approximately 100,000 construction workers to design and build the facilities to produce highly-enriched uranium and high-quality plutonium.

Both the Hiroshima and Nagasaki bombs weighed about 5000 kg. The Hiroshima bomb (a gun device) used about 50 kg of U-235 in the form of uranium metal enriched to have about 80 per cent U-235. Somewhat less than 1 kg of U-235 actually fissioned to provide the approximately 15 kilotons of explosive yield; thus the efficiency in the use of the fissile material was less than 2 per cent.

In contrast, the Nagasaki bomb (an implosion device) used only about 6 kg of plutonium metal in the form of a solid sphere. The weapon had a slightly higher yield than the Hiroshima bomb (20 kt) so that about 1 kg of plutonium was fissioned in the explosion. The efficiency here was therefore about 15 per cent.

Estimates of the effort required for a country with no prior nuclear weapon experience to duplicate the US achievement of those years are necessarily imprecise. Carson Mark [1] estimates that at least one year would be needed to design, fabricate and assemble a weapon. This assumes "*a fairly large and competent staff with diverse experience and capabilities*" which is well supported, as we assume a serious nuclear weapons effort would be. The number of scientists and engineers required would probably be in the order of one hundred. This does not include the personnel required to develop and implement the processes required to produce significant quantities of plutonium and/or weapons-grade uranium--an effort that might require thousands of professionals.

Plutonium: Weapons-Grade and Reactor-Grade

The plutonium isotope of mass 239 is the preferred plutonium isotope for weapons. However, in the plutonium production process other isotopes, particularly plutonium-240, are unavoidably produced. The neutrons emitted from the spontaneous fission of plutonium-240 can initiate a chain reaction before the time designed for optimal yield, resulting in both poorer and more uncertain performance. This effect can be minimized by use of 'weapons-grade' plutonium (produced in so-called production reactors) having over 93 per cent plutonium-239 and only about 6 per cent plutonium-240 rather than 'reactor-grade' plutonium (normally produced in power reactors) which may consist of about 55 per cent plutonium-239 and about 25 per cent plutonium-240. Nevertheless, reactor-grade plutonium is usable for even simple fission weapons and has only a slightly higher critical mass than weapons-grade plutonium. For example, if reactor-grade plutonium were used in the Nagasaki implosion device, the expected yield would have been of the order of one kiloton rather than the 20 kilotons actually realized by using weapons-grade plutonium.

The performance penalty in using reactor-grade rather than weapons-grade plutonium decreases and can be made quite small for weapons using more advanced implosion techniques that involve a very rapid rate at which the assembly goes critical, and for boosted fission weapons. Thus, in terms of weapons performance the use of reactor-grade plutonium would mainly be a problem for less advanced non-nuclear states without access to advanced designs. [2]

But it should be noted that reactor-grade plutonium, containing a much larger fraction of the less stable isotopes of plutonium, is substantially more hazardous to work with than weapons-grade plutonium, which in turn is considered a far more hazardous material than uranium. All existing nuclear-weapon states utilize weapons-grade plutonium as much to minimize the radiation exposure to personnel involved in weapons fabrication and field operations (particularly on submarines) as it is to optimize performance.

More Advanced Designs

It is reasonable to assume that the arsenals of both the declared and undeclared nuclear-weapon states no longer contain any Nagasaki or Hiroshima-type bomb designs. Advances in fission-weapon design, involving the use of, e.g., levitation, hollow rather than solid spherical cores, and devices to provide precise timing of the initiation of the chain reaction, have made possible great improvements in fission weapons performance. Also, in advanced designs, reactor-grade plutonium can be used effectively in bomb fabrication with the difficulties mentioned in using this material.

Gun weapons could also be made to have much better performance than the Hiroshima bomb. By using weapons-grade uranium and efficient (non-uranium) tamper/reflectors they can be made light enough to be deliverable by missiles and also artillery.

Designing weapons based on more advanced techniques adds some risk in the development programme, and requires more laboratory and theoretical preparatory work, but is not beyond the capability of even moderately advanced industrial states. For example, there is evidence that Iraq was working on more advanced bomb designs.

Beyond this are boosted and multi-stage thermonuclear devices. Boosted weapons include a small amount of a deuterium/tritium mixture that 'ignites' in a thermonuclear reaction and releases a large quantity of neutrons when raised to a sufficiently high temperature by the fission reaction. The rapid addition of high energy neutrons 'boosts' the chain reaction substantially, increasing the efficiency of the nuclear explosion. However, the thermonuclear reaction by itself adds relatively little to the total yield.

Thermonuclear nuclear bombs involve fusion of hydrogen isotopes which is triggered by a relatively small fission explosion. In a true multi-stage weapon, fusion usually provides a substantial fraction of the total yield of the explosion. All the current declared nuclear powers have developed boosted weapons and thermonuclear weapons for their stockpiles.

Although the basic concepts involved in boosted and thermonuclear weapons are well-known, these represent a major step in technology and are well beyond the initial capability of all countries, except those with prior weapons design and test experience, or those with access to design and test data and who also have sufficiently advanced technology to understand and use these data.

Testing and Readiness

Simple fission weapons can be designed and produced with

confidence after only 'zero-yield' tests. Prototypes of weapons can be tested in their final design configuration with all their components in place but using only a fraction of the necessary quantity of fissile material, so that only a very small amount of nuclear energy is released. In this way, all components of a weapon can be tested to see how well they work when integrated. By increasing the released radiation and comparing it with calculated values, understanding of the nuclear processes involved can be confirmed. A great deal of nuclear weapons expertise can be developed this way, without large and observable testing of nuclear devices. [3]

Full yield tests would of course provide real design confirmation but are not necessary for most applications of simple fission weapons where some uncertainty in yield is tolerable.

However, ignition and burning of thermonuclear fuels adds a level of complexity to nuclear weapons design. Despite sophisticated computer simulation now possible, it would be quite risky for any nation to embark on a programme of *producing* boosted or thermonuclear weapons without at least some testing at substantial yields to measure and confirm the expected thermonuclear reactions under realistic conditions. [4] We can assume that such tests would, with high probability, be detected and identified as such.

But it is not necessary for advanced industrial states to have a large number of tests, or take a great deal of time to progress from simple fission weapons to boosted weapons and on to thermonuclear weapons. Forty years ago the Soviets required only three fission explosions before testing a thermonuclear device. Somewhat later, China exploded a thermonuclear device after only a few nuclear tests. It is quite conceivable that an advanced industrial state, even without prior weapons experience, would test a prototype of a boosted weapon or a thermonuclear weapon in its first real nuclear test and be prepared to produce such weapons soon thereafter. Nations experienced with thermonuclear weapons can forgo any tests if enough 'institutional memory' of the design and production of such weapons remains.

Facilities

Any nation can go a long way in developing indigenous

expertise in weapons-related scientific disciplines without having an explicit weapons programme. However, the development of nuclear weapons would require a well-organized and structured programme, but which can in principle be carried out covertly in laboratory facilities. Zero-yield testing can also be carried out without having observable and identifiable indicators.

The existence of operating facilities for the production of components and the assembly of nuclear weapons would be harder to keep secret for long periods of time, but we can have no assurance that such facilities can be detected and identified as such without quite intrusive inspection procedures.

Production of Weapons-Usable Fissionable Materials

Our basic assumption is that the use of weapons-usable nuclear materials, particularly plutonium, as well as the facilities that produce such materials for peaceful nuclear activities, primarily power generation, will be under strict international control. Some people would go further to argue that any use of plutonium in nuclear fuel cycles should be eliminated. The counter argument is that concern about the consequences of greenhouse warming will inhibit the burning of fossil fuels, particularly coal, so that nuclear power will inevitably play a major role in energy supply, and that this implies the use of plutonium breeder reactors.

For example, if nuclear power-generated electricity were used to displace 25 per cent of *current* fossil fuel use--including both fossil-generated electricity and production of synthetic gasoline via hydrogen generation by electrolysis of water--the required nuclear capacity would be approximately 3000 GWe. This compares to current nuclear capacity of about 300 GWe. If this capacity were to be supplied by light water reactors operating on a once-through fuel cycle, it could be sustained for about 50 years using current OECD/IAEA estimates of the terrestrial uranium resource base (24 million tonnes, recoverable at a price of $130/kg U or less, a large fraction of which are speculative, undiscovered resources). Thus, to have nuclear contributions of the order of 3000 GWe which can be sustained for hundreds of years or more, one needs breeder reactors. However, this implies very large flows of plutonium or uranium-233. For example, the plutonium throughput of a conventional 1 GWe fast breeder reactor is of the order of several tonnes per year, so that plutonium flows of the order of several thousand tonnes of plutonium per year would be required if an appreciable fraction of the assumed 3000 GWe nuclear capacity came from plutonium breeder reactors. Comparing this with the several kilogrammes of plutonium required to make a nuclear weapon illustrates the severe requirements placed on the international control regime.

On the other hand, critics of nuclear power make the case that in an energy-efficient world, renewable sources in various forms could provide for a substantial fraction of energy end-uses; hence, nuclear power need play, at most, only a minor role, and therefore its use can be restricted to once-through fuel cycles using low-enriched uranium. While inefficient in the use of uranium, such fuel cycles are much more 'proliferation-resistant' than plutonium breeders. Moreover, if more nuclear power is needed, it may be possible to 'mine' economically the large uranium resource in seawater, and thus considerably increase the potential nuclear contribution using once-through fuel cycles.

We do not pursue this idea here. Our basic point is that having any dangerous materials and facilities under national ownership and control is incompatible with a stable NWFW. Perhaps optimistically, we assume that the international control of such materials and facilities could be managed so as to eliminate essentially the risk of diversion of such materials, and also minimize the risk of overt seizure by a nation state. Under these conditions, a country wishing to break out in a militarily meaningful way would have to build clandestine facilities to produce plutonium and/or high-enriched uranium, and possibly fusion materials such as tritium.

Thus, it can be assumed that the major obstacle to breakout for all states will be the production of significant amounts of weapons-usable materials without detection. Both plutonium and tritium for weapons are conventionally made in production reactors, and can be separated by well-known chemical processes. Enriched uranium for weapons and reactor fuel can now be produced by a variety of technologies.

A comprehensive open-literature assessment of the resource requirements for building plutonium production reactors and centrifuge enrichment plants, as well as considerations relevant to the detection of such facilities, was prepared in 1976 for the US Office of Technology Assessment by Science Applications International (SAI).[5] This study is still useful, but more for its qualitative insight than the quantitative estimates of costs, time and personnel requirements. The reason for this is that various country-specific factors which could significantly affect the given estimates are not accounted for. These include: the relative amount of imported materials and equipment required, the need to create new basic industrial processes, transport routes, and service capabilities, and the level of secrecy and security deemed necessary.

The main limitation of the SAI report is in the area of uranium enrichment. In particular, events over the past ten years have demonstrated that, under current conditions, potential proliferators can build small gaseous diffusion plants (Argentina) and large electromagnetic isotope separation (EMIS) facilities (Iraq) in a clandestine manner. Both of these technologies are mentioned in the SAI report, but were not considered to be attractive for practical implementation in the near term. On the contrary, the experience in Iraq demonstrated that although the EMIS process is highly capital, labour and energy intensive, it is nonetheless attractive because of the relatively low-tech nature of the technology and the fact that all aspects of the process, including detailed blueprints, were declassified by the USA soon after the war. Finally, although the possibility of laser enrichment is also noted, this technology was in its early infancy at the time of publication of the report; the same is true of two chemical enrichment techniques which have now been demonstrated at the pilot-plant level in Japan and France.

The major proliferation concern about laser enrichment, specifically the atomic vapour laser isotope separation (AVLIS) process under development in the USA, France, and Japan, is that the high selectivity of laser enrichment leads to the potential for a very compact facility and a low power requirement per unit of separative work (comparable to the gas centrifuge, and approximately 5 per cent that of gaseous diffusion). Thus, a clandestine AVLIS facility might be particularly difficult to detect on the basis of physical size and energy supply. On the other hand, the AVLIS process involves the successful integration of several advanced technologies, and it has not yet been demonstrated for production of low-enriched uranium (LEU) except on a laboratory scale.

However, if AVLIS is successfully deployed for LEU production, its potential efficiency may make it an attractive means for production of highly-enriched uranium for weapons. An additional factor which would favour such a development is that ongoing advances in laser science and technology, driven by work on AVLIS as well as by other military and civilian applications, should make it less difficult to re-invent the AVLIS process as compared to the initial effort. An example of this is the rapid advance in semiconductor diode laser technology which offers a more reliable and efficient means for providing laser pump power for the AVLIS process from current technology.

A full, open literature discussion of the proliferation implications of the AVLIS process was prepared for the US Arms Control and Disarmament Agency (ACDA) by one of us (MM) [6].

Some Relevant Case Studies

This section discusses briefly what is known about two countries that have embarked on nuclear weapons programmes: Iraq and Sweden. Our aim is to gain some understanding about the extent of their accomplishments, how much dependence there was on outside help and how much was known and when to the outside world. In each case there were some early and clear indications of the existence of ongoing nuclear weapons programmes, but to this day much remains unknown.

The Iraqi Nuclear Weapons Programme

As of March 1992, the International Atomic Energy Agency (IAEA), acting as the agent of the United Nations Special Commission on Iraq, had carried out ten nuclear inspections in Iraq in order to identify, and then either destroy, remove, or render harmless, as appropriate, all materials, facilities and equipment that might be used to construct nuclear weapons. The findings and conclusions of the IAEA inspection teams have been documented in a series of reports issued by the Security Council;

there has also been extensive media coverage of the Iraqi programme, based on information, misinformation, disinformation, and speculative opinions supplied by the Special Commission, the IAEA, various intelligence services, and various 'experts'.

In sum, the findings to-date indicate that soon after the Israeli destruction of the Iraqi Osiraq reactor in June 1981, Iraq began a major programme whose goal was the production of substantial amounts of weapons-grade uranium, as well as development of both nuclear weapons and means for their delivery. Various methods of uranium enrichment were investigated, and two of these, electromagnetic isotope separation and the gas centrifuge, were chosen for full-scale production. The basis for the former choice was that, despite the fact that EMIS is highly capital, labour, and energy-intensive, it is known to work--most of the enriched uranium for the Hiroshima bomb was produced using this process. Also, if it uses rather low technology compared with other enrichment methods, and has been extensively documented in the open literature. Another advantage was that most proliferation analysts considered EMIS to be an unattractive technology compared with other enrichment technologies, particularly centrifuges. The advantages of the latter method compared with EMIS is its much smaller scale and energy intensity, which makes it easier to hide, and the fact that despite extensive international and national controls on its export, centrifuge hardware and expertise was readily available on the international market, particularly in Western Europe.

By January 1991, the EMIS enrichment programme had progressed beyond a significant research and development effort, including production of small amounts of enriched uranium, to the start of construction of full-scale enrichment facilities, as well as plants for both the manufacture of EMIS hardware and the required uranium feedstock. In particular, on the basis of data provided by Iraq, the IAEA inspectors estimated that the EMIS enrichment plant at Tarmiya would be operational within one to two years and could produce up to 15 kg of weapons-grade uranium per year.

A major investment had also been made in the centrifuge programme, and research and development had progressed to the point of the testing of various machine types, based on designs by Urenco, the European enrichment consortium. In addition, large quantities of centrifuge materials and components, as well as manufacturing technology adequate for the production of more than 2000 intermediate technology machines per year, made from high-tensile strength maraging steel, had been acquired from outside suppliers. About 1000 of such machines running at full capacity could produce about 20 kg of weapons-grade uranium per year. A major centrifuge manufacturing and test facility at Al Furat was under construction at the time of the bombing.

In addition, R&D was also devoted to chemical exchange methods for uranium enrichment and to gaseous diffusion. Presentations by Iraqi scientists to IAEA inspection teams indicate that work on the exchange methods had not progressed very far, while the diffusion effort had been abandoned in 1987 after five years of work because of a lack of the industrial infrastructure necessary for a large-scale plant.

The other major activity of the Iraqi nuclear weapons programme uncovered to date was weaponization. Based on the questioning of Iraqi authorities, as well as progress reports, equipment, and facilities uncovered to date, the IAEA has concluded that the main effort in weaponization was concentrated on developing an 'intermediate' implosion-type design in which a solid sphere of uranium was surrounded successively by a natural uranium reflector, an iron tamper, and an explosive lens system. To this end, both theoretical calculations and experiments had been conducted in all the required areas, e.g., core design, high-explosives, neutron initiators, and the detonator and firing system. The IAEA concluded that this work appeared "*somewhat superficial*", and that Iraq "*still had a long way to go*" to develop a workable weapon design.

Unfortunately, this conclusion is almost certainly based on incomplete information and, quite likely, also disinformation. Since the beginning of the inspection effort, Iraq has persistently impeded access, and destroyed relevant equipment and facilities. Indeed, there is a widespread concern that a major piece or pieces of the programme, e.g., a plutonium production reactor, a centrifuge cascade with hundreds of machines, or even significant quantities of weapons-grade uranium, remain undiscovered. What is now clear is that Iraq in the 1980s mounted a major programme to produce nuclear weapons. It involved the efforts of thousands of scientists, engineers, and technicians, and the expenditure of billions of dollars on the construction of major R&D and production facilities at many dispersed sites, as well as the procurement of significant outside assistance. According to statements by senior US government officials, e.g., Defense Secretary Richard Cheney, major aspects of this project, in particular the EMIS programme, were only discovered after the end of the Gulf War, based on information supplied by Iraqi defectors. How can this failure be understood, and what are its implications for the future detection of other clandestine weapons programmes, particularly in a NWFW? Was Iraq a failure of intelligence or policy, or both?

The official explanation of the US failure to detect major aspects of the Iraqi nuclear weapons programme was based on two factors: the repressive nature of the Iraqi regime, which made it easy to limit knowledge of the programme, and the relative ease of hiding such an effort in a country with many uninhabited areas.

This seems plausible, but also incomplete as a rationale of what occurred. Obviously this failure is a sensitive matter, of which there has been little public discussion. However, based on what is known publicly, it seems plausible that several factors may have also played a role. (1) The US political 'tilt' towards Iraq during the Iran-Iraq war may have led to a reduced level of intelligence collection in Iraq, and biased both the analysis based on such collection, and the policy based on such analysis to an overly benign view of the Iraqi nuclear programme. (2) This tilt also led the USA to share intelligence information with Iraq about Iran. Even if such information were sanitized, it could have given Iraq valuable insights into US intelligence capabilities, and hence into methods for evading or deceiving such capabilities. (3) Iraq undoubtedly had studied the export regulations of states whose companies could supply both the nuclear and the dual-use technology and materials that Iraq wanted; Iraq became adept at evading these regulations, with, unfortunately, the support or acquiescence of many companies and governments, based on both greed and the aforementioned political tilt on the part of the USA and many other countries. (4) Information which indicated that Iraq was engaged in a serious nuclear weapons programme could have been deemed unimportant or not credible; this could be especially true in the case of information which goes against what was expected by the analytical community, e.g., data pointing to the existence of an EMIS programme for uranium enrichment. (5) The lack of 'human' intelligence in Iraq. Obviously, the prospect of swift and severe punishment undoubtedly deterred would-be Iraqi defectors until after the war. Moreover, if the ability of a country like Israel to staff its covert operations with men and women who can pass convincingly as Arabs is in serious decline,[7] the situation in this regard can be expected to be even worse in the USA and other Western nations.

In sum, it seems plausible that a complex set of factors, involving both the political policies and intelligence systems of the USA and other interested countries, as well as Iraqi manipulation of these policies and intelligence systems, contributed to the failure to appreciate the scale of the Iraqi nuclear effort.

Over time, we expect that the sophistication of the various technical means which can be used to detect clandestine nuclear programmes will increase. Unfortunately, the ability of potential nuclear break-out states to master the technical problems involved in making weapons using indigenous expertise will also increase. The latter is particularly true with regard to weaponization; however, the production of significant amounts of weapons-usable materials, the major technical barrier today, should also be easier even without any significant technical advances, e.g., the development of a reliable method for uranium laser isotope separation.

Thus, the technology for making nuclear weapons will become available to an increasing number of states; preventing breakout depends on international control of stocks of weapons-usable materials and their production facilities for peaceful use, and on making it more difficult to hide significant weapons programmes. The major lesson of Iraq in the latter regard is that reliance on technical means for detection may not suffice; 'human' intelligence is also important. It may also be essential to have a global norm which encourages 'whistle blowing' by scientists, engineers, indeed, everybody who would be involved in violating the commitment of nations not to produce nuclear weapons in a NWFW. (For a discussion of this issue, see Chapter 6).

The Swedish Nuclear Weapon Programme

Within a year after the USA exploded the first nuclear

weapons in Hiroshima and Nagasaki, the Swedish government embarked on a nuclear programme of its own. The ostensible aim of the programme was to pursue a nuclear energy option. But right from the beginning, Swedish efforts reflected a strong interest in nuclear bomb technology as well.

The main source of information on the technical aspects of the Swedish weapons programme comes from a report published in a Swedish technical journal (*Ny Teknik*) in April 1985; it included recently declassified Swedish government documents dating back to the start of the programme and, equally important, several revealing interviews with leading participants in the programme.[8] Unfortunately the report does not provide a coherent, consistent description of the full programme. But there are enough authoritative and detailed fragments to provide a good picture of its size and technical accomplishments, as well as the bottlenecks that were encountered.

The Swedish nuclear programme was carried out by two organizations: AB Atomenergi (ABA)--a semi-public corporation-- and the Institute for Defence Research (FOA). ABA was responsible for research and development relating to civilian use-- primarily development of nuclear reactors; FOA had responsibility for research relating to 'protection' against nuclear weaponry. In fact, the FOA programme focused on weapons technology which went far beyond what was necessary for 'protective' (i.e. civil defence) research, and the ABA effort programme was as much, if not more, concerned with developing a capability for producing weapons-grade plutonium as with power production for civilian use. The two programmes were fully co-ordinated, guided by a common plan.

What is particularly interesting about the Swedish programme is that so many individuals at the highest political level of government (including the Parliament) were either unaware of the true nature of the weapons programme or chose not to know too much about it.

Not surprising, it was the Swedish military and the conservative political leaders who were most interested in having Sweden acquire nuclear weapons. At the same time there was substantial pressure from the public and from the liberal elements in Parliament for Sweden to renounce any interest in nuclear weapons acquisition. The government in its formal decisions equivocated; it never 'approved' a programme explicitly directed towards weapons acquisition--this would not have been politically viable--nor renounced outright its interest in nuclear weaponry, thereby closing the nuclear option. However, a research programme for 'protection' against nuclear weaponry seemed politically safe and was authorized.

Technically, it is hard to define a boundary between research and development directed at ultimate weapons acquisition, and research and development directed at 'protection', as well as the boundary between reactor development for nuclear power and development for plutonium production. However, for a select group of political leaders, the top military leaders as well as those working at the technical levels, there was little ambiguity about what was really going on. The FOA programme was focused on the technology of nuclear weapons, and the ABA programme was aimed at producing a sufficient quantity of fissile material to maintain the option. An explicit decision to *produce* nuclear weapons was not yet necessary.

In 1966, when the military budget was in jeopardy, the Swedish military began to lose interest in nuclear weapons. Military leaders assumed that continued pursuit of the nuclear option would only be at the cost of conventional military capability--a trade-off they were unwilling to make. Finally, in 1968 the Swedish government decided to phase out its nuclear weapons programme and this led to the complete termination of maintaining a nuclear weapons option.

Based on the *Ny Teknik* report, it is clear that FOA went quite far in its nuclear weapons technology effort. A great deal more relevant technical data, instrumentation and special materials (other than fissile material) needed for the development of fission weapons was available to Sweden in the 1950s and 1960s than was available to the USA early in its first nuclear weapons development programme. Further, FOA's achievements were quite impressive. Their understanding of nuclear weapon designs were substantially more advanced than those of the first US efforts. FOA moved confidently to the design of an implosion device using a hollow plutonium pit, an 'electronic' initiator of their own design and construction, and a non-spherical chemical implosive geometry to reduce the bomb's diameter.

The first FOA weapons were designed to have a yield of

about 10 kilotons--about the same as the first US implosion bomb, but were to weigh only about one-tenth as much.

When, later in the programme, in the 1960s, it became clear that the weapons-grade plutonium would not be available to the weapons programme for some time, serious studies and experimentation took place for a bomb designed to use reactor-grade plutonium. This meant accepting a lower yield. Swedish calculations demonstrated that the maximum yield for such a weapons might be about 1 or 2 kilotons and the technical challenge was to design such a weapon with the minimum amount of plutonium.

The FOA effort also included zero-yield testing with all bomb components in place, except for the fissile material being replaced by inert material. By 1965, a full-scale test would have been possible, had about 5 kg of plutonium been available to FOA. The total bomb R&D programme at FOA involved about two hundred scientist and technicians.

On its part, ABA designed and constructed Sweden's first reactor, a 1 MW heavy water research reactor that went critical in 1954. This design was chosen to avoid any need for uranium enrichment and to facilitate plutonium production. Sweden later acquired a 30 MW light water reactor from the USA that required enriched uranium for fuel. The USA supplied the uranium fuel and required controls and inspection. This reactor went critical in 1960. A third reactor, of Swedish design and construction, had the dual purpose of producing kilogramme quantities of plutonium for the weapons programme and also power for civilian use; it came on line in 1963. However, it too ended up using low enriched US supplied fuel and thus subject to safeguards.

An unsafeguarded 200 MW heavy water reactor was later designed. It was to provide a supply of plutonium adequate for about ten weapons per year, as well as to provide thermal output for civilian use starting in 1968. It never reached operational status because of the combination of high operating costs, severe technical problems and waning interest in weapons production. Besides, for reasonable performance it would have required foreign-supplied low enriched uranium and consequently would be safeguarded too.

In summary, producing plutonium in a domestic, unsafeguarded reactor proved to be an impossible job for

Sweden's bomb project. Even for simple experiments to measure the physical and chemical properties of plutonium, FOA depended on gramme quantities imported from the United Kingdom and France.

However, before complete abandonment of the weapons programmes, FOA realized that to have such a programme it would have to design and construct a heavy water reactor, to be fuelled by a domestic supply of natural uranium and be totally dedicated to supply plutonium for weapons production. ABA also planned a reprocessing plant with a throughput of enough plutonium for about ten weapons per year. Neither facility was constructed.

What is clear from the Swedish experience is how relatively easy it is for even a small industrialized country to design and fabricate sophisticated fission weapons clandestinely if an adequate supply of fissile material were available. But obtaining substantial quantities of fissile material for a clandestine bomb programme was the technical bottleneck for Sweden.

Summary

Based on our review of the literature on nuclear weapons technology and the production of fissionable materials, and our own consideration of the problems involved, we conclude that many states can acquire the requisite technology and expertise to develop and *produce* nuclear weapons and, if they have possession of a sufficient amount of fissionable materials, can do so clandestinely. The only real control of breakout in a NWFW is strict international control of all facilities for the production of fissionable materials that could be used in nuclear weapons. We do not address the political feasibility of such controls.

From a technical perspective, breakout could be particularly rapid and simple if, under a NWFW regime, nations insist on maintaining or acquiring production facilities for weapons-usable materials or stockpiles of such materials. Breakout would of course be relatively easy for advanced industrial states, especially if they had prior nuclear weapons experience and retained an 'institutional memory' (expertise, experimental data, designs etc.) of their nuclear weapons programmes.

References

1. J. Carson Mark, "Some Remarks on Iraq's Possible Nuclear Weapon Capability in the Light of Some of the Known Facts Concerning Nuclear Weapons", Nuclear Control Institute, April 5, 1991.

2. J. Carson Mark, "Reactor-Grade Plutonium's Explosive Properties", NPT At The Crossroads, August 1990. Amory B. Lovins, "Nuclear weapons and power-reactor plutonium", *Nature*, Vol.283, 28 February 1980.

3. Theodore B. Taylor, "Nuclear Testing Is A Pandora's Box", FAS Public Interest Report, Volume 39, No.10.

4. Jack Worlton, "Some Myths about High-Performance Computers and Their Role in the Design of Nuclear Weapons", Los Alamos National Laboratory, 1990.

5. D. Rundquist and E. Straker, "Technical Description of Fuel Cycle Facilities and Discussion of Diversion Potential", *Science Applications International*, November 8, 1976.

6. "Fiscal Year 1989 Arms Control Impact Statements", US Government Printing Office, Washington, April 1988.

7. Ian Black and Benny Morris, *Israel's Secret Wars, A History of Israel's Intelligence Services*, p.500, Grove Weidenfeld, New York, 1991.

8. Christer Larssen, "Build a Bomb!", *Ny Teknik*, April 25, 1985, p.83. (A translation of the article has been made by The Congressional Research Service.)

6

Societal Verification

Joseph Rotblat

Introduction

The end of the Cold War and the subsequent collapse of the communist regime and the Soviet Union have eliminated the main rationale for the retention of huge nuclear arsenals. But even if these arsenals are greatly reduced, the threat of the use of nuclear weapons will obviously exist as long as nuclear weapons exist, and many people are led to the belief that a world with nuclear weapons is bound to be an unstable world.

Among them are some who--while convinced that a nuclear-weapon-free world is desirable--are not convinced that it is feasible; they are concerned about the effectiveness of the treaty to eliminate all nuclear weapons in protecting against cheating, such as concealment of a clandestine nuclear arsenal, or undetected production of weapons later on (see Chapter 5).

The chief protection against possible violation of the treaty is a regime of verification of compliance with the terms of the treaty. The main component of such a regime--technological verification, which uses methods such as physical inspection, instrumental detection, ground surveillance or aerial reconnaissance--is discussed in Chapter 4. This chapter deals with another component, societal verification. It is shown that the simultaneous employment of both these components would provide adequate protection and satisfy the legitimate concerns about the effectiveness of the treaty.

Role of Societal Verification

Societal verification is here defined as a system of monitoring compliance with treaties, and detecting attempts to violate them, by means other than technological verification. As the name implies, societal verification is based on the involvement of the whole community, or broad groups of it, in contrast to the employment of highly specialized teams of experts required for technological verification. In that sense societal verification can be viewed as being part of the political requirements for the disarmament process.

Even at the present state of the art, technical verification is sufficiently developed to protect treaties aiming at reducing nuclear arms down to very low levels, of the order of a few per cent of the present arsenals. But it is asserted that technology alone would not be an adequate safeguard for treaties aiming at zero, the complete elimination of nuclear weapons. The effectiveness of verification techniques is likely to be greatly improved in the future, if more research effort is put into it, particularly if the weapon designers themselves were given the task of seeking such improvements, as part of the process of conversion of military research establishments to peaceful applications. Nevertheless, these techniques are unlikely to become 100 per cent effective, or to come near enough to this figure to satisfy the concerns of national security organs. For non-nuclear weapons, a 90-95 per cent effectiveness is generally acceptable, but the enormous destructive power of nuclear weapons makes it necessary to reduce the error to very nearly zero, if a treaty to eliminate these weapons completely is to have a chance of being universally accepted. In a NWFW, the illegal retention of even a few nuclear weapons, or their clandestine production after the treaty has come into force, might give the transgressing state considerable power and the capability to exert political blackmail. This is the reason why an additional system of verification is needed.

Like the technological element, societal verification will have to be an integral part of the step-by-step disarmament process. As will be shown, its implementation requires a change in certain attitudes of the general public, which may take time. On the other hand, the technological element, even the mere physical destruction of nuclear armaments, will also take some years to complete. As has been pointed out elsewhere [1], the two aspects of the disarmament process, the technological and the political, are both not only necessary but reinforce each other in a process of positive feed-back. The side-by-side implementation of both aspects will significantly accelerate the achievement of a NWFW.

Citizen's Reporting

The main form of societal verification is by inducing the citizens of the countries signing the treaty to report to an appropriate international authority any information about attempted violation going on in their countries. For this system of verification to be effective it is vital that all such reporting becomes the right and the civic duty of the citizen. This right and duty will have to become part of the national codes of law in the countries party to the treaty. The adoption of such laws would be greatly facilitated if this was made an integral part of the treaty on the elimination of nuclear weapons, and explicitly expressed in a specific clause of that treaty.

The concept of citizen's reporting has been discussed in the literature for many years, under different names, such as 'inspection by the people', or 'knowledge detection'. The idea was introduced in the late 1950s by Lewis Bohn [2] and Seymour Melman [3] and incorporated in the classic *World Peace Through World Law* by Grenville Clark and Louis Sohn. [4] Leo Szilard, in his quixotic *The Voice of the Dolphins* [5] also considered it an important part of the disarmament process.

The early 1960s were the period of intense debate on 'general and complete disarmament', when many detailed studies, including concrete proposals for the implementation of GCD, were much on the United Nations agenda (see Chapter 1). After it became obvious that the political climate was not ripe for such a radical remodelling of the world's security system, and with the intensification of the Cold War and declining stature of the United Nations, the subject of citizen's reporting ceased to be a topic of interest, although papers elaborating certain aspects of the concept appeared in various journals from time to time. [6]

The momentous events since the end of the 1980s have made it possible to bring back from the cold many ideals and aspirations; objectives that were previously dismissed as Utopian can now be brought to the fore. Among these is citizen's reporting. This appears to be an idea whose time has come. The recent dramatic changes in the political arena, especially the restoration of the United Nations to its primary role of maintaining global peace and security, justify a re-examination of the concept of citizen's reporting, at least as applied to the more restricted aim of nuclear disarmament.

In relation to general disarmament, Clark and Sohn [4] proposed a revision of the UN Charter that envisaged a UN Inspection Service with direct responsibility for supervision over the fulfilment of obligations by nations and individuals in respect to all phases of disarmament. Two sections of the relevant Article deal with citizen's reporting:

> *Any person having any information concerning any violation of this Annex or of any law or regulation enacted thereunder shall immediately report all such information to the United Nations Inspection Service. The General Assembly shall enact regulations governing the granting of rewards to persons supplying the Inspection Service with such information, and the provision of asylum to them and their families.*

> *No nation shall penalize directly or indirectly any person or public or private organization supplying information to the United Nations with respect to any violation of this Annex.*

The granting of rewards for supplying information--as an encouragement to fulfil this duty--was also recommended by Szilard [5]; writing in 1961, he suggested an award of one million dollars, free of tax, to be paid by the government accused of a violation, but returnable if the information later turned out to be invalid. Lewis Bohn [7] also approves of financial and other rewards, but goes further than this: he calls specifically for *a provision in the original arms-control agreement requiring all participating governments to pass laws making it a crime, punishable by domestic law, to violate the provisions of the arms-control agreement or to keep secret from the agency for international control any information of such a violation. Moreover, these provisions of the law of the land should be publicized by each government and failure to support them by such publicity (or by other ways) should be declared to be a major violation of the control treaty.*

As already mentioned, these proposals were put forward in the context of general and complete disarmament, but they can also be applied--with a better chance of success--to the treaty on the elimination of nuclear weapons. The fundamental point is that the duty of the citizen to supply information about any violations should be an integral part of the treaty on the elimination of nuclear weapons, and be spelled out clearly in the terms of the treaty. Thus, disclosing to an outside--albeit international--body information about sensitive security matters inside one's country, would not only cease to be considered as a crime, an act of treason, but would in fact become part of the law of one's country.

The inclusion of a clause in an international treaty demanding the enactment of new national laws may be viewed as an infringement of sovereignty, but surrender of some sovereignty is implicit in every international treaty. In any case, the currently accepted concept of the nation-state as the supreme power--which can compel obedience from the population within its territory, deny the right of others to interfere in its internal affairs, but would expect others to come to its rescue if its territorial integrity is assailed--would have to be abandoned, since it is not compatible with world security.

In this interdependent world, there can be no room for a multitude of absolutely sovereign states. Indeed, the very tendency to break up into smaller and smaller units makes sovereignty a nonsensical notion. The Russell-Einstein Manifesto [8] stated *"The abolition of war will demand distasteful limitations of national sovereignty."* Thirty seven years later, the political and technological developments have made this imperative.

Moves in this direction are already afoot. Simultaneously with the separation of states into smaller units, some long-established independent states are coming together and forming large communities. Even one of the oldest of parliaments, the British House of Commons, has conceded that, once the UK had signed the Treaty of Rome, the laws of the European Community took precedence. Such limitations on national sovereignty as have been accepted in Europe will have to be applied widely, to all nations of the world.

Effectiveness of Citizen's Reporting

Even if governments were persuaded to pass laws to make reporting legitimate, this goes so much against traditional loyalties that it would require a considerable educational effort to induce people to act on it voluntarily. This raises the question: how effective would citizen's reporting be, if it were legitimized and safeguarded by a clause as discussed above?

In considering the answer to this question one needs to be reminded of the assumption implied in this chapter, namely that a political climate has been generated in which the elimination of nuclear weapons is being considered as a realistic and desirable goal for world security. During the Cold War era, with all the mistrust, fear and hostile propaganda that it engendered, a treaty to eliminate nuclear weapons would have had no chance. An atmosphere of trust, and willingness to elaborate and collaborate on a global security system, are essential conditions for starting negotiations on such a treaty. But the changed political situation has brought us a long way towards meeting this condition. Another essential condition is the existence of an international authority capable of ensuring compliance with the terms of the treaty. In this respect too, the recent events augur well. The greatly enhanced stature of the United Nations makes it likely that an agency under its aegis would command the necessary degree of confidence about its effectiveness, although this effectiveness would have to be boosted by providing the United Nations with the machinery both for peace keeping and peace enforcing, so that it would be able to exercise its authority in a demonstrably independent manner. The measures proposed by the UN Secretary-General, [9] if implemented, will go a long way towards this objective.

There are good reasons for expecting that citizen's reporting would be more effective in relation to nuclear than to other types of weapons. By the very nature of its technology, the maintenance of a concealed nuclear arsenal, or the preparation for making such weapons, requires the involvement of many people with specialized skills, and complex facilities. A government intending a violation would thus face the considerable risk that the attempt would be detected at an early stage and reported to the international authority by its own citizens, thus incurring the reprisals provided in the treaty, well before being in a position to reap the fruit of the contemplated violation. Another reason why the probability of exposure of such attempts is greater in relation to nuclear weapons is because in the minds of the public a nuclear war carries with it the threat of global destruction, possibly the end of civilization, and people are likely to do their utmost to prevent anything that may lead to such an outcome. If properly operated, citizen's reporting would provide the necessary supplement to technological verification, and thus allay the fears that a violation of the treaty on the elimination of nuclear weapons would go undetected.

Data in the literature justify the belief that there will be enough people willing to overcome the taboo on reporting upon their own government.

In 1958, a public opinion poll was carried out in six countries to determine the attitude of citizens towards disarmament and inspection by the public. [10] The poll was conducted by the American Institute of Public Opinion and its affiliates in other countries.

Table 1 contains the text of the three questions posed in the poll and the replies in terms of percentages. The sizes of the samples (shown in the table) were sufficiently large (especially in the UK and USA) to give statistically meaningful answers. They matched, by sex and age, the total populations in the countries.

As is seen, in all six countries the opinion was decisively in favour of making it a citizen's duty to report attempts to make nuclear weapons secretly. Similarly, at least half of those interviewed expressed a willingness to report any knowledge of such attempts.

A breakdown by sex showed no difference in the responses by males and females, but there was a significant difference between

TABLE 1

Opinions About Disarmament Inspection in Six Selected Nations

	USA	UK	France	India	FRG	Japan
(size of sample)	(1610)	(1000)	(287)	(250)	(282)	(200)
	%	%	%	%	%	%

Would you favour or oppose setting up a world-wide organization which would make sure—by regular inspections—that no nation, including Russia and the United States, makes atom bombs, hydrogen bombs, and missiles?

	USA	UK	France	India	FRG	Japan
Favour	70	72	85	78	92	91
Oppose	16	10	6	1	1	8
No Opinion and No Answer	14	18	9	21	7	1

If this inspections organization were set up, would you favour or oppose making it each person's duty to report any attempt to secretly make bombs, hydrogen bombs, and missiles?

	USA	UK	France	India	FRG	Japan
Favour	73	54	74	71	86	80
Oppose	11	15	13	2	4	16
No Opinion and No Answer	16	31	13	27	10	4

If you, yourself, knew that someone in (name of country) was attempting to secretly make forbidden weapons, would you report this to the office of the world-wide inspection organization in this country?

	USA	UK	France	India	FRG	Japan
Yes	80	50	63	63	73	83
No	6	17	18	6	11	5
No Opinion and No Answer	14	33	19	31	16	12

professions: scientists and engineers (about 1.5 per cent of the samples) did show a greater willingness to report violations (84 per cent in the total survey) than the other groups (69 per cent). This difference is significant, and singles them out as the key group for citizen's reporting.

It might be of interest to repeat the survey at the present time, after the momentous changes in the world, and to include, in particular, the countries of the former Soviet Union as well as those with ambitions to become nuclear powers.

All the countries canvassed in the 1958 survey had democratic regimes. In non-democratic countries, with little respect for individual human liberties, citizen's reporting is likely to be ineffective. This is a general view, but it merits closer examination.

Consider the case of a country like Iraq, under the heel of a Saddam Hussein. What is the probability that a citizen of that country would report preparations to manufacture a nuclear weapon? In answering this question one has to be reminded that we are looking not at the situation as prevails now, but at a future stage, when the vast majority of nations had agreed to sign a treaty to eliminate nuclear weapons, and as part of it, had agreed to make the right and duty of citizen's reporting an integral part of national law. There would then be two alternatives for Iraq: (a) to accede to the treaty with all its ramifications; (b) to refuse to join it. Choosing the latter alternative would be deemed by other states as a declaration by Iraq that it intends to acquire nuclear weapons, and this would make it subject to all the rigours, such as economic sanctions and strict import controls, designed to make it impossible for Iraq to achieve its aim.

Should Iraq choose the first alternative, then it would have to accept the terms of the international safeguarding regime, including the setting up of monitoring offices in the country, and this would make it easier for citizens to report attempts to violate the treaty. This would greatly reduce the chances of a violation going on undetected, particularly since one needs only a few reports of genuine attempts at transgression to initiate an investigation and thwart the attempt.

Various ways have been suggested to encourage and remind people of their duty, such as frequent advertisements on television and in newspapers, or the provision of detailed information about how to get in touch with the relevant UN authority. The suitability of offering financial rewards (except for expenses incurred) is debatable. In some cases it may be a useful inducement. On the whole, reporting should be a response to one's deeply felt moral obligation. Financial rewards might indeed be counter-productive and encourage false reporting.

This leads to another difficult problem, how to prevent trivial reports or deliberate hoaxes. A continuous flood of alleged violations would not only saturate the system but could lead to embarrassing situations and even international crises. Indeed, discrediting the reporting regime by such action could be the deliberate aim of a government (or group of terrorists) intending to violate the treaty. In a somewhat different context, this is the kind of problem that faces the community all the time in many countries, where hoax calls of bombs hidden on aircraft or in other public places often result in the disruption of the normal way of life. But just as the community is learning to deal with these nuisances, it should be possible to devise a system of scrutinizing reports to distinguish between genuine and bogus information. For example, any anonymous report would be disregarded; the *bona fides* of the 'reporter' would be investigated before any action is taken; penalties might be imposed for deliberately false information. There is a need for more study of this problem, as well as of the detailed procedure for checking and verifying reports of attempted violations of a treaty, when and how a government should be confronted with the evidence, and the type of sanction to be applied.

Whistle Blowing

Apart from citizen's reporting, which relies upon members of the general public finding out, in one way or another, about attempts to rebuild nuclear weapons in a NWFW, the preparation for such actions could also be monitored systematically by workers in the relevant disciplines or industries. Any serious attempt to violate the treaty would require the involvement of highly specialized scientists and technologists. Monitoring the movement and change of employment of such experts would provide an important clue and lead to early detection. For this purpose the community of scientists and technologists would need to be alerted and their help enlisted.

It should be pointed out that one of the requirements in the agreement to abolish nuclear weapons would be the closure--or conversion--of research establishments, such as Livermore or Chelabinsk, whose main task is the design and development of nuclear weapons and the means of their delivery. The closure--or conversion--of these establishments will remove the existing legitimized secrecy of scientific research, a pernicious practice that goes against the very basis of science, openness. Openness in science means that the outcome of research work is published in journals or books, and is available to anyone interested. It also means that projected and ongoing research is widely known. Under openness in science there would be much more communication among scientists, and therefore greater awareness in the scientific community about the whereabouts, and the type and scope of the work carried out by their colleagues. This would make it particularly difficult for key people, those who would have to be in charge of a breakout attempt, to carry out such attempts undetected.

Apart from relying on sporadic observations, organizations of scientists and technologists could be set up for the specific purpose of acting as a watchdog of compliance with treaties, by monitoring the activities of individuals likely to become involved in illegal projects. Such monitoring can be done, without appearing to spy on one's colleagues, by keeping a register of scientists and technologists, and by noting changes of place of work or pattern of publications (or their absence). Other 'give aways' of attempted clandestine activities include the start of new projects at academic institutions without proper justification; the recruitment of young scientists and engineers in numbers not warranted by the declared purpose of the project; or the large scale procurement of certain types of apparatus, materials, and equipment.

Special attention would have to be paid to institutions with nuclear facilities, such as processing of spent fuel elements from nuclear reactors, storage of such elements, plants for enrichment of isotopes, or management of intense radioactive sources. With the halt of military uses, all the establishments dealing with the above will have to be opened and made subject not only to monitoring by IAEA safeguards, but also to the scrutiny of the watchdog organizations. The disclosures from Iraq have demonstrated the inadequacy of the present IAEA safeguard regime, and the need for a much tighter and effective system. The needed changes should be such as to ensure better monitoring of all activities in nuclear facilities.

In countries with an open democratic regime, the measures described above could ensure that no clandestine activities would go on undetected, thus easing the task of the inspectorate supervising the compliance with the terms of the treaty. In countries with non-democratic regimes much more vigilance by the inspectorate would be necessary. But even in these countries there are bound to be many scientists with a social consciousness ready to carry out the task of monitoring and whistle-blowing, particularly if this became a legal duty.

A Loyalty to Mankind

One of the most difficult aspects of societal verification is that it carries with it the taint of disloyalty, the stigma of spying on one's colleagues or fellow-citizens; this would make it distasteful to many well-meaning people, although this stigma would be removed if reporting were sanctioned in international and domestic laws.

Loyalty to one's group is a natural condition for the stability of the group; it is essential to ensure its continuity. For this reason it has, over the years, become enshrined with codes and taboos. Disloyalty is equated with dishonour and, in addition, may carry penalties of various kinds. The more aggressive, or less scrupulous, members of the group often exploit this for their own gains; weaker members are bullied and subjected to various forms of mistreatment, and the codes ensure that this will not be disclosed by the victims. This happens in all groups, starting with the family where children will not squeal on their siblings; in schools, where 'telling tales' is not done on the penalty of being ostracized; and it extends to trade unions--where disclosure of unfair practices carries with it the threat of being 'sent to Coventry'--and to other fraternities and associations.

The increasing interdependence of everyone in modern society--mainly resulting from ever-increasing specialization-- inevitably leads to new, larger groups coming into being, and demanding new loyalties. These new loyalties are usually an extension, not a replacement, of the loyalties to the smaller communities. We still have our loyalty to our family, to our local community, to our professional group, on top of the loyalty to our nation. The necessity for larger groups is unquestioned, since they are able to provide greater security for all their members, and therefore loyalty to them takes precedence over that to the smaller groups.

At present, loyalty to one's nation is supreme, generally overriding the loyalty to any of the subgroups. Patriotism is the dogma; 'my country right or wrong', the motto. And in case these slogans are not obeyed, loyalty is enforced by codes of national criminal laws. Any transgression is punished by the force of the law: attempts by individuals to exercise their conscience by putting humanitarian needs above those dictated by national laws are denounced by labelling those individuals as dissidents, traitors or spies. They are often severely punished by exile (Sakharov), long-term prison sentences (Vanunu), or even execution (the Rosenbergs).

The time has now come to develop, and recognize consciously, loyalty to a much larger group, loyalty to mankind. In this nuclear age the very existence of the human species is no longer assured. It has been put in peril not by the threat of external or natural forces, such as a collision with a large meteorite, or an enormous eruption of a volcano, but by the action of man; the end of civilization can now be brought about either abruptly, in a nuclear war, or slowly, by the continuous degradation of the environment.

Nothing unites people more than the threat from a common enemy. All our national differences would have been forgotten in an instant, if the planet Earth were attacked by 'Martians'. The fact that the threat is man-made, the outcome of our own developments and actions, should not make it less of a common enemy, demanding common efforts. The Russell-Einstein Manifesto [8] recognized this when it said: "*We are speaking on this occasion, not as members of this or that nation, continent, or creed, but as human beings, members of the species Man, whose continued existence is in doubt*".

Among scientists, the group to whom the Manifesto was especially directed, the feeling of belonging to mankind is already well developed. Science has always been cosmopolitan in nature; its methods and ethics are universal, transcending geographical frontiers and political barriers. Because of this, scientists have developed the sense of belonging to the world community, of being citizens of the world. There are also other groups which 'speak the same language', such as musicians or artists. What is now urgently needed is to develop the same sense of feeling in everybody. We need to foster and nurture in each of us a new loyalty, an extension of the loyalty to our nation, to embrace the whole of mankind.

This new loyalty is necessary for the protection of the human species, whether nuclear weapons are eliminated or not. But the recognition of the necessity of this loyalty, and the education of the general public about this need, would be of momentous importance in ensuring compliance with a treaty to eliminate nuclear weapons. It would contribute towards this by overcoming national taboos, and by making societal verification a natural expression of one's concern for mankind. It would make it an effective instrument for achieving such a treaty, since it would allay the fears that many have about the stability of a NWFW.

Summary

The end of the Cold War has further reduced the need for nuclear arsenals. The dramatic events in the Middle East and the former Soviet Union have brought home to everybody the grave dangers of the spread of nuclear weapons. Such proliferation cannot, however, be prevented, if some states consider the retention of nuclear weapons to be necessary for their security. This emphasizes the desirability of the complete elimination of nuclear weapons.

The feasibility of a nuclear-weapon-free world depends largely on the existence of an effective regime of verification. Due to the enormous destructive potential of nuclear weapons, such a regime would have to be nearly one hundred per cent effective. Further intensive research work--involving the designers and makers of nuclear weapons--needs to be carried out urgently, in order to improve the effectiveness of technological verification.

In parallel with this, there is the equally urgent need to evolve a system of societal verification, in which all members of the community, or large groups of it, would have an active role. The main form of such verification is citizen's reporting, in which all citizens will have the right and the *duty* to provide information to an international authority about attempts to violate the terms of the treaty on the elimination of nuclear weapons. This right and the civic duty of citizens would have to be safeguarded by a clause in the treaty, requiring the passing of relevant national laws in the countries party to the treaty.

The passing of such laws may not be as difficult as is feared by some; after all, it would simply mean the underwriting of an agreement entered into by the government on behalf of its citizens. The surprising thing is that it has not been done before. In order to test the acceptability of such a step, a clause as mentioned above should be introduced into any treaty negotiated henceforth.

In addition, organizations of scientists and technologists should be set up with the task of serving as watchdogs and whistle blowers, to monitor the activities of individuals and groups likely to become involved in projects contravening international treaties.

The implementation of societal verification would be greatly facilitated by a modification of the concept of sovereignty of states and by the development of a new loyalty, a loyalty to mankind. This is in any case essential in the ever increasing interdependence of all peoples on the globe, and the threat to the continued existence of the human species. The fostering and nurturing of this new loyalty should be a specific task for the groups, such as scientists, that are already cosmopolitan, because they 'speak' the same language.

References

1. J. Rotblat and V.I. Goldanskii, "The Elimination of Nuclear Arsenals: is it Desirable? is it Feasible?" in *Verification: Monitoring Disarmament* F. Calogero, M.L. Goldberger and S.P. Kapitza eds., Westview Press, Oxford, 1991, pp.205-23.

2. Lewis Bohn, Rand Corporation Memorandum, 1956.

3.   Seymour Melman ed., *Inspection for Disarmament*, Columbia University Press, New York 1958.

4.   Grenville Clark and Louis B. Sohn, *World Peace Through World Law (2nd ed.)*, Harvard University Press, Cambridge, 1960, p.267.

5.   Leo Szilard, *The Voice of the Dolphins*, Simon and Schuster, New York, 1961.

6.   see B.M. Portnoy, "Arms Control Procedure: Inspection by the People - A Revaluation and a Proposal" *Cornell International Law Journal*, vol.4, No.2, 1971.

7.   Lewis Bohn, "Non-Physical Inspection Techniques", in *Arms Control, Disarmament, and National Security*, D.G. Brennan ed., Braziller, New York, 1961.

8.   see J. Rotblat, *Scientists in the Quest for Peace*, MIT Press, Cambridge, MA, 1972, pp.137-140.

9.   Boutros Boutros-Ghaili, *An Agenda for Peace*, United Nations, New York, 1992.

10.   W.M. Evan, "Inspection by the People", in *Inspection for Disarmament* (ref. 3 above)

7

A NWFW Regime:
Treaty for the Abolition
of Nuclear Weapons

Maxwell Bruce, Horst Fischer,
and Thomas Mensah

Introduction

A radical shift in international relations, such as the establishment of a NWFW, requires, in accordance with the political practice established in this century, an international treaty, as a permanent and binding structure. Such a treaty would formulate the rights and obligations of the states parties. It would define violations, the method of determining them, and the modes of enforcement.

The Treaty for the Abolition of Nuclear Weapons would of course be the end-product of a long process of negotiation. The formulation of possible provisions of the Treaty does not solve the many political problems likely to be encountered in those negotiations; however, it may help to indicate where the main problems lie.

There are certain clear pre-conditions for the successful completion of such a treaty. The first is that all the five declared nuclear-weapon powers would have to be persuaded that such a treaty was in their interest. As they come to realize that the main threat to their security is likely to be from the proliferation of nuclear weapons to many more countries, they could well reach this conclusion. Secondly, they--and other states--would also have to be persuaded that adequate guarantees exist against the re-emergence of nuclear-weapon states. This is discussed extensively elsewhere in the book. That means, so far as the Treaty is concerned, that its provisions would have to be binding on all states, and there could be no right to withdraw.

The Treaty, when in force, would supplant and make obsolete a number of treaties, e.g. the Partial Test Ban Treaty, the Tlatelolco Treaty, the Non-Proliferation Treaty, the Anti-Ballistic Missile Treaty, the Sea-Bed Treaty and the Rarotonga Treaty (see Chapter 10). Indeed, it would put into effect the words of the Preamble to the NPT, which speaks of facilitating the cessation of the manufacture of nuclear weapons, the liquidation of existing stockpiles, and the elimination from national arsenals of nuclear weapons. The NPT was, after all, only an intermediate stage on the way to global denuclearization.

An international law regime for nuclear weapons (as the Treaty here proposed would be) must, in the words of Richard Falk [1], be based on broad public support for the idea that any use, and especially the first use, of nuclear weapons would constitute a crime against humanity. Present international treaty law tacitly accepts the legality of nuclear weapons, prohibiting their emplacement only in certain (arguably unimportant) places, such as the sea-bed and outer space.

A clear approach to the problem was taken in Protocol I to the 1949 Geneva Convention [2] which prohibits indiscriminate attacks, thereby including the use of weapons of mass destruction. But three of the five nuclear-weapon states have not ratified this Protocol. The USA and the UK have signed Protocol I with reservations as to nuclear weapons, and have not ratified it. France has not signed it. The USSR and China have ratified Protocol I without reservations as to nuclear weapons. Some NATO members have ratified with a reservation about nuclear weapons.

In these circumstances, a strong political will is required for such a fundamental change in international law as the Treaty here proposed. With the rapid shifts in the international scene experienced in recent years, the time, since Hiroshima, has never been more propitious.

Universal Membership

Given the necessary precondition that all the five declared nuclear-weapon states are in favour of the Treaty, it may be reasonable to expect rapid general adherence. All non-nuclear-weapon states parties to the NPT should be eager to join; the Treaty would give them all the progress on nuclear disarmament which they have long demanded; it would completely fulfil the requirements of article VI of the NPT. For the states that had not joined the NPT, the main argument, that it discriminates between nations, would no longer apply. Thus, the process of adherence should be rapid and general.

If any difficulties remained in achieving universal (or as near as possible universal) participation in, and speedy adoption of, the Treaty, a mechanism exists for attaining these objectives. This is to use a variation of the procedure currently used by some agencies, such as the International Maritime Organization and the International Civil Aviation Organization to bring international regulations into force, notwithstanding that the NWFW Treaty would greatly exceed these regulations in importance.

Under this procedure, regulations enter into force on dates pre-determined at the time of their adoption, without requiring express acceptance or ratification by states. Furthermore, the regulations apply to *all* the states involved, except those states which specifically declare that they do not wish to be bound. This procedure ensures a high likelihood that the regulations will become applicable at a given time, and apply to a fairly predictable number of states.

It should be possible, by using a variation of the 'expedited entry into force' and 'tacit acceptance' procedures, to bring the proposed NWFW Treaty into force with minimum delay and also ensure that all states will be bound by it--except those states which find it necessary to declare publicly that they are unwilling to be bound. There should be provision that states coming into existence after the Treaty has come into force shall be deemed automatically to be parties to the Treaty, unless they similarly make a specific declaration that they are not willing to be parties. In view of the negative implications of such a declaration it can be assumed that very few, if any, states would wish to take advantage of that option.

Parties to the Treaty should be all States Members of the United Nations, or of any other of the specialized agencies, such as the International Atomic Energy Agency, or Parties to the Statute of the International Court of Justice, as well as states invited to send representatives to a Conference on a Nuclear-Weapon-Free World, a necessary first step towards enactment of the Treaty.

There was a suggestion that the Treaty should provide for the taking of measures against states which decide not to become parties to it; this could be based upon a resolution of the Security Council stating that the principles and obligations in the Treaty will be applicable to all states, including any states which decide not to participate in the Treaty. It has, however, been pointed out that this would be contrary to the general rules of international law. Furthermore, a study of disarmament agreements concluded that violations are more likely to occur in imposed agreements than in those freely entered into. [3]

Prohibitions

The Treaty would make illegal the possession or use (with the possible exceptions discussed below) of nuclear weapons or other nuclear explosive devices. Research into production of, or the manufacture, testing or deployment of new systems of such weapons or devices would, without exception, also be illegal. [4]

Any exceptions to the foregoing would be of limited duration and degree and in respect of nuclear-weapon states as defined in the NPT. The purpose would be to provide deterrence and assurance during the period after nuclear weapons had been denounced but before a NWFW had been brought about. During this run-down period, the nuclear-weapon states would be permitted either to retain their existing nuclear weapons or other nuclear explosive devices for a limited time, perhaps ten years, and to cede control of them to the Security Council--dismantling and destroying a certain proportion of them each year--or possibly to transfer a small number to a UN agency at once (see below). A like programme of dismantlement and destruction would exist for the remaining national arsenals, and those of the UN agency would be dismantled and destroyed last.

It has been suggested by Gerard C. Smith [5] that during this period only airborne delivery systems should be allowed and ballistic missiles abolished. It is also suggested (Chapter 14) that all overseas nuclear weapon systems should be withdrawn to their home territories. A more rapid rate of run-down by any nuclear-weapon state or the UN agency during one or more years might also be provided for in the Treaty.

Upon completion of the run-down, which would be of equal maximum duration under both options, specific research into, or the manufacture, possession, testing or use of nuclear weapons or other nuclear explosive devices would be declared to be uniformly and globally illegal for all states or agencies as a matter of positive law.

Enforcement

A collective enforcement system, including military measures, is outlined below as the most appropriate to sustain the Treaty for the Abolition of Nuclear Weapons. It would allow the necessary measures to be implemented quickly and effectively. The critical period is when non-nuclear-weapon states already possess a nuclear-weapon capability or (as seen in the case of Iraq) they attempt to acquire that capability. Up to the present it has not been argued that the mere possession of such a weapon is a threat to peace. It is not clear that the Security Council resolutions imposing disarmament measures on Iraq portend a wider interpretation of Article 39 of the UN Charter. It could be argued that the Iraq situation is unique. However, the Security Council has subsequently clearly stated that the proliferation of weapons of mass destruction is a threat to international peace and security.[6]

There is, of course, no intention of applying Article 39 to the nuclear-weapon states; under the foregoing proposals for a treaty they would be exempted from any such application so long as they conformed to the phased reduction of nuclear armaments within the agreed time scale. A further point is that the Security Council has been reluctant in the past to apply Article 39 in general. Moreover, there are only a few resolutions defining a situation as a 'threat to the peace'. State practice is far from clear as to the agreed interpretation of Article 39 with regard to the possession of weapons.

The way forward may be for the Treaty not only to make illegal (with the exceptions noted below) all relevant research and manufacture, testing, possession, deployment or use of nuclear weapons, but, in addition, to declare that any of these acts would constitute a threat to the peace within the meaning of Article 39. The run-down arrangements, outlined in the following sections, with respect to the nuclear-weapon states, would be the subject matter of the exemption, limited as it is both quantitatively and temporally. One should be aware that problems may arise of judging when research and production activities--which may be equivocal--are embraced by these formulations.

The Run-Down Period

On the road to the abolition of nuclear weapons and whilst the nuclear-weapon states are running their numbers down to zero over a period of years, two alternative proposals are made in the following sections of this chapter. These are Security Council control or control by a UN agency. The premise of both alternatives is that it would be undesirable to leave the decision about the use of a nuclear weapon to an individual nuclear-weapon state--as it is at the moment. There should be a transfer of decision to an international authority of some kind. This may not be ideal but would be better than leaving the decision to any individual state.

The Treaty should, however, establish that the only function of these residual nuclear weapons is that of deterring the use of nuclear weapons by any state. There should be no question of any internationally-authorized first use of a nuclear weapon.

There are a number of problems in the international control of nuclear weapons. Should just the decision to use be transferred, leaving the operational procedures in the hands of the existing nuclear-weapon states? Or, should there be an actual transfer of operational authority to an international agency? One possibility is for the Treaty to require that any decision to use a nuclear weapon must be that of the Security Council. The possibility of a veto then arises: it would hardly be acceptable to face a potential veto by any of the five permanent members of the Security Council (who are themselves the five nuclear-weapon states), for a transgressor might conceivably be one of the five themselves. But it would be a very large surrender of sovereignty for the nuclear-weapon states to delegate such a decision to an external body.

The Treaty might provide for a rapid response: if any state were to use a nuclear weapon on any other state, there could be retaliation with a nuclear weapon. However, the precise nature of that response is left open. This indicates the great utility of the UN Agency idea, whereby such an agency is required by the Treaty to provide a nuclear response to the use of a nuclear weapon by any state. It is difficult to envisage an agreement to remit this decision to any single individual, hence the proposal suggested below for an independent commission of specialists. It should be again recalled that such a decision would occur in a world of very substantial nuclear disarmament, and consequently where the idea of the use of a nuclear weapon had become exceedingly remote. Consequently, arrangements might be feasible which at present seem to be beyond political possibility.

Some of those who have considered this matter envisage an internationally controlled nuclear-weapon capability for a long time, until there is absolute assurance that the possibilities of national nuclear-weapon capabilities have disappeared. There are those who envisage it as a virtually permanent institution, or likely to continue to the limit of our time horizon.

There are those too who find the whole idea of a UN nuclear-weapon capability unpalatable and unacceptable. The answer to them is, surely, that at least it is better than leaving the decision to an individual nuclear-weapon state, which is the present situation.

Security Council Control

Whilst the nuclear-weapon states are running the number of nuclear weapons down to zero over a period of years, these states could continue to manage their own forces, but could cede control of them to the Security Council. Their use would be solely for deterrence and not for war fighting or first use. The establishment of an integrated command and control system would, of course, be necessary.

The Security Council, in accordance with its powers under the Charter of the United Nations, could--it has been suggested--assign responsibility for decisions on substantial operational questions (i.e. prompt retaliation in case of the unauthorized use of a nuclear weapon, which would be declared an act of aggression) to an independent commission of specialists who would be appointed in their personal capacity and would not represent any government. The decisions of this commission would, therefore, involve no political consultation and would not be subject to the veto of any Member of the Security Council. The 'order to fire' would be assigned to one designated individual, but with appropriate safeguards. A model of such an independent body is to be found in the International Civil Service Commission whose members are appointed by the General Assembly but are required to operate independently of both the Assembly and their own national governments. However, this model may not be relevant. The importance of the decisions of the proposed body would be orders of magnitude greater than those of the International Civil Service Commission, and furthermore it might create a dangerous precedent in this context. An alternative decision-maker could be the existing Military Staff Committee established by Article 47 of the UN Charter.

Alongside any such arrangement and operating concurrently with it would be the dismantlement and destruction programme already outlined. This would need to be co-ordinated between nuclear-weapon states and with the Security Council so that an appropriate deterrent was in place world-wide, albeit of a continually diminishing size. During the run-down period improved technological and societal means of verification would be developed and put into place.

The Security Council would throughout, of course, have its existing and enduring right under Articles 41 and 42 of the Charter of the United Nations to take military or other measures to give effect to its decisions concerning the maintenance or restoration of international peace and security. Such decisions could be expected to pertain to any infringement of the Treaty, including, for example, refusal to allow inspections.

UN Agency Control

Joseph Rotblat and Vitalii Goldanskii at one time proposed the creation of a new organ of the United Nations as a keeper of a small number of nuclear weapons and means of delivery. [7] A somewhat similar proposal has been made by Gerard C. Smith [5] (see also Chapters 11 and 12). It should be noted, however, that some authors of this book (including Joseph Rotblat, private communication) do not agree with this idea. It would correspond to Security Council control just outlined, in that a similar dismantlement and destruction programme with a like time-dimension would be established.

It would differ in that a minimum number of nuclear weapons would be assigned to a special UN Agency, and these would be the last to be dismantled and destroyed. The agency would be an independent legal entity, established under the Treaty. Questions of governance, staff, financing and dispute settlement would have to be addressed. It would report to the Security Council. The Treaty should provide for the dissolution of the Agency when its purpose has been fulfilled.

As with the Security Council control proposal, decisions on substantial operational questions could be assigned to an independent commission of specialists not representing governments or to the Military Staff Committee. The Agency would need to enter into agreements with all nuclear-weapon states whereby the title and the exclusive right to control the relevant weapons were vested in the Agency, but the weapons and their delivery systems would be manned, maintained in operational order and operated on behalf of the Agency by the transferring state. An integrated command and control system would also be required.

Violations and Verification

The Treaty should specify violations and the sanctions for such violations. The means of redress for violations would be action by the Security Council pursuant to its general powers under the Charter of the United Nations, to maintain or restore international peace or security. The enforcement character of the responses is thus clear. This role of the Security Council would last throughout the run-down period.

The question of enforcement is dealt with in Chapter 8. It would be a mistake to equate enforcement with the use of nuclear weapons. It, therefore, should be stressed that, under the Treaty regime, nuclear weapons would *never* be used unless some state had used them first. During the run-down period leading to the abolition of nuclear weapons, any such weapons would be internationally controlled and would be used only for deterrence.

The aftermath of the Gulf War exposed violations of the NPT by Iraq, to which it is a party. This clearly shows that the existing powers and procedures of the International Atomic Energy Agency to monitor compliance with that Treaty are insufficient and ineffective. It would be necessary, therefore, to expand the authority of the IAEA and strengthen its procedures. With such enhanced authority and improved procedures, the IAEA would be the appropriate body to verify compliance with the proposed Treaty for the Abolition of Nuclear Weapons. The nature of the necessary inspection and verification regime is discussed in Chapter 8. The IAEA would need to retain this role indefinitely, along with its concern with non-military uses of atomic energy. There should be a permanent and verifiable ban on all nuclear secrecy, with full public disclosure of the character and purpose of the peaceful uses of nuclear energy.

The technology of verification is dealt with in Chapter 4 and a substantial part of the Treaty would perforce be concerned with verification. Inspection 'anytime, anywhere' would be paramount, and this would mean the total abolition of the idea of military secrecy in relation to the possession or attempted possession of nuclear weapons. There is also the need for prompt action to prevent the illicit movement of nuclear weapons-usable material. It is not enough just to verify that such material is not improperly moved from its containment site, but that there is adequate force available to prevent any attempt to move it. Whether these security requirements should be met by the state concerned or by some kind of international force is still to be resolved.

Societal Verification

Chapter 6 sets out the case for societal verification both to enforce and to complement conventional verification procedures. The Treaty itself should contain a provision to buttress societal verification. All states parties would undertake to enact in their domestic law stipulations whereby all citizens and residents would be required and empowered to report any observed breaches of the Treaty to the IAEA or another special agency, and be protected from prosecution or any other penalty or disability for so doing.

These treaty provisions would remove a basic criticism of early proposals for societal verification: that is was advancing an idea that would be politically unacceptable to most governments. The adoption of a Treaty for the Abolition of Nuclear Weapons would carry with it consent to societal verification. Fear of retaliation by one's own government should disappear.

An observer of international politics has recently commented [8]

the possibilities of enlisting the cooperation of citizens in monitoring the activities of their own government are much more realistic. (Even in terrorized Iraq, a defector informed UN inspectors of the whereabouts of some of Saddam Hussein's previously unknown nuclear facilities).

The same writer continues:

some hope that, in an age of democratic yearning, people can be encouraged to put principles of democracy and dedication to an open society ahead of blind obedience and false patriotism. ... the presence of millions of citizens who are no longer terrorized by their own governments can serve as an added deterrent to cheating on a disarmament agreement. ... In a demobilizing world in which democratic aspirations are virtually universal and democratic practice is expanding, it will be harder to conceal violations of any disarmament arrangement.

Here, of course, concern is solely with the abolition of nuclear weapons, not with general disarmament, so the goal may be more easily achieved.

Reparation and Satisfaction

Up to now there has been no multinational arms regulation or disarmament agreement dealing with the general aspects of state responsibility. Nevertheless, the draft presented by different rapporteurs in the International Law Commission has gained widespread acceptance.[9] The main rights of the injured state are embodied in Article 6 of the Fifth Report of 1984, whereby the injured state may *inter alia* require that the state which has committed an internationally wrongful act should "*discontinue the act ... re-establish the situation that existed before ... [and] provide appropriate guarantees against repetition of the act*".

Article 8 of the Fifth Report lists some rights for the injured state, including the right to suspend the performance of its obligations towards that state which has committed an internationally wrongful act, if such obligations correspond to, or are directly connected to, the obligation breached.

Whilst application of the principle in Article 8 above to the Treaty for the Abolition of Nuclear Weapons is hard to envisage, the principles in Article 6 might be embodied, *mutatis mutandis*, in the Treaty.

Withdrawal and Amendment

The Treaty should be of indefinite duration, with no right of withdrawal and without conflict with the UN Charter. Many treaties contain withdrawal provisions. It is not necessary, however, that they do so. Indeed the Vienna Convention on the Law of Treaties[10], Article 60, which provides that a breach of a treaty may be a ground for terminating or suspending the operation of the treaty, expressly states that it is without prejudice to any provision of the treaty in question applicable in the event of a breach. Thus, a provision in the proposed Treaty for the Abolition of Nuclear Weapons which denies to parties the right to terminate or suspend the operation of the Treaty, or to withdraw from the Treaty, would not appear to be contrary to international treaty law.

Amendment and review clauses would be appropriate, modelled perhaps on those found in the Charter of the United

Nations, or in existing agreements on multilateral arms regulation and disarmament. International treaty law has already developed models of these and many of the other necessary provisions of a Treaty for the Abolition of Nuclear Weapons. It requires political will to bring such a treaty into being.

References

1. R. Falk, "Toward a Legal Regime for Nuclear Weapons" in A.S. Miller & M. Feinrider, *Nuclear Weapons and Law*, London 1984, p.124.

2. Protocol Additional to the Geneva Conventions of 12 August 1949, and relating to the Protection of Victims of International Armed Conflicts (Protocol I) Article 51 (4) (c).

3. R.D. Burns, *Disarmament in Perspective: An Analysis of Selected Arms Control and Disarmament Agreements Between the World Wars, 1919-1939*, 1968, p.20.

4. See, "Outlawing Nuclear Weapons", a letter from Lloyd G. Shore in *Bulletin of the Atomic Scientists*, March 1992, p.47.

5. G.C. Smith, "Take Nuclear Weapons into Custody", *Bulletin of the Atomic Scientists*, December 1990, pp.12-13.

6. UN Security Council Declaration, 31 January 1992, S/PV.3046.

7. In, *Verification: Monitoring Disarmament*, F. Calogero, M.L. Goldberger, & S. Kapitza eds., Westview Press, Boulder 1991, pp.205-218.

8. Richard J. Barnet, "Reflections: The Disorders of Peace", *The New Yorker*, 20 January 1991, p.62.

9. Draft Articles on State Responsibility adopted by the International Law Commission on First Reading, *Year-book ILD 1980* Volume II, part two, pp.31-2.

10. See, *International Legal Materials*, 1969, pp.679 *et seq.*

8

Verification and Enforcement in a NWFW

James Leonard, Martin Kaplan, and Benjamin Sanders

Verification and enforcement are related but not the same thing. The objective of the former is to ascertain whether a commitment--in this case, a promise not to develop or otherwise acquire nuclear weapons--is being faithfully observed. If it is not, then enforcement is needed to correct the problem.

Verification

The technical body that would be given the task of monitoring compliance might be part of the UN Secretariat, or be a semi-autonomous entity within the UN family of organizations. The verification of a treaty to ban nuclear weapons could be part of a larger verification organization, which was charged with the verification of all or most disarmament and arms control agreements, including such multilateral instruments as a chemical weapons convention or a comprehensive test ban, and perhaps even with observer functions pursuant to regional agreements on military disengagement or confidence-building. Such a body would be useful in providing central administration for all verification activities; it might also have a common data collection and analysis service, but it should have a separate technical unit with a specialized staff for each treaty-specific form of verification it is asked to perform. Each such unit could recruit its staff from the stated parties to the disarmament measure in connection with which the unit carries out its verification task.

States that have their own sophisticated means of collecting and analysing data would no doubt continue to use them. Any information they share with the verification body will be so formulated as to avoid giving an insight into the way they collect and analyse their data. They would also be reluctant to share information that might give the verifying organization an insight into weapon production or testing procedures, lest doing so might contribute to proliferation. It is likely, therefore, that verification of compliance with disarmament undertakings of the kind discussed here will always have to rely on a combination of national technical means and international monitoring measures, based both on direct observation and pre-digested data derived from national technical means.

Clearly any new organization would draw on the experience--which is now beginning to build up--of verification of past arms control agreements. The next two sections consider, first, the case for the International Atomic Energy Agency (IAEA) taking on the verification of a NWFW Treaty, and second, the ideas that can be transferred from the long negotiations about methods of verification of the Chemical Weapons Convention.

The IAEA

Should the International Atomic Energy Agency be entrusted with verification functions in respect of the elimination of nuclear weapons? It is the one international body in the UN system now in existence with experience in monitoring nuclear activities to ensure that they do not serve the production of nuclear weapons. Given the wide expertise the Agency has gained in this respect, it would seem logical to involve it in the process. There are objections, mainly based on three arguments: first, that being a promotional body in the nuclear field, the Agency cannot effectively carry out a monitoring and potentially restrictive function; secondly, that the Agency's inability to deter Iraq from embarking on an ambitious weapon-production programme shows that its verification system would not be up to the task; and thirdly, that the Agency is not authorized by its Statute to do that kind of job anyway.

All three arguments are based on misunderstandings. While it is one of the two principal tasks of the IAEA to provide assistance in the development of nuclear energy for peaceful purposes, it may do so only upon assurance that such assistance is not used for proscribed ends. Its verification ('safeguards') system is the basic condition for its promotional activity. That system has been applied too restrictively in the past, which gave Iraq a chance to profit from legalistic loopholes, but still delayed its vast effort to a large degree. The system is now being tightened and the loopholes will be closed.

The issue of statutory appropriateness calls for a little more comment. The IAEA arose from the 1953 *Atoms for Peace* initiative of President Eisenhower, which was based on the idea that the peaceful uses of atomic energy and nuclear disarmament could be furthered by the transfer of nuclear material from military to civilian uses. To this end, an international agency would be set up through which all international cooperation in nuclear matters would be channelled. It would have stocks of nuclear material for peaceful use that would be withdrawn from military use, and it would be given the means to ensure that the material was only used for peaceful purposes. In this way, the Agency's promotional activities would become an effective instrument of nuclear arms limitation.

This provides an additional answer to the contention that there is a conflict of interest between promotion and restriction. On the contrary: that very approach is laid down in the IAEA's Statute, among other things in the provision for international storage of surplus nuclear material, under the Agency's aegis. It foresees precisely the situation that now faces us: the withdrawal of nuclear material from military use. It would indeed be appropriate if, forty years after its inception, this visionary plan should come to fruition.

Lessons from the Chemical Weapons Convention

Negotiations for a Chemical Weapons Convention (CWC), now successfully completed, have for many years struggled to reach agreement on the formulation of a suitable organizational structure. A major component of this structure is the technical secretariat charged with ensuring compliance with a treaty totally banning these weapons and including highly intrusive inspection procedures. Many of the problems involved with regard to nuclear weapons are similar, but would be much less complicated than those which arise with chemical weapons. Much helpful groundwork is contained in the Pugwash Monograph on Verification. [1]

Administrative Structure. Using the CWC as a model, one can envisage a scheme for the administrative structure of the Verification Agency for nuclear weapons. It would have three major organs: a General Assembly (one vote per member country); an Executive Board; and a Technical Secretariat, the head of which would be elected by the General Assembly on the recommendation of the Executive Board.

The *Assembly* could meet annually unless special sessions are convened on urgent matters requiring their decision. Decisions on matters of substance would be taken as far as possible by consensus. It is the principal organ of the Agency and supersedes in authority the Executive Board and Technical Secretariat. It considers and adopts the programme and budget of the Agency. A Scientific Advisory Board would be required to provide independent and specialized advice to the Agency in areas of science and technology.

The *Executive Board* would promote the implementation of the agreement establishing the Agency, supervise the Technical Secretariat, deal with matters of compliance with the agreement, draft the programme and budget for submission to the Assembly, and perform any other functions relegated to it by the Assembly.

The *Technical Secretariat* would carry out international verification measures noted in the basic agreement, address and receive communications from the members states, inform the Executive Board of any problems concerning its function, provide technical assistance to its member states, and establish an Inspectorate as a special unit under the supervision of the Secretary-General of the secretariat. As a general principle, the Secretary-General, the inspectors and other staff members should not seek or receive instructions from any Government, or from any other source external to the Agency.

Inspection Procedures. In a NWFW, a major activity will be inspection, either routine or 'challenge' in nature, to ensure compliance with the Agency agreement banning research, development, manufacture or stockpiling of nuclear weapons or the transfer of any information in this connection. This would be the primary activity of the Inspectorate. Various inspection procedures have been worked out both on a bilateral basis (INF), and as a multilateral activity (IAEA). The INF calls for verification of the complete elimination of the weapons concerned. The treaty for a Chemical Weapons Convention bars all research (except of a limited nature for protective purposes), development, and stockpiling of these weapons. The provisions are close to those needed with regard to nuclear weapons, although those for chemicals are far more extensive than would be needed for zero nuclear weapons. The relatively non-contentious points governing the Inspectorate can be referred to in the 27 August 1991 Report on Chemical Weapons prepared for the Conference on Disarmament. [2] This subject would have to be considered in detail when the functions of the Inspectorate of the Enforcement Agency was elaborated in the course of reaching a final agreement, to deal with such matters as precursors of nuclear weapons material, steps for the development of a nuclear device, weapons-grade chemicals (enriched uranium, the plutonium cycle, destruction procedures, and so on).

Routine and Challenge Inspections. Negotiators for a CWC have essentially agreed on principles and practices that would govern routine inspections. These have been accepted by the chemical industries, despite the intrusiveness of some of the measures. There have been considerable difficulties in the negotiations for challenge inspections for suspected violations of the CWC, which were first advocated by President Bush in 1984 *"any place, any time without the right of refusal"*. During continued negotiations on this point the USA retreated from the former Bush position and tabled a series of proposals negating the concept, but subsequently it accepted a modified inspection role, labelled 'managed access'.

However, for the verification of a NWFW Treaty, there is no doubt that an 'any place, any time without the right of refusal' rule for challenge inspections would be needed. In a NWFW, it would not be acceptable for a state to retain any military secrecy for any operations which might be relevant to a nuclear-weapon capability. No state would be permitted to declare that any building was off bounds for inspection.

Enforcement

This analysis starts with the assumption that an agreement not to possess nuclear weapons has been accepted by the entire international community, with perhaps insignificant exceptions, and that the Security Council has been charged with enforcing the agreement. In addition to this ban on possession, it is assumed that a prohibition on use of nuclear weapons has been established either in conjunction with, or prior to, the treaty barring possession. In connection with enforcement, one can imagine that regional and other organizations will also have been given roles, but action there would be skirmishing, relating mainly to verification or to preliminary political manoeuvres. The real focus of enforcement for a long time to come will certainly be in the Council. Moreover, it will be a Council much like the present institution. Its composition and some procedures should, and probably will, be improved, but its powers--and the veto provisions--are not likely to be too different in 2010 or 2020 from what was established in 1945.

If ten or twenty years from now there is a ban, and the verification machinery sounds an alarm that some government may have violated the ban, or may be preparing a violation, what can the international community or its members do in response? The first duty of the Council will be to assess the seriousness of the problem. If the case has moved through preliminary screening in the IAEA or elsewhere, then there probably will have been some fault on the part of the accused. In one scenario, the basic charge may be without merit; the accused, indignant at being falsely put in the dock, may have rejected some of the procedures that it was obliged to accept. If this is how most of the Council assess the case, they presumably will try to use diplomacy--special representatives and bilateral contacts, for example--to persuade the accused to demonstrate his innocence.

If such efforts fail, the Council should then move to sanctions, but certainly not to military measures. It is dealing with a breach of good order, not a breach of the peace. It should take the matter seriously in order to avoid setting a bad precedent for a case in which a violation is involved, but it can afford to proceed quite deliberately, giving time for sound counsel and second thoughts to take effect. Any sanctions imposed should be designed for political impact and should avoid driving the accused into a defiant mode. Once the case had dropped off the front page, it is hard to imagine that ways would not be found to assist the accused in exculpating himself and turning the tables on the accuser.

A second and far more serious scenario will unfold if major accusations are made and major powers believe that they have a real basis. Again, an assessment must be made of the gravity and urgency of the problem. Is the accused likely to have a bomb rather soon? Does he perhaps already possess one or more? How is he likely to use his capability: in an offensive or only in a defensive or political mode? Are other states likely to move to pre-empt? What kind of leaders are involved? Is this a crisis which must be resolved at once or is there time to negotiate, time to let economic pressures work on the accused?

It is evident that a very wide variety of situations could develop under this general heading. The international community should and surely would take the matter seriously. Having worked its way out of a nuclear world and into one free of nuclear weapons, the community would rightly be outraged at any government that tried to destroy or to take advantage of that achievement. It could be expected that the Security Council would have little difficulty enacting, step-by-step, an almost total and effective isolation of the violator, on the lines of what was done against Saddam Hussein before the Gulf War.

If the danger appears imminent, and political pressures combined with economic isolation seem too slow or ineffective a response, then military measures will certainly be considered.

Again one can imagine a wide range of possibilities, depending on whether the violator is large and relatively invulnerable, or is small and rather vulnerable.

If the violator is a large and powerful state, one must hope that large-scale military measures will be rejected. It hardly makes sense to initiate a large and inevitably bloody war in such circumstances. If other major states are convinced that the violator can become a threat to their security, one or more of them will re-nuclearize, taking us back to the world of mutual deterrence. That is not an ideal world, but it is far less terrible than one embroiled in a major war. And it is a world that can again evolve into a world free of nuclear weapons, once the violator has seen that he gained nothing by his re-nuclearization. The task of the Security Council in this scenario will be to maintain political pressures, economic sanctions, and perhaps military harassments against the violator for as long as may be necessary.

This analysis will fail to satisfy many people who, not unreasonably, want clear answers to clear questions. The matter should, however, be seen in perspective. The re-nuclearization of a large state is only one of a large class of problems of international security for which we do not now have, and may never develop, thoroughly satisfactory general solutions. It may be some consolation to reflect that it is also a quite unlikely danger, since large states are inherently much less vulnerable to aggression than small states and thus are less likely to feel a need for nuclear weapons. (We have been badly misled by the special circumstances after World War II which led five powerful states to build large stocks of weapons which they did not, in fact, need to ensure their security. The model for a new nuclear state in a 21st century world free of nuclear weapons, is likely to be Israel or Iraq rather than the Soviet Union or India.)

Major states are unlikely to re-nuclearize for another complex of reasons. If a world free of nuclear weapons is realized early in the next century, as seems possible, it will be precisely the largest and most powerful states, which now have nuclear weapons, that will have gone through the process of determining that they are more secure in a world with no nuclear weapons. That will be in each case an extended, intense debate, producing a national consensus which will not readily be annulled or subverted. These states are, therefore, not likely to reverse course unless there is a catastrophic decline of world order--a disintegration descending far below the present imperfect level. Nor are large states like Brazil, Nigeria, or Indonesia likely to face security threats for which nuclear weapons would have any relevance.

In sum, it can be said that the enforcement of a ban on nuclear weapons against a very large violator of the ban is a difficult, perhaps in some sense an insoluble problem. It is also one which the international system is not likely to face.

The considerations if a small state violates the ban are rather different. It was suggested above that Iraq or Israel might be a model which some state or other would be tempted to follow even after the attainment of a world free of nuclear weapons. The examples are not chosen at random. The first, Israel, has a serious security problem for which a nuclear capability appears to offer at least a partial and temporary answer. The other, Iraq, is about as 'pure' an example as one is likely to see of an aggressive despot interested in intimidating or defeating his neighbours for ignoble purposes. Israel's weapon capability is a last resort, designed to avert a catastrophic defeat by conventional forces. (Its acquisition may have been unwise; that is another matter.) Iraq's desired capability may or may not have been intended for offensive use. At the least, it was sought as an umbrella, a deterrent, under which Saddam could carry out political intimidation or military aggression without having to fear a nuclear response.

In a world free of nuclear weapons, the way in which the Security Council would deal with a small country which threatened to go nuclear should be calibrated to the position of that country on the spectrum between Israel and Iraq. If the state going nuclear is in a situation like Israel's, the international system will have the right to interdict, but only if it can provide alternative, better solutions to that country's security problem. What might be the form of security guarantees, how to make them convincing both to the endangered nation and to its adversaries, which states would stand behind a Security Council dictum--all these are precisely the problems of organizing an effective peace in a world still full of dangers. The nuclear case is one important example of the problems that the next several generations will have to wrestle with.

If, on the other hand, the Council faces a situation rather like Iraq, it is to be hoped that it will use the measures enumerated in

Article 42 of the UN Charter, up to and, if necessary, including the use of force, in order to halt the nuclear-weapon programme it faces. This repertory of non-military measures, and preparation of modest means of military intervention, both by forces dedicated to the UN and by national forces available to back up the UN troops, are likely to undergo a considerable development over the next twenty or thirty years, quite apart from whether a world free of nuclear weapons is or is not realized. This is because the world is surely not going to be free of wars, aggressions, and threats of aggression, and the Council will have to work through, in real life, a variety of crises which will equip it with at least a certain number of precedents, both successes and failures, on how to handle threats to international security.

Readers of this chapter who come from small states will have noted a certain unfairness in the enforcement machinery being described. Large states should not, we argue, be the object of all-out military measures to deal with a violation of a ban on nuclear weapons. Small states might be. There can be no disputing the charge of unfairness.

The obvious response is that the world is unfair, not the authors of this chapter. It is clearly not morally defensible to urge the sacrifice of thousands of lives in a war against some large state for the sake of avoiding the charge of a double standard. Nor should the international community shrink from sacrificing lives if it can thereby avert the danger that a petty despot will commit aggression which would be far more costly.

Two other comments may soften the sharpness of the contrast. Even against a very powerful state there may be measures of a military character, a blockade for example, which the Security Council could order without putting large numbers of lives at risk. If the case were sufficiently grave and the necessary military coalition could be organized by the Council, even more extensive measures could be considered. The violator's navy could be attacked if it sailed from its home ports. His airforce could be ordered not to fly in part or all of his territory under penalty of coming under coalition attack. These are cited as examples of what was above referred to as a repertory of measures, and they could be used as appropriate to the particular situation, whether the violator was large or small. When the Security Council is pondering what to do about a violation it has more choices than an all-out land invasion versus doing nothing at all.

The second comment on 'unfairness' is that small states, though they might have better reasons than large states to want a nuclear weapon, are still most unlikely to try to get one. They have been the strongest supporters of the 'unfair' Non-Proliferation Treaty, and they are today the strongest advocates of the complete elimination of nuclear weapons. This is not out of some altruistic idealism, but flows from a hard-nosed assessment of their security interests. Many small states have, or fear they will have, an aggressive neighbour. They have thought it through and have decided that they are more secure if neither has nuclear weapons than if both do.   They have, therefore, committed themselves to non-nuclear status, usually through the NPT. This preference of small states for a nuclear-free neighbourhood can only be enhanced by the realization of a NWFW. The problem cases that the Security Council will face are, therefore, likely to be few in number, a megalomaniac here and there who will need to be brought into line, most often for human rights violations as well as nuclear ambitions. Cases analogous to Israel are likely to be very rare; in fact most of the candidates are readily identified today: Taiwan, for example. New possibilities can emerge when heterogenous states break up--for example, Armenia and Croatia; it will be important to give them confidence that their security will be protected by means other than nuclear.

The number of potential violators, large and small, is thus quite limited. The image, so widely accepted in the nuclear-weapon states, of a vast jungle of dark-skinned, irresponsible military dictatorships longing to get their hands on these symbols of power and modernity, is simply false. The few states, like Saddam's Iraq, which do fit that stereotype, are generally vulnerable to a military intervention or even to pressures short of military action.

A world free of nuclear weapons will not be a fragile, unstable structure, doomed to collapse at the first major crisis, dangerously at the mercy of the first despot who develops his own bomb. Neither will it be a world from which war and the danger of war have been eradicated. There will be more than enough ancient hatreds and twisted egos to require a much more effective security system than exists today. The danger that some evil leader may go for a bomb is one, but only one, of the serious contingencies with which the Security Council may have to deal.

The danger is greatest if that leader commands substantial conventional strength and is relatively free of internal constraints. Hence the importance to a world that wants to remain free of nuclear weapons of maintaining stringent controls on conventional weapons and of fostering human rights and democratic structures.

Since the world without the bomb will remain dangerous--though less dangerous than with the bomb--it is important that the Security Council has a substantial potential to bring military force into play. It is not likely that anything more than small detachments comparable in size to classical peacekeeping units will be made permanently and continuously available to the Council and the Secretary-General. Whether governments are or are not permanent members of the Council, they will wish to retain their sovereign veto on the risks to which they permit their armed forces to be exposed. What the Council is likely to have for enforcement actions are small rapid-reaction units backed up by major national forces of large powers under national (or an agreed coalition) command. Under current conditions, which are not likely to alter rapidly, US leadership in any such enforcement action is obviously a *sine qua non*.

US leadership in bringing the nuclear-weapon states to eliminate their nuclear weapons is also essential; once it has been exercised to carry through the de-nuclearization process, it can be expected that the USA will go to considerable lengths to prevent any backsliding.

If a violator of the ban is just too large for the international community to take on militarily, there will be no choice but to rely on political and economic pressures. No consideration should be given to the idea that a small stock of nuclear weapons should be put under the control of the Security Council to use if necessary. Even the smallest nuclear weapon is too indiscriminate in its effects. Far worse, it would break the taboo which has continuously grown stronger since Nagasaki, and it would open the way to re-nuclearization. Just as one should not launch a world war to prevent a world war, so one should not use a nuclear weapon to prevent the acquisition of a nuclear weapon or even to punish its use.

If it is not possible for the Council to cut short promptly an effort to go nuclear, it must as a minimum warn the violator, large or small, that any use of his weapon will be dealt with in a truly drastic manner. It should perhaps be part of the agreement that formalizes the nuclear-free status of the world community that the development and possession of a nuclear weapon is designated as an international crime, to be punished as the community may decide. If that is the case, then any *use* of a weapon would be a far greater crime. The entire leadership of any state that might be guilty of such a crime should be on notice that it will have made itself an outlaw band, to be pursued and punished in the most severe way. The people of that nation as well, though they may be helpless and even, in a sense, innocent, should still be made aware that if a weapon is used their motherland will inevitably suffer heavy consequences in what follows.

In order to deal with the contingencies that may arise, whether or not they have a nuclear component, it will remain important for the states which have substantial conventional forces, and the political freedom to use them, to be willing to despatch their forces under Security Council mandate. This means that the principal enforcement arm of the Security Council will be the armed forces of the USA and some of its close allies, supplemented in certain cases by regional friends.

No-one is comfortable with this 'world policeman' arrangement, but it is impossible to get away from the facts. The more broadly this policeman role is shared the better, both for the USA and for the development of a true security community. But for some time to come the USA will be the Sheriff and its friends will be the Deputy Sheriffs. How well they carry out those roles will have a decisive significance for the development of a decent, fair and peaceful international order, and on the place the USA makes for itself in the history of the Twenty-First Century.

References

1.   *Verification: Monitoring Disarmament*, F. Calogero, M.L. Goldberger and S.P. Kapitza eds., Westview Press, Boulder 1991.

2.   CD/1108, pp.136-172.

9

International Security in a NWFW

Shalheveth Freier

Introduction

As far as my imagination goes, international security in a NWFW should not be much different from the maintenance of internal security in a Western democracy, of which I recognize the following ingredients: an overwhelming consensus on the rule of law, on permissible conduct, and on the obligations of citizens; on the existence of an enforcement agency (the police), able to deal with trespasses; and on an educated electorate able to give vent to its desires and dissatisfactions in periodic elections. Moreover--and I believe this to be important--these countries have a sense of pride which reposes largely on their intrinsic performance and achievement. Having said this, I do not wish to imply that the Western democracies are always virtuous in their international behaviour. Not at all--look only at their lucrative arms trade, with little concern where and when those arms will be employed. But I claim the ingredients of a Western democracy are still the best we have, in trying to contemplate a livable world, made up of many countries.

It is immediately apparent that the ingredients of a democracy are completely lacking in the community of nations, as compared with a community of citizens--a democratic nation. It seems therefore, however unpalatable the thought is to a citizen of a democratic country, that the community of nations needs to pass through some intermediate states, in which some nations will lead, and some will have to be led, before all will share those norms which make peaceful cohabitation possible: that is, in which international security is assured. Of course we have much of this inequality even now. The General Assembly of the UN--with one country, one vote--is a complete fiction, and hundreds of resolutions against war have not prevented a single one.

Much more power resides in the permanent members of the Security Council, certainly not so democratic an arrangement, and more power still in understandings between the heads of government of the major nations. It pays to face these facts soberly and acknowledge them. This is necessary if we wish the transitory period, in which some nations lead and some are led, to result in a community of nations which share the norms on which the maintenance of international security must rest.

There is some comfort in the fact that there are no more than about 200 sovereign states in the world. This is a number which permits individual study of each one. On the other hand, there is the disturbing fact that many of these states lack the coherence, internal stability and the popular support which make for a reliable partnership and a coherent policy in the quest for a secure world.

In the following sections an attempt will be made to address some of these problems, in the hope of advancing a little the discussion of international security in a NWFW.

Assumptions

The thoughts presented in this chapter build on three assumptions.

First, nuclear weapons are bad, for five reasons:

*   they are so destructive that irreparable damage can have been done, once they have been employed, and second thoughts cannot redress the damage; conventional weapons are not as indiscriminately destructive, and second thoughts might limit the extent of the damage they cause;

* they effect lasting and pernicious injury to people and the environment;

* they tend to proliferate also to countries which might feel less inhibited in contemplating their use than the recognized and veteran nuclear-weapon states;

* once the threshold has been passed, and a nuclear weapon has been employed in an actual conflict, there is no credible barrier to their escalation in number and destructive power;

* there is the possible loss of control over such weapons by a government whose authority is contested--or which is not otherwise in complete charge of military hardware, installations and personnel on its soil; this could have devastating consequences. This contingency has assumed a measure of likelihood with the break-up of the USSR, the internal instabilities in some of the republics and the uneasy relations between some of them.

Secondly, a NWFW can only be attained in passing through some intermediate stages, some of which need necessarily be concurrent.

Before nuclear weapons are eliminated, their numbers need be reduced and a residual nuclear arsenal be set up under multinational--not international--control. This residual arsenal cannot be eliminated and must be in place until two conditions are fulfilled: a credible verification regime is instituted which ensures that nuclear weapons and their carriers are not developed or produced anywhere, and a mobile military force is established for speedy intervention in order to halt the outbreak of hostilities between states, anywhere, at an early stage. A third condition, of course, is the commitment on the part of the major powers--those which control the residual arsenal--not to use military force in the settlement of any claim pertaining to their individual interest.

Thirdly, a verification regime and a mobile military force address only a very limited, though indispensable, aspect of the transition to a NWFW, and its eventual establishment. Policing actions are credible only if an overwhelming consensus exists all round that wars are an unprofitable way of settling conflicts. The creation of such a consensus and such a climate must be addressed, in parallel, with commensurate vigour.

Security in a NWFW: Problems and Proposals

The problems of a NWFW can be divided into two categories: those which concern the coercive aspects of a NWFW--verification and a mobile intervention force--and those which can create the appropriate international setting and climate.

Recent experience suggests that international verification, as practised by the IAEA, can at most serve as a useful back-up to regional verification, as embodied in Nuclear-Weapon-Free Zones (NWFZs). It is, after all, one's neighbour which most often constitutes a military threat. Regional negotiation of a NWFZ, and mutual, rather than international, inspection of each other's installations are much more reassuring than an international team of inspectors, whose sense of mission is necessarily limited in motivation and subject to extraneous considerations, such as being welcome to the inspected party.

I therefore suggest that the practice of negotiating NWFZs regionally be encouraged, and that the IAEA serve not as a substitute for them but rather as an instrument of technical expertise and overall assurance that the NWFZs are established, and function, in conformity with their purpose. The Non-Proliferation Treaty is useful only when you do not intend to cheat.

A mobile intervention force poses two problems: who controls it and what size should it be. In the matter of control it is evident, as is the case with the Security Council, that some countries will make the decision, and some will not. The countries which should make the decisions must be such as are relatively immune from yielding to venal or particular interests, have a sense of global responsibility, and have publicly renounced recourse to war in the pursuit of their national interest.

Such a sense of global responsibility can only reside in countries which are militarily and economically powerful and can afford not to think of their own interests each time they are called upon to make unpalatable decisions. Their judgement must be tempered by the association of other countries in their councils, which have equally renounced recourse to war in the settlement of such problems as they might have with their neighbours. The controlling body, moreover, must address itself to the identification and settlement of conflicts before they erupt into war.

In fact, the controlling body should publicly and periodically survey the state of the world. This survey could increase our awareness of conflicts which do or may lead to wars, destruction and destitution. The UN has been highly selective in this matter. Irrespective of Iraq, it would seem that arraigning Israel--at least in the past--has been its major contribution to the identification and 'settlement' of conflicts in the Middle East.

The size of the mobile intervention force is something to be thought about; it must have the capability to halt military conflicts. This in turn implies that in a NWFW there cannot be unfettered arms races. Arms reductions must be negotiated between potential adversaries, especially those which have a powerful military establishment at their disposal. There is a clear correlation between the size and credibility of the mobile intervention force and the forces at the disposal of potential adversaries in a military conflict. Moreover, speed is of the essence. Kuwait was largely destroyed before the Iraqi army was rolled back.

This survey of the coercive measures which would have to be a part of a NWFW is of necessity partial and does not do justice to the problems which stem from the fact that the world is anything but uniform in its values and circumstances. At the same time, an appropriate international setting and climate must be generated in parallel with the introduction of the coercive measures.

Indeed, coercive measures by themselves have only a limited life-span, unless they are supported by norms of behaviour which are willingly accepted, such as the rule of law and its enforcement within national states.

Creating the climate and the setting in which international security can be built must take account of the following problems:

* some nations are powerful militarily and economically, and dispose of a vast human and resource potential; others are bereft of any power to influence their destinies;

* states differ widely in their sense of identity and pride; some

take pride in their military prowess and sense of power; some in their economic, social and scientific achievements; some are preoccupied with their internal struggles--with no sense of being part of the international community; some just wish to be left alone with their co-nationals, with whom they share a common history; and some have religious affinities which determine their transcendent sense of belonging. This division is not neat: some states combine a mixture of these attributes.

Under these circumstances, it is difficult to inculcate the overwhelming interest all states should have in eliminating the scourge of war. This will take time, but two approaches commend themselves: the organizational and the educational approach.

The Organizational Approach

This approach should take advantage of the experience of those regions of the world where--within the region--there is security: it has become inconceivable that military force would be used to settle disputes within such a region. This is true of the Scandinavian countries, for example, and also now of the countries of the European Community. What organizational approaches have helped to bring this result about? At the political level, the Ministers in the various countreis are in constant contact, and have built up a habit of collaboration. It is assumed that sooner or later points of difference will be solved and that compromise solutions will be found. There is a great deal of intra-trade, and people are free to move from one country to another. As part of the general background, all the states are democratic, and that was a necessary condition: Spain could not have joined while Franco was in power.

The approach, therefore, should emphasize in thought, speech and action the growing interdependence of states, and eventually its all-inclusive character. Especially, economic planning and industrial development supported by international funds should pay heed to creating interdependence between states which are potential adversaries. This should be done also in thought and speech, because it is also necessary that the sense of interdependence be brought into relief, at a high profile.

Regional groupings should be promoted, in order to offset the artificial and incidental nature of many small states. Such regional groups may guarantee economic and social viability to such small states without infringing their sense of identity. In an interdependent world, such regional groups are in fact inevitable.

The common hazards we face are a compelling argument in favour of common action--certainly regional common action. Their recognition, and the need for joint action to deal with them, largely transcend the particular sensibilities of individual states, and can help in adjusting the sense of priorities of states which otherwise desire to go it alone.

If regional collaboration of this kind becomes more widespread, that will certainly help to smooth the path for developments such as the outlawing of nuclear weapons. However, progress towards a NWFW should be possible even while there are still some regions of the world where conflicts are likely to break out. A fully peaceful world is not a necessary condition for abolition of nuclear weapons.

The Educational Approach

This is conceptually the most challenging. It requires sustained effort.

We should try to create a sense of national identity which does not derive from an accrual of power, but from distinction in those areas which constitute the contribution of a state to the common international weal.

This goal does not contradict the reality which has become manifest in recent times, that common history is a bond which reasserts itself within nations which have been forcibly amalgamated in bigger unions. There seems much to be said in favour of recognizing these communal identities and not promoting unnatural uniformity. The regional groups can take care of the practical--rather than emotional--interests, common to the states of a region.

In the realm of education proper, we must acknowledge that vast populations are suffering and will continue to suffer from the conditions created by the industrial and scientific nations. It is not conceivable that in the long run, there will be populations deprived of access to the occupations and preoccupations of the more affluent and successful nations of the world.

This is easily said, but daunting as a challenge. It demands education in all spheres and on all levels, in order to increase popular participation in national decision and to enhance the potential of individual people to chose and lead lives satisfactory to them.   It tacitly assumes that the ideas that Western democracies have about themselves reflect in fact desirable values and criteria. This is not at all certain, but I can see no other way of trying to attend to the problems of a world which must be increasingly integrated, viable and free from conflict.

This recipe is not one for linear progress. It will be full of inconsistencies--such as the aberration of Communism trying to create wealth, rather than distributing wealth which only capitalism could produce, according to the much maligned Karl Marx, and the terrible and protracted consequences of this aberration. Progress may even require cherished values in the Western countries to be modified in favour of a manageable world. But I see no loadstar in education, other than the one proposed.

Problems and proposals relating to international security in a NWFW, as touched upon in this essay, are surely not exhaustive, but they are pertinent.

As a last suggestion, I believe, these problems can move centre-stage only if they become a permanent feature of summit meetings of heads of governments. The UN and its agencies are no substitute. The UN can prepare valuable studies and help to implement decisions arrived at by heads of governments. Experience shows that international dispositions of consequence still flow from meetings of heads of governments.

10

Making Nuclear Weapons Illegal

Jozef Goldblat

Introduction

Efforts to reduce brutality in war, motivated by humanitarian and religious as well as practical considerations, have a long history. Over centuries, a body of rules and principles guiding the behaviour of belligerent states has developed as customary law. Custom is a widespread repetition, over a long period of time, of a specific type of conduct in the belief that such conduct is obligatory and should be respected by all. It has thus been generally recognized that weapons and war tactics must, in their application, be confined to military targets; that they must be proportional to their military objectives, as well as reasonably necessary to the attainment of those objectives; and that they should not cause unnecessary suffering to the victims, or harm human beings and property in neutral countries.

Since the second half of the 19th century, customary law has begun to be codified and supplemented by conventional law in the form of multilateral treaties. Rules prohibiting or regulating the use of weapons or methods of warfare form part of the law of armed conflict. Those restricting or banning the possession of weapons belong to the law of arms control and disarmament.

Law of Armed Conflict

The agreements regarding the use of specific weapons are as follows:

*   the Declaration of St. Petersburg of 1868 prohibiting the use of a projectile having a weight below 400 grammes, which is explosive or charged with *"fulminating or inflammable substances"*;

*   the Hague Declaration IV, 2, of 1899 prohibiting the use of projectiles for the diffusion of asphyxiating or deleterious gases;

*   the Hague Declaration IV, 3, of 1899 prohibiting the use of so-called dum-dum bullets expanding or flattening in the human body;

*   the Hague Convention IV of 1907 prohibiting the use of poison or poisoned weapons;

*   the Hague Convention VIII of 1907 prohibiting the laying of unanchored automatic contact mines, except when they are so constructed as to become harmless one hour at most after the person who laid them ceases to control them, the laying of anchored mines which do not become harmless as soon as they have broken loose from their moorings, the use of torpedoes which do not become harmless when they have missed their target, and the laying of automatic contact mines off the coast and ports of the enemy with the sole objective of intercepting commercial shipping;

*   the Hague Declaration XIV of 1907 prohibiting the discharge of projectiles and explosives from balloons or by other methods of a similar nature;

*   the Geneva Protocol of 1925 prohibiting the use of asphyxiating, poisonous or other gases, and all analogous liquids, materials and devices, as well as the use of bacteriological methods of warfare;

* the Environmental Modification Convention of 1977 prohibiting military or any other hostile use of environmental modification techniques as the means of destruction, damage, or injury;

* the Inhumane Weapons Convention of 1981 prohibiting or restricting the use of certain conventional weapons which may be deemed to be excessively injurious or have indiscriminate effects--fragmentation weapons, booby traps, mines and incendiary weapons.

None of the above-enumerated agreements deals explicitly with nuclear weapons. The 1977 Protocol I, additional to the 1949 Geneva Conventions and relating to the protection of victims of international armed conflicts (Protocol II deals with the protection of victims of non-international armed conflicts), is interpreted by some participants in the Diplomatic Conference, which has led to the conclusion of the Protocol, as prohibiting the use of nuclear weapons. They refer to the 'basic rules' governing the use of methods and means of warfare, as embodied in Article 35 of Protocol I, and to Article 51 of the Protocol dealing with the protection of the civilian population. The latter provision bans all forms of indiscriminate attacks, and in particular those which employ a method or means of combat *"the effects of which cannot be limited as required by the Protocol"*. However, in signing Protocol I, the Governments of Great Britain and the United States declared that in their understanding the rules established by Protocol I were not intended to have *"any effect on and do not regulate or prohibit the use of nuclear weapons"*. (US Army Field Manual on the Law of Land Warfare affirms that the use of nuclear weapons by itself does not constitute a violation of international law.) Also France stated that it did not consider Protocol I as applicable to nuclear weapons. It is, however, generally recognized that the humanitarian rules of armed conflict, which have been re-affirmed by Protocol I, apply to *all* arms.

Laws of Arms Control and Disarmament

The agreements--in force or under negotiation--banning the

possession of non-nuclear weapons are as follows:

* the 1972 Convention on the prohibition of the development, production and stockpiling of bacteriological (biological) and toxin weapons and on their destruction;

* the Convention on the prohibition of the development, production and stockpiling of chemical weapons and on their destruction, recently adopted.

As distinct from the Biological and Chemical Weapons Conventions, which provide for comprehensive bans, the agreements dealing with nuclear weapons provide only for partial arms control. They limit the testing of nuclear explosive devices, or prohibit the presence of nuclear weapons in certain geographical areas, or restrict the deployment of nuclear weapons in certain environments, or forbid the manufacture and import of nuclear weapons by non-nuclear-weapon states, or provide for cuts in the nuclear weapons arsenals.

* Nuclear testing is limited by the 1963 Partial Test Ban Treaty, the 1974 Threshold Test Ban Treaty, and the 1976 Peaceful Nuclear Explosions Treaty.

* The presence of nuclear weapons is proscribed in Antarctica by the 1959 Antarctic Treaty, in Latin America and the Caribbean by the 1967 Treaty of Tlatelolco, and in the South Pacific by the 1985 Treaty of Rarotonga.

* The deployment of nuclear weapons is banned in outer space by the 1967 Outer Space Treaty, on the moon by the 1979 Moon Agreement, and on the seabed and the ocean floor by the 1971 Seabed Treaty.

* The acquisition of nuclear weapons by non-nuclear-weapon states is forbidden by the 1968 Non-Proliferation Treaty (NPT).

* The nuclear arsenals of the United States and the former Soviet Union have been or are about to be reduced by the 1987 INF Treaty, the 1991 START Treaty, and the June 1992 Washington agreements.

The arms control agreements concluded so far may have had a constraining effect on the acquisition, spread or use of nuclear weapons. However, the possession of these weapons and their employment have not been outlawed.

The Need to Determine
the Legal Status of Nuclear Weapons

In the Cold War atmosphere of nuclear confrontation between the superpowers, an authoritative international inquiry into the legal status of nuclear weapons could not be carried out. Since the political developments of recent years, especially in Europe, have rendered a major international conflict highly unlikely, the role of nuclear weapons in maintaining the security of states has been considerably reduced. Hence the relative ease with which even unilateral cuts can be made in the nuclear arsenals of the superpowers. The departure from the NATO strategic doctrine, based on early use of nuclear weapons, may be taken to mean that the option to employ nuclear weapons at the outset of hostilities started with conventional arms has been abandoned, and that the employment of nuclear weapons by NATO is now envisaged only as a last resort, that is, when all other means to repel an armed attack have failed. Moreover, competent studies about the effects of nuclear weapons have made it obvious that nuclear destruction would outweigh any political interests which are meant to be served by nuclear weapons. Prevailing or winning in a nuclear war is generally recognized as impossible. For all these reasons, the present conditions are favourable for an objective examination of the relevance of international law to nuclear weapon issues.

Applicability of Existing Law to Nuclear Weapons

One can envisage the following situations in which the use of nuclear weapons might be initiated: in a surprise pre-emptive attack aimed at disarming an adversary who may or may not be nuclear-armed, or in the course of escalating hostilities started with conventional means of warfare.

First Strike

The first situation, usually referred to as 'first strike', is covered by the fundamental rule of international law enshrined in the UN Charter. The threat or use of force against the territorial integrity or political independence of any state is prohibited unconditionally, irrespective of the type of weapon employed-- nuclear or non-nuclear.

First Use

The second situation, usually referred to as 'first use', applies to the use of nuclear weapons in war in response to the use of conventional weapons by an adversary. It involves the right to self-defence, which is also enshrined in the UN Charter. If an armed attack occurs against a member of the United Nations, all states may defend themselves, individually or collectively, until the UN Security Council has taken measures necessary to maintain international peace and security. The Charter does not specify which weapons may or may not be used by states in such a situation. However, there is no rule of law which would justify a departure from the laws of war on the ground that a state had committed an act of aggression. In other words, the inherent right of self-defence is limited under international law.

In discussing these limitations, one should start from the rule, which is embodied in the 1907 Hague Convention IV on laws and customs of land warfare, and which prohibits the employment of arms causing "*unnecessary*" suffering, or the destruction of the enemy's property, unless such destruction is "*imperatively demanded*" by the necessities of war. This rule seems to have little practical value, because no suffering caused by weapons or war can be deemed necessary, and because military necessity is a subjective notion. Nevertheless, the 1868 St. Petersburg Declaration was already quite specific in this respect. It proclaimed that the only legitimate objective which states may endeavour to accomplish during war is to weaken the military forces of the enemy, and that, consequently, the employment of arms which uselessly aggravate the suffering of disabled men, or render their death inevitable, is contrary to the laws of humanity. Since nuclear explosions could produce uncontrollable environmental consequences and cause massive injury to people and massive damage to property, and since mass destruction can hardly be a necessity, it would be nearly impossible to observe the relevant rule of war in a nuclear war. It is conceivable that a small tactical nuclear weapon might be used against a selected military objective without causing indiscriminate harm to the civilian population or irreparable damage to the environment. However, once the nuclear threshold has been crossed, there can be no guarantee that nuclear warfare would be kept limited in scope. There will always be a risk of uncontrollable nuclear escalation on the part of the attacker, as well as on the part of the attacked nation if the latter, too, possesses nuclear weapons. Thus, a single use, irrespective of motivation, could start a large-scale nuclear war.

In any event, it is not the targeting that should be decisive in an attempt to determine the legality of the first use of nuclear weapons. It is rather the destructive potential of these weapons, which exceeds many times the destructive properties of any other weapons, that should render their first use illegal. Even the 1925 Geneva Protocol dealing with chemical and bacteriological weapons, which are considerably less devastating than nuclear weapons, does not differentiate between targets or between more or less severe effects caused by the use of the banned weapons. It has never been suggested that allowance should be made for some degree of harm to human life or destruction of property with the use of weapons covered by the Geneva Protocol.

Customary international law, reiterated in the 1949 Geneva Conventions for the protection of war victims, makes a clear distinction not only between military and non-military objectives, but also between combatants and non-combatants. The belligerents are under strict obligation to protect the civilians, not taking part in hostilities, against the consequences of war. However, the indiscriminate nature of nuclear weapons also renders this rule very difficult to comply with. Even if exclusively military targets were aimed at, civilian casualties would be an important by-product; in many cases they might outnumber the military ones.

Yet another iniquitous aspect of nuclear warfare is the inability of the belligerents to comply with the demand of the world order to respect the inviolability of the territory of neutral powers. It is impossible to confine the effects of nuclear explosions, particularly radioactive contamination, to the territories of states at war.

Non-nuclear-weapon states which have nuclear weapons deployed on their territories would not even be in a position to declare themselves neutral in an armed conflict between the nuclear-weapon powers.

Furthermore, nuclear radiation and radioactive fall-out produced by nuclear explosions inflict damage on the biological tissue of humans, animals and plants. It can therefore, for the purpose of international law, be compared to poison, the use of which as a method of warfare is prohibited by the 1907 Hague Convention IV and the 1925 Geneva Protocol.

It is worth noting that, in placing limitations on the conduct of hostilities, the 1907 Hague Convention IV included (in its preamble) the so-called Martens Clause, which was subsequently re-affirmed in several treaties of the laws of war. This Clause makes usages established among civilized peoples, the laws of humanity, and the dictates of the public conscience obligatory by themselves, even in the absence of a specific treaty prohibiting a particular type of weapon. It was this legal yardstick that the International Military Tribunal, convened in Nuremberg to prosecute Nazi leaders after World War II, applied in concluding that the law of war is to be found not only in treaties, but also in customs and practices of states, and that, by its continual adaptation, this law follows the needs of a changing world. Thus, it is also the case that weapons and tactics, which may be resorted to in the exercise of legitimate self-defence, must not be violative of the existing norms of international law, whether or not these norms are spelled out in formal international agreements.

Existing No-Use Pledges

In 1982, the Soviet Union formally pledged itself not to be the first to use nuclear weapons, but it added a caveat that in the formulation of its policy it would take into account whether other powers followed its example. This pledge complemented the declaration, made by the Soviet Union four years earlier, that it would never use nuclear weapons against states which had renounced the production and acquisition of such weapons and did not have them on their territories. China has been committed, since 1964, not to be the first to use nuclear weapons at any time and under any circumstances; its undertaking not to use or threaten to use nuclear weapons against non-nuclear countries and nuclear-free zones is unconditional.

The remaining nuclear-weapon powers maintain that they cannot assume a sweeping non-use obligation as long as there is a threat of war. They have renounced the first-use of nuclear weapons only under certain circumstances. Thus, the United States said that it would not use nuclear weapons against any non-nuclear-weapon state which is party to the NPT, or any comparable internationally binding agreement not to acquire nuclear explosive devices, except in the case of an attack on the United States or its allies by a non-nuclear-weapon state allied to or associated with a nuclear-weapon state in carrying out or sustaining the attack. A similar statement was issued by the United Kingdom. France said that it would not use nuclear arms against a state that does not have these weapons and has pledged not to seek them. However, France, too, made it clear that its unilateral no-use obligation would not apply in the case of an act of aggression carried out in association or in alliance with a nuclear-weapon state against France, or against a state with which France has a security commitment.

The reservations attached by the Western nuclear-weapon powers to their no-use pledges were clearly addressed to a situation in which a non-nuclear-weapon member of the Warsaw Pact (say, the former German Democratic Republic) attacked a non-nuclear-weapon member of NATO (say, the Federal Republic of Germany) with the support of the Soviet Union. Since the Warsaw Pact no longer exists, it is difficult now to think of a contingency which would warrant the use of nuclear weapons against a non-nuclear-weapon country in Europe. The reservations have become untenable.

In joining Additional Protocol II of the 1987 Treaty of Tlatelolco prohibiting nuclear weapons in Latin America--the first international agreement relating to non-use of nuclear weapons, which has been signed and ratified by all the five nuclear-weapon states--China, France, the Soviet Union, the United Kingdom and the United States made interpretative declarations. The declarations by the Western powers contained reservations analogous to those contained in their unilateral statements. The Soviet interpretative declaration was originally similar to the

Western declarations, but it may have been superseded by the 1978 and 1982 non-use pledges referred to above. China maintained its unconditional no-use commitment against nuclear-weapon-free zones.

Protocol 2 of the Treaty of Rarotonga which has established a nuclear-free zone in the South Pacific also provides for assurances to be given by the nuclear-weapon powers not to use or threaten to use nuclear weapons against the parties to the Treaty. The Protocol was signed by China and the Soviet Union, with qualifications which were not concordant with the unilateral non-use commitments previously assumed by both states. These qualifications were not referred to at the time of ratification. The Western nuclear-weapon powers have declined to join any of the protocols attached to the Treaty of Rarotonga.

Efforts to Reach Further Non-Use Agreements

Since the failure of the Baruch Plan (see Chapter 1), repeated efforts have been made to ban or restrict the use of nuclear weapons against all states, or only against non-nuclear-weapon states, or only against those among the latter that have joined the NPT. Relevant proposals have been discussed in the United Nations, at the Conference on Disarmament, and at the conferences reviewing the operation of the NPT.

In 1961, by a vote of 55 to 20, with 26 abstentions, the UN General Assembly adopted a declaration stating that the use of nuclear weapons was contrary to the spirit, the letter and the aims of the United Nations and, as such, a direct violation of the UN Charter. The resolution went on to proclaim the use of nuclear weapons to be "*a crime against mankind and civilization*". The United States and other NATO countries opposed the resolution, contending that in the event of aggression the attacked nation must be free to take whatever action with whatever weapons not specifically banned by international law. In addition to the pronouncement of the illegality of nuclear weapons, the UN General Assembly asked the Secretary-General to ascertain the views of the governments of UN member states on the possibility of convening a special conference for signing a convention on the prohibition of the use of nuclear weapons. The Secretary-

General's consultations proved inconclusive and the requested conference was never convened.

Resolutions calling for a ban on the use of nuclear weapons have also been considered at subsequent sessions of the UN General Assembly. All were opposed by the Western nuclear powers and have remained a dead letter.

The 1978 UN General Assembly Special Session devoted to disarmament called upon the nuclear-weapon states to take steps to assure the non-nuclear-weapon states that no use or threat of use of nuclear weapons would be made against them. Accordingly, the Geneva-based Conference on Disarmament has tried to develop a uniform formula of non-use, which would be free of limitations, conditions or exceptions contained in the unilateral declarations of the nuclear-weapon powers, and which would be legally binding. Since these efforts have yielded no result, a proposal was made to adopt different formulae for different categories of non-nuclear-weapon states, depending on their participation or non-participation in a military alliance, presence or absence on their territory of nuclear weapons belonging to a nuclear-weapon power, as well as adherence or non-adherence to the NPT or to another relevant international instrument. However, such a categorization could be construed as legitimizing the use of nuclear weapons against at least some non-nuclear-weapon states, and could even adversely affect the existing security assurances. It proved, therefore, unacceptable to many.

The question of non-use of nuclear weapons has been extensively discussed in the context of nuclear non-proliferation. Those who have formally renounced claims to nuclear weapons under the NPT are demanding formal assurances that nuclear weapons would not be used against them. Various ideas have been put forward to meet this concern. In particular, the following proposal was submitted at the 1990 NPT Review Conference. The nuclear-weapon states should undertake, under an international agreement, not to use or threaten to use nuclear weapons against any non-nuclear-weapon party to the NPT, which does not belong to a military alliance and does not have other security arrangements with a nuclear-weapon state, as well as against any non-nuclear-weapon state party to the NPT, which belongs to a military alliance or has other security arrangements with a nuclear-weapon state, but has no nuclear weapons stationed on its territory. Non-nuclear-weapon states belonging to the latter category would, for their part, undertake not to participate in, or contribute to, a military attack against any nuclear-weapon state or its allies, parties to the NPT, except in self-defence.   To conclude such an agreement, a special international conference would be convened.   This proposal appeared to be deficient in that it failed to apply to all non-nuclear-weapon states.

Even if some compromise formula for non-use of nuclear weapons against non-nuclear-weapon states were eventually found, the assurances sought would be of questionable value and in practical terms may not be necessary. All generally recognized nuclear-weapon powers possess conventional armed forces quantitatively and/or qualitatively superior to those of their potential non-nuclear adversaries and might not need to have recourse to nuclear weapons to stop an aggression launched by the latter. Under all imaginable circumstances, the use of nuclear weapons by the great powers against non-aligned countries not having such weapons on their territory--and these are the countries most insistent on obtaining security assurances--is unlikely.

Only a formal assurance of no-first-use of nuclear weapons, given to *all* countries, whatever their status--nuclear or non-nuclear, aligned or non-aligned--would carry real weight. Such a new norm of the international law of armed conflict might even have arms control implications, because it could lead to changes in the composition, characteristics and deployment of nuclear forces and, in the first place, to the renunciation of those nuclear weapons that have war-fighting functions. The role of the remaining nuclear weapons would be reduced to deterring the use of such weapons by others. The fire-break separating conventional and nuclear warfare would be reinforced, and the risk of nuclear war minimized. A no-first-use commitment valid *erga omnes* would enhance the security of all nations, and would better serve the cause of nuclear non-proliferation than would assurances accorded selectively as a 'reward' for membership of the NPT.

The Doctrine of Nuclear Deterrence

Were the first use of nuclear weapons to be formally

prohibited, the very threat of such use would become unlawful. Consequently, the doctrine of nuclear deterrence, which consists in threatening a nuclear attack in response to *any* armed aggression, would have to be declared invalid.

As a matter of fact, even in the absence of a generally accepted no-first-use commitment, it is legally dubious for states to retain the option of causing unlimited and indiscriminate destruction of an enemy population and of its industrial base, should deterrence fail. It is considered indefensible from the moral point of view as well. For example, the 1983 Pastoral letter of the American Catholic Bishops argued that non-nuclear attacks must be resisted by other than nuclear means, and that deterrence based on the balance of nuclear forces could be judged morally acceptable only if it were a step in progressive disarmament. A statement made by the British Council of Churches in 1980 went even further: it characterized the doctrine of deterrence as offensive to the Christian conscience.

The Problem of Retaliatory Use

If no-first-use were generally recognized as a norm of international law, and if this norm were generally and strictly observed, *any* use of nuclear weapons would be practically excluded. However, like all laws of war agreed in time of peace, a no-first-use rule may not resist the pressure of military expedience generated in the course of hostilities. Some governments may be prepared to resort to any means, including nuclear means, in order to avoid defeat in a war affecting their vital interests. This, in turn, may lead to reprisals.

Belligerent reprisals are usually considered to be legitimate, if they are proportionate to illegitimate practices, and if they are adopted with the sole purpose of inducing the guilty party to desist from these practices. They do not need to be of the same kind as the original illegal act, but they must bear a reasonable relationship to the degree of violation committed by the enemy. The right to such reprisals is limited only by the prohibition on attacking the civilian population and other targets protected by international law.

It is clear that the use of nuclear weapons as a reprisal for 'ordinary' violations of the laws of war, would be excessive. It is less clear whether a victim of a nuclear aggression should not have the right to retaliate in kind by using the same weapon. One can argue, however, that, given the particularly inhumane nature of weapons of mass destruction, their second-use must be considered to be as illegal as their first use. Many countries have adopted this attitude with regard to chemical and/or biological weapons by recognizing the prohibition on their use to be absolute and valid under any circumstances.

Conclusions

The cumulative effect of the generally accepted restraint on the use of weapons is such that nuclear war cannot be initiated with obedience to the rules of customary international law. This may be why, in 1963, in the Shimoda Case, the District Court of Tokyo concluded that nuclear attacks on Hiroshima and Nagasaki had violated international law as it existed in 1945.

In its judgement of 1986, in the case concerning military and paramilitary activities in and against Nicaragua, the International Court of Justice recognized that customary humanitarian law has the same standing as treaty law. Nonetheless, in view of the special character of nuclear weapons, a ban on their first use cannot be simply deduced from restrictions regarding other types of weapon or from an isolated court decision. This reasoning must have guided those who in 1925 decided to sign the Geneva Protocol banning the use of chemical and bacteriological means of warfare, even though the use of these means had already been condemned by the "*general opinion of the civilized world*", as stated in the Protocol itself. In other words, a prohibition concerning a specific weapon must be unambiguously stated in positive law, and a binding international document is preferable to easily reversible unilateral declarations.

To be meaningful, the required document should specify that the first use of nuclear weapons in response to, or in anticipation of, a prior non-nuclear armed attack, would gravely violate international law. The possession of nuclear weapon systems having first-strike characteristics would also have to be declared illegal, and the persons associated with such weapons would have to be treated as engaging in illegal activities.

Second-use of nuclear weapons cannot be ruled out as long as the weapons remain in the arsenals of states. Nonetheless, second-use must be subject to constraints specified in the humanitarian rules of armed conflict relating to belligerent reprisals. A retaliatory nuclear strike, carried out solely as an act of vengeance, without obvious military justification, should be forbidden.

At present, mere possession of nuclear weapons is not considered illegal. It would not become illegal even if the first use of nuclear weapons were universally banned. The situation would be different if an absolute prohibition on the use of nuclear weapons--both first and retaliatory--were adopted. Possession would then imply preparation for a prohibited act and could, therefore, according to the 1946 Nuremberg Charter, be considered a violation of international law. Logically, an unconditional ban on the use of a weapon, whether nuclear or non-nuclear, should be followed by a treaty banning its development, production and stockpiling, as the regimes of non-use and of non-possession of weapons are mutually supportive. The prohibition on possession of nuclear weapons would, at first, be binding only on states which have become parties to the treaty but, with the passage of time, it might become a customary rule of law binding on parties and non-parties alike. In a nuclear-weapon-free world the ban on nuclear weapons would have to be policed by an international authority having the power to impose sanctions on violators.

Sources

G. Schwarzenberger, *The Legality of Nuclear Weapons*, London Institute of World Affairs, Stevens & Sons Ltd., 1958.

N. Singh, *Nuclear Weapons and International Law*, Indian Council of World Affairs, New Delhi, Stevens & Sons Ltd., 1959.

S.D. Bailey, *Prohibitions and Restraints in War*, Royal Institute of International Affairs, OUP, 1972.

B.V.A. Röling and O. Sukovic, *The Law of War and Dubious Weapons*, SIPRI, Almqvist & Wiksell, 1976.

D. Schindler and J. Toman, *The Laws of Armed Conflicts*, Sijthoff & Noordhoff, Henry Dunant Institute, Geneva, 1981.

J. Goldblat, "The Laws of Armed Conflict", *Bulletin of Peace Proposals* Vol.13, No.2, 1982.

R.J. Lifton and R. Falk, *Indefensible Weapons*, Basic Books, Inc. Publishers, 1982.

F. Blackaby, J. Goldblat and S. Lodgaard (eds.), *No-First-Use*, SIPRI, Taylor & Francis, 1984.

J. Dewar, A. Paliwala, S. Picciotto and M. Ruete (eds.), *Nuclear Weapons, the Peace Movement and the Law*, Macmillan Press Ltd. 1986

I. Detter de Lupis, *The Law of War*, CUP, 1987.

Y. Sandoz, Ch. Swinarski and B. Zimmerman (eds.), Commentary on Additional Protocols of 8 June 1977 to the Geneva Conventions of 12 August 1949, International Committee of the Red Cross, Martinus Nijhoff Publishers, 1987.

A. Roberts and R. Guelff (eds.), *Documents on the Laws of War*, Clarendon Press, Oxford 1989.

G. Darnton (ed.), "The Bomb and the Law", London Nuclear Warfare Tribunal: A Summary Report, published by Alva and Gunnar Myrdal Foundation & Swedish Lawyers Against Nuclear Arms, Beyronds Tryck AB, Malmo, 1989.

PART D

Alternative Routes to a NWFW

11

Nuclear Weapons for the
United Nations?

Richard Garwin

Introduction

As this chapter is being written in July, 1992, after 40 years of enormous growth in the numbers and capabilities of nuclear weaponry, the world is witnessing a precipitous decline in weapons numbers, by agreement and example. Tens of thousands of nuclear warheads are being disabled, transported, and will be dismantled and many of them destroyed, according to commitments of the USA and Russia. However, there are many costs and difficulties associated with this process, which is not expected to be complete for at least another decade. Indeed, those contributing to this volume and those reading this volume may have considerable influence on the pace and assurance of this process.

Nevertheless, numbers discussed are on the order of 3000 strategic nuclear weapons to be retained by the USA, and a similar number by Russia, a number which has been considered to be compatible with essentially no change in the deterrent strategy. [1]

I have previously proposed levels of 1000 strategic nuclear

weapons (and zero tactical nuclear weapons) for the United States and the Soviet Union, and a reduction to 300 each for France, the UK and China. [2] These numbers were attractive as a lesser evil in the days of 50,000 nuclear weapons worldwide, and avoided the difficult analysis as to what smaller number would actually 'suffice', and what precisely would be the targets and the conditions for potential use of such nuclear weaponry.

There is clearly no justification for the position that some individuals or nations are entitled to the possession of nuclear weaponry, while others are not; on the other hand, it is conceivable (and to my mind even quite likely) that the world as a whole (and even its poorest member) benefits from an unequal distribution of power.

The critical need is for a world structure such that power serves the greater good, without being used to deny the rights of others.

There could hardly be an activity or motivation more evil than that we see taking place in Yugoslavia, with individuals being murdered by armies simply because they are of the wrong ethnic background or religion, and that is only one example of the problems against which nuclear weapons are impotent.

The motivation of an individual actually involved in a process--the researcher in physics, the police officer, the doctor--may be quite different from the purpose of the society or business or larger organization in employing that individual. Quite literally, the world would be a poorer place if one insisted that all doing a job think alike as well as act in the prescribed fashion. For the same reason, one should resist the tendency to discard one option or another simply because one of the practitioners may state a position which is repugnant, thoughtless, or just plain wrong.

It is essential that the power to create and to change lie with the organization as a whole (the individual or the world society), rather than with the practitioner's--hence 'civilian control of the military', which ought to be honoured as much in reality as it is in principle.

In the modern world of advertising and electoral campaigns, paradoxically it is the freedom of choice of the consumer or the citizen that leads to such detailed and costly deception with which we are familiar, and for which there was little need in an era in which a mass of individuals had little choice or power. We should expect to see specious and self-serving arguments created, selected, and widely disseminated.

But our scepticism about such arguments and the recognition that highly capable and intelligent individuals are involved in the process should not lead to a total rejectionism.

In my view, it is possible that the existence of a modest nuclear force serves all of humanity, given certain conditions for its maintenance and use. [3] It is this position on which I will now expand a bit for the present purpose, for comparison with the contributions in this volume by Vitalii Goldanskii and Stanislav Rodionov (Chapter 12) and by Francesco Calogero (Chapter 13)

It would be desirable if one individual could provide a comparison of a set of possible options--zero nuclear weapons, nuclear weapons for the United Nations, nuclear weapons for individual nations willing to commit them only to support for the UN, widespread possession of nuclear weaponry, and the like. An interesting early view of a UN missile force armed with nuclear weapons for preventing aggression was proposed by Arthur C. Clarke [4].

In principle, one might lay out all possible futures, sort them into these categories, evaluate against all possible hazards, and choose one or another. But there would be no reason for the reader or independent thinker to accept the various probabilities, so that individual might make a different choice unless one approach so dominated all others that it was robust against a wide range of assumptions.

The practical best, in my opinion, is for individuals who have some interest (not necessarily self-interest) in a given position to evaluate it as honestly as they can (concealing nothing of relevance) and to report on their assumptions and conclusions. Where some assumption cannot be proved, it should be stated as an assumption or an explicit precondition. But one approach or another should not be rejected simply because of inadequate presentation.

We are involved now in a process of vast reductions of nuclear weaponry. We should not let disagreements about the ultimate fate of nuclear weapons and the organization of the world interfere with a process that almost all of us support and that *requires* broad support if it is to go forward. Advocates of a

NWFW should not imagine that their task is to persuade those who advocate the retention of a few weapons on behalf of the UN; their mission lies instead with the much larger and more influential group who do not engage in the discussion at all.

A Four Step Programme

Step 1

The United States and Russia essentially eliminate their tactical nuclear weapons, commit irrevocably all nuclear weapons, above a certain number of designated strategic weapons, to the process of dismantlement and destruction, and transfer all weapons-usable plutonium and uranium to the civil energy sector under international safeguards.

Note that the existing commitments need to be substantially extended, since there is as yet no binding commitment to a cut-off of production of fissile material or to transfer of existing stock of the military plutonium or uranium to the civil inventory.

Step 2

In parallel with the reduction in warheads and transfer of material, the change in the status of nuclear weaponry should be institutionalized. It is almost universally accepted now that any legitimacy of nuclear weapons comes solely from their use in deterring the use of nuclear weapons by others, or in responding to that use. To some extent, this is a reflection of the current political and military situation, in which the armies of the Soviet Union and the Warsaw Pact pose no conceivable organized threat to NATO, but it cannot be predicted that nowhere in the world in the next century or more would arise a potential conflict of that nature.

The increment in security provided by nuclear weapons (if any) must be shared with others if one is at the same time going to achieve a goal parallel to that of reductions--that of preventing the proliferation of nuclear weaponry. Of course, a commitment to the non-use of nuclear weapons except in response to nuclear attack automatically provides 'negative guarantees' of non-use against non-nuclear states; but a non-nuclear state has no benefit parallel to that of a nuclear state in the potential to respond with nuclear weapons to nuclear attack.

I believe that non-nuclear nations should be encouraged by the UN to seek guarantees from the individual nuclear states that nuclear weapons would be used by the guarantor on behalf of the victim state, if a non-nuclear state were attacked with nuclear weapons. Such guarantees could be legitimized by being registered with the United Nations while there remained national possession of nuclear weaponry, but with use prescribed and limited by agreement.

Note also that a literal no-first-use (NFU) policy would prevent the use of nuclear weapons in response to a devastating attack on population by the use of biological weapons (BW). It is not clear to what extent nations have refrained from BW programmes because they recognized that they might incur a nuclear response, but an airtight NFU policy would remove that particular impediment to the acquisition of BW capability.

Step 3

In addition to institutionalizing and exercising in the next few years the powers provided in Article 43 of the UN Charter, as regards armies, ships, aircraft, and the like, the UN should take seriously the eventuality that nuclear weapons might have to be used in support of a UN cause. Any use of nuclear weaponry anywhere in the world is fraught with consequences, but that would be especially true of a first use of nuclear weaponry. I would reserve this to the United Nations by a mechanism which will, of course, involve the Security Council. The UN would in this stage be the instigator, steward, and executor of the nuclear guarantees, but would not actually possess nuclear weapons.

During this era, nuclear testing is likely to be eliminated worldwide, beginning, for instance, in 1996. Nations retaining some numbers of nuclear weapons, on their own behalf and on behalf of the UN, will conduct a vigorous non-nuclear inspection programme and a non-nuclear test programme, with the ability to remanufacture nuclear weaponry in case problems are encountered with chemical deterioration, deformation, and the like. It cannot be excluded that remanufacture would be required

at intervals of about 20 years and it would certainly be necessary
to maintain some modest, dedicated facilities with specialized
tools and procedures for this work.

I do *not* believe that such facilities and laboratories should
continue to design new kinds of nuclear weapons or pursue non-
weapon applications of nuclear explosions. This point requires
further attention, in view of the fact that most, if not all, of the
existing nuclear-weapon establishments have in the last year or
so suddenly emphasized the scope and value of the pure science
that can be done with nuclear explosions. For instance, Edward
Teller in a speech of 16 October 1991 advanced four arguments
for the continuation of US nuclear test explosions: first, to
improve the safety of nuclear weaponry; second, to develop a
nuclear-explosion-powered X-ray laser to improve the
effectiveness of defence against ballistic missiles; third, to develop
and explore the utility of nuclear weapons that might weigh 50
kg and have a yield of five tons of high explosive, to be used, for
instance, against armoured vehicles; and fourth, to do interesting
physics, such as learning how to compress iron tenfold while not
heating it excessively. [5]

On the other hand, Minister of Atomic Power V.N.
Mikhailov, in a presentation in Rome, 17 June 1992, stated
explicitly that although the Russian nuclear test moratorium will
expire in October 1992, and military testing is likely to resume at
Novaya Zemlya, Russia has no plans for 'peaceful use' explosions
and no programme either. He stated that he was confronted
with such proposals when he first took office, but that not one of
them was well justified. Indeed, there are many opportunities
for pure research with nuclear explosions, and some of them (the
Halite-Centurion programme in the United States) have played a
useful role in exploring the feasibility of inertially confined fusion
(ICF), for instance. But I believe the elimination of nuclear
explosions is necessary for maximum non-proliferation impact; in
an era free of fission tests, the result of Halite-Centurion would
need to wait for the development of sufficiently powerful lasers,
for instance, to carry them out.

It is suggested (Chapter 12) that a UN international team of
scientists and engineers gain their own experience for design and
production of even third-generation nuclear explosives, and
further to have designs and the ability to construct a very high

yield thermonuclear explosive device which might be assembled, integrated into a spacecraft and launched within a few weeks, in order to intercept a substantial asteroid before it can strike the Earth. Although such a risk is no fantasy, since there are believed to be some 400 Earth-crossing asteroids 2 km diameter or larger and the collision probability with Earth is on the order of two collisions per million years, the proposed remedy is probably even worse than the threat. If the damage produced by such a collision were some $100 trillion (for instance, one billion people killed with a personal loss of $100,000 per person) this would be an ongoing annualized tax of $200 million per year. It is certainly true that we will be smarter in the future, and in addition to strong arguments for delay based on the present value approach, there is every reason to wait until we have better tools for the job.

A further problem defining a programme to counter such catastrophe is that money and resources spent now are far more valuable than an equal amount of damage prevented a long time in the future. Furthermore, other means may very well prove more effective that the use of nuclear explosions.

It should be noted that the proposed remedies for asteroid impact are associated with hazards of their own. One such (non-nuclear) proposal is to gently divert small asteroids in such a way as to keep them in orbit where they would be handy for further diversion to actually collide with asteroids too large to handle by nuclear explosions. But long before that capability is available, one will have practised asteroid diversion and guidance to the point where a city or region could be destroyed essentially on demand, although typically with some extended delay. In the United States, such capabilities were apparently considered explicitly by some, in response to assumed activities by the Soviet Union to create a weapon that US enthusiasts called "*Ivan's hammer*". [6] It is not at all clear that there would be a net benefit to the world to create such a powerful tool until we became a lot wiser and better behaved.

In similar fashion, the use of underground nuclear explosions in the former Soviet Union to quench runaway gas and oil wells was never necessary in the United States, where the technique of accurate drilling and intercept at depth was well developed as a means of last resort. Although the use of nuclear explosives was mentioned early in conjunction with controlling the 800 wells sabotaged by Iraqi forces in Kuwait, every one of these wells was brought under control by conventional means within seven months.

These considerations are of interest for:

Step 4

At this stage, at least some of the nuclear-weapon states transfer their nuclear weaponry and relevant information to an appropriate agency of the United Nations for maintenance and possible use. They would do this if they had sufficient confidence in the integrity of the UN and its ability to act to protect the interests of the former nuclear-weapon state, as one of the nations of the world. Presumably they would need to judge also that there was a significant probability of a threat arising that could be handled by the use or threat of use of nuclear weapons and which could not be handled in some other way, and if they felt that there were positive benefits, such as non-proliferation associated with holding of nuclear weapons by the UN instead of by individual nations.

Of course, once all nuclear weapons had been transferred to the UN, there would be no assurance that they would be preserved indefinitely. There would also be important questions of security and safety, including a restriction on knowledgeable UN employees sharing nuclear weapons design information in a fashion other than that required by the job.

Nuclear weapons storage, inspection, monitoring, and refabrication facilities would have to be available to the UN, and appropriate restrictions placed upon these facilities to prevent access by others.

Discussion

Against what threat does one propose to take this possibly interim step (of UN nuclear forces) between national possession of nuclear weapons and the elimination of nuclear weapons?

One possibility would be the acquisition of nuclear weapons by a nation in violation of its undertaking not to do so ('cheating'). Another would be the overt rejection of the NPT and further non-proliferation treaties, together with an open programme to develop nuclear weapons.

The second threat could presumably be handled by sanctions, and, if necessary, concerted non-nuclear military action.

But in a world in which the NPT were universally accepted and in which international agreements required publication of the agreement domestically, and domestic enabling legislation that requires each person within the borders (and every agent and citizen outside the borders) to comply with the international undertaking and to report infractions, as emphasized by Joseph Rotblat in Chapter 6, cheating and rejectionism would be less likely; that era would also provide the basis for UN sanctions and military action.

Problems with Deterrence

If a weapon or means for harm exists, a society will wish to have a perfect defence, especially if it does not cost very much. Nuclear weapons have such an enormous potential for destruction that any reasonable evaluation concluded that there was no potential for perfect defence, but Bernard Brodie and others observed that under many circumstances the use (and even the acquisition) of nuclear weaponry could be *deterred* by the promise of retaliation, against which a perfect defence was also not on the cards. But the *combination* of potential retaliation with defence (including the partial destruction of one's retaliatory weapons before they can be launched) encouraged the US-Soviet arms race, particularly since each side in reality toyed with goals that went far beyond the inhibition of nuclear attack by the other side.

This is not the place to argue that nuclear deterrence is in fact compatible with a very modest number of nuclear weapons and a reduced dependence and concern for nuclear weaponry. [3]

Nuclear deterrence does have genuine deficiencies. Some are concerned that an intelligent and adamant opponent will follow out the logical argument that would lead an intelligent victim, in full command of a retaliatory force, not to use that force. Others will judge that the expectation of loss exceeding potential gain is not sufficient to deter attack, unless that 'loss' is equivalent to annihilation. Still others argue that some actors have as primary goal the annihilation of their opponents, and that it is only a minor matter whether the actor survives, himself, or not.

All of these are questions dealing with the *effectiveness* of a deterrent structure. Of greater importance to many is the *acceptability* of deterrence. Some find it repugnant to threaten retaliation even against intentional attack by another individual. In the model of two individuals with differing values, I, personally, have no trouble at all with the principle of deterrence; I do not believe it excludes friendship and cooperation to create a system such that if one individual is intentionally destroyed by the other, then the other is destroyed as well. In fact, such a system would eliminate a lot of expenditure and concern over what the other side might be doing. My view of deterrence is entirely compatible with a formulation of the *'Golden Rule'*--I believe it acceptable for me because I am willing to give similar capabilities to others.

A bigger question arises because the 'side' is not an individual actor, owning all and risking all. Paradoxically, deterrence would still appear to 'work' and to be justified between democratic societies, in which the majority, at least, could be held personally accountable for their collective actions. But even between democracies, what about the minority that may have opposed the attack?

The acceptability of deterrence is posed most starkly in the case of confrontation with a dictatorship or autocracy such as that of Saddam Hussein. If he had actually achieved a nuclear-weapon capability with deliverable nuclear weaponry, a no-first-use policy would have kept the UN or other nuclear states from destroying Iraq's nuclear weapons by nuclear weaponry, and Iraq could have promised to launch their weapons in case of conventional attack. Would that launch have been deterred by even the certainty of destruction of Iraq, including its leader and most of its military might? Where is the moral basis for destroying or threatening to destroy people, the vast majority of whom had no influence on building the imagined nuclear capability or threatening to use it?

Two answers can be given, neither of them totally

satisfactory. The first is that the threat, though immoral, is effective and is therefore in the interest even of those who are threatened. The second depends on the potential of the masses actually to depose their leader if they cared enough to do so.

The question of nuclear weapons for the UN is not whether it is preferable to a world in which no nuclear weapons exist or can ever exist. It is whether it is preferable to and would avoid a world in which many nations retain virtual nuclear capabilities in order to build actual nuclear weapons in response to the acquisition of nuclear weaponry by another power. The question is whether nuclear weapons for the UN can hasten the elimination of national nuclear weapon forces. It is whether a UN role in nuclear weaponry (even before actual possession of nuclear weapons by the UN) can provide additional incentives against the use of nuclear weapons by those who have them and against the acquisition of nuclear weapons by those not possessing them.

The primary barrier to acquisition of nuclear weapons by individuals or nations must be first and foremost a legal structure by which most abjure the possession or acquisition of the requisite fissile material, and access to material is forcibly denied to others. In such a regime it would not seem helpful that transfer of a nuclear-weapon capability to the UN should be accompanied by the detailed revelation worldwide of the precise design and fabrication plans for those nuclear weapons. This is true whether the nuclear weapons are at the cutting edge of modern technology, or are 1960s style, for instance. A city can be destroyed just as well with a 1960-vintage nuclear weapon, and the stability of the world shattered, as with nuclear weapons that are still on the drawing boards.

Individuals selected to serve on the UN Nuclear Force will have to agree not to reveal information to their own nations or to others, and there will need to be a security, investigatory, and enforcement mechanism to guarantee this. The UN force will need not only the competence to carry out its job over many decades, but it will need the organization to ensure that this job is performed by an inherently multinational team that may contain, overtly or covertly, individuals antagonistic to a particular action or to the whole scheme.

Epilogue

In a world in which nations are likely to persist and conflicts of various kinds continue, the devastating power of nuclear weapons will long be of concern. Serious wars are likely to take place in the future, perhaps among adversaries not now foreseen. The acquisition or covert retention of nuclear weapons might give a decisive advantage to one side, which might not be overcome even by conventional forces of nations supporting a world free of nuclear weapons. The discussion in this paper of some of the considerations that would be involved in the UN retaining a residual but reliable nuclear-weapon capability may help to compare this option with that of several nations retaining such a capability on behalf of the UN, and to compare with the option of an explicitly (if temporarily) nuclear-weapon-free world.

References

1.   "The Future of the US-Soviet Nuclear Relationship", a report by the Committee on International Security and Arms Control (CISAC) of the National Academy of Sciences, Washington D.C. 1991.

2.   R.L. Garwin, "A Blueprint for Radical Weapons Cuts", *Bulletin of the Atomic Scientists*, March 1988.

3.   R.L. Garwin, "Reducing Dependence on Nuclear Weapons", *Nuclear Weapons and World Politics*, McGraw-Hill Book Company, New York, 1977.

4.   A.C. Clarke, "The Rocket and the Future of Warfare", Prize Essay in *RAF Quarterly*, March 1946.

5.   R.L. Garwin, "Science, technology and national security in an era of democracy and human rights", 'Guest Comments' *American Journal of Physics*, Vol.60, No.5, May 1992, pp.395-396.

6.   C. Sagan, "Between Enemies", *Bulletin of the Atomic Scientists*, May 1992.

12

An International Nuclear Security Force

Vitalii Goldanskii and Stanislav Rodionov

Introduction

The choice between a world with nuclear weapons and a world with none, may appear at first sight a clear, black-or-white choice: either nuclear weapons exist, or they are totally eliminated. However, particularly in the later stages of reductions in the number of nuclear warheads, certain 'grey areas' emerge. The purpose of this chapter is to discuss some of these grey areas. There is the question of an international nuclear security force to ease the transition from a world with national nuclear forces to a world in which there are no nuclear weapons at all. There is also the question of various forms of civil research which might still need some low-yield nuclear explosions, and the possibility that there could be some other peaceful uses for such explosions. In particular, there is a small but finite danger that the Earth might be struck by an asteroid, and the only method of preventing a major disaster might be the projection of a high-yield thermonuclear device into the path of the incoming body.

One initial question concerns timing--how long it would be before a NWFW could become possible. It would be wrong simply to extrapolate the rate of reduction which is implied by the recent statements of the Presidents of the United States and Russia. Once the two powers have reduced the number of their warheads to a figure of around 2000-3000 each, further reductions will become more difficult, since the other nuclear-weapon states will have to be brought into the negotiations. In any case, the reductions presently envisaged will need at least 10-15 years for their implementation.

There is another time-related aspect: to what extent can nuclear weapons be totally eliminated so long as civil power plants are producing large quantities of plutonium as by-products of the nuclear power industry. [1] It is very much more difficult to construct adequate safeguards against illicit production of nuclear weapons if production of plutonium or enriched uranium for peaceful purposes is permitted, while its use for nuclear warheads is forbidden.

Nuclear reactors produce about 20 per cent of the world's electrical energy. Various proposals have been made for designing nuclear power systems that are much less prone to diversion of nuclear materials for weapons than present nuclear plants and their supporting fuel cycle operations. None of them avoid the production or use of heavy isotopes that would be much easier to extract from fresh or spent fuel than it would be to enrich natural or low enriched uranium sufficiently to become weapons-grade.

A long-term alternative to nuclear energy could be controlled thermonuclear fusion as a new and more powerful source of ecologically clean energy (without radioactive fission products). The recent success of British scientists with a Tokomak experimental device is a rather encouraging indication that controlled fusion might possibly be achieved within 30-50 years. This could be used as a rough estimate of possible timing for complete nuclear disarmament.

Another relevant period of time is the connection with the average life-time of new nuclear warheads, which reportedly is about 20-30 years (for thermonuclear warheads that could be explained by the lifetime of the tritium used in the warhead).

So there can be no question of a transition to a NWFW during the remaining years of the 20th century. Whether we like it or not, we will be obliged to reconcile ourselves to the existence of nuclear weapons well into the first half of the 21st century.

The process of nuclear weapon elimination should begin now by banning the production for nuclear weapons of highly enriched uranium, plutonium and tritium; by large reductions in the number of warheads; and by developing technologies for the treatment of fissile materials. It seems reasonable to assume that, down to a certain total of nuclear warheads, five states (USA, Russia, UK, France and China), will continue to have national nuclear forces. In addition, there are the covert possessors of nuclear weapons--for example, Israel, India, Pakistan, and some others, possibly including a few of the former Soviet republics. There is a risk, which is not negligible, that nuclear weapons might fall into the hands of criminal groups--for example, under the conditions which now exist in some parts of the former Soviet Union. The smallest models of modern tactical nuclear weapons weigh only approximately 50 kg., have a diameter less than 20cm,--so they can be considered portable devices--and explode with a yield equivalent to approximately 1000 tons of TNT.

Safety

This raises the question whether a nuclear weapon could be detonated without the involvement of those who know the safety and code systems. For example, US nuclear warheads are designed so that:

> in the event of a detonation initiated at any one point in the high explosive systems (rather than multiple points, which would occur providing the authorization codes were properly entered and the environmental sensors registered the design launch-to-target sequence), the probability of a nuclear yield greater than 1.8 kilogrammes of TNT equivalent shall not exceed one in a million. [2]

However, there is another danger--that a 'one-point' explosion would result in the dispersal of very tiny particles of highly toxic, radioactive plutonium into the atmosphere. This problem has been investigated quantitatively. [2] It has been estimated that a one-point explosion would convert about 30 per cent of the plutonium contained in the warheads into a PuO_2 aerosol of respirable size. If we assume an accident involving a single warhead, and that this warhead contains about three kilogrammes of plutonium, then the resulting aerosol would contain around one kilogramme of PuO_2.

The warheads probably contain 20-50 kg of high explosive (HE). Since normal HE is nearly twice as powerful as TNT, an accident could result in an explosion equivalent to 40-100 kg of TNT. The corresponding initial cloud sizes are: cloud-top height: 200-300 metres; cloud radius: 20-30 metres. The main risk from exposure to plutonium aerosol is from inhalation; the external radiation from the passing cloud and from plutonium deposited on the ground can be neglected. Health effects from radiation can be divided into two categories: illness and death due to high doses, occurring within a month or so after exposure, and cancers occurring during the remainder of the lives of the exposed population, starting a few years after exposure to low doses. High dose effects would result from exposure within about a hundred metres from the explosion point. The estimate of low-dose effects suggests that under worst-case weather conditions and for high population density an accident with a single plutonium warhead-- that is, detonation of HE with no nuclear yield--could result in a few thousand fatalities during the remainder of the lives of the exposed population. This is just the effect of the passage of a cloud of plutonium aerosol. To avoid more casualties, there would have to be evacuation procedures and a cleaning-up of the area.

However, inside a pressurized chamber a one-point explosion of HE in any warhead can be used to obtain a critical mass of any fissile material after some chemical manipulation. In this way, any state--or indeed a terrorist group (with the help of appropriate specialists)--could convert normal safe warheads into nuclear feedstock for the construction of a new nuclear weapon, which might be more primitive but which would still produce an explosion.

UN Nuclear Security Forces

Once nuclear warhead numbers have been substantially reduced, the next step should be a qualitative one. Instead of national nuclear forces, there should be international nuclear safeguard forces in order to keep some stability during the transition to a NWFW. It should not be particularly difficult for the five nuclear powers to put their nuclear forces under international control. However, there could be a number of problems with the members of the 'international underground'. For example, Israel and some Arab countries might refuse to reveal their nuclear secrets unless the political crisis in the Middle East is in some way solved. There could be the same problems with India-Pakistan relations, or in the Korean peninsula. These examples show that progress in nuclear disarmament is highly dependent on the general world political situation. In many parts of the world an improved political climate is a necessary condition for the process of reduction of nuclear forces.

The idea of an international nuclear police force under UN auspices has been a matter of discussion for a number of years. [3] The proposal was to create a new UN organ, which would keep a small number of nuclear weapons and means of delivery. This would seem to be an inevitable stage in the nuclear disarmament process--for the Security Council and the Military Staff Committee would have the capabilities for the immediate and effective use of this force against any aggressor possessing nuclear weapons or any other weapon of mass destruction. These international nuclear forces could be called the UN Nuclear Security Force (NSF). This force would be created against the background of massive reductions in the nuclear weapon stockpiles, the guaranteed and controlled total destruction of chemical and biological weapons, considerable reductions in conventional arms, progress in creating effective European and Asian-Pacific security structures, and general and effective international means of conflict prevention and resolution.

Even under these favourable conditions it might be possible for some criminal groups or even governments to use clandestine stocks of nuclear materials, or new low-scale devices for isotope separation (which could not easily be verified by international inspection) for the construction of a few nuclear explosive devices; these might then be used for blackmail. Similar attempts could be made to produce other weapons of mass destruction. What should be the role of the NSF in these cases? Should its role simply be that of deterrence? The question then arises whether in all cases deterrence would be effective.

History suggests that deterrence works in relations between developed countries, where the adversaries have a rather large number of nuclear warheads and a developed political and economic superstructure. However there are historical examples with developing countries where deterrence was ineffective--for example the Korean War and, in part, the Gulf War. Deterrence would not work against fanatical religious groups, or possibly even against some developing countries with low population density. So there could be cases where the NSF had to use nuclear weapons for a preventive or retaliatory strike. Of course this should be the last resort for dealing with a threat to world security. There should first be political and economic pressure, and probably an attempt to deal with the matter by the use of conventional weapons.

International problems arising from a NWFW Treaty should not in general call for immediate action by the UN Nuclear Security Force. There should be lengthy attempts to manage such situations without resort to the use of nuclear force. So the delivery systems which might be more relevant to this 'slow response' policy would be either air-launched or sea-launched cruise missiles. Both are highly accurate weapons, and with further development their accuracy could be improved still more.

It should not be necessary for the NSF to conduct any nuclear tests (though later in this chapter it is suggested that there may be scientific reasons for permitting some low-yield tests). For purposes of weapons production, *"nuclear weapons that derive all their energy from fission can now be developed with a high confidence, without any nuclear tests"*. [4]

A 'slow response' strategy would make it possible to take a succession of steps which could serve as a warning to violators: a declaration that the 'first-use' of a NSF nuclear weapon might be necessary; the installation of a cruise missile on a UN aircraft or ship; the movement of the delivery vehicle to a base which was within cruise missile range of a potential target, and so on. The arrival of a nuclear armed ship or aircraft should result in additional psychological pressure on the violator.

Any actual use of nuclear weapons by the NSF should be structured to specific ground-based or underground targets; a high degree of targeting precision would be needed. It could well be that in time non-nuclear explosives could be substituted for nuclear ones, as the risk of any violation of a NWFW Treaty decreased. A situation could be reached in which all highly enriched uranium and plutonium, which had been produced before nuclear power was phased out, had been rendered incapable of sustaining an explosive chain reaction, and in which detailed inspection gave a hundred per cent guarantee that there were no hidden stockpiles of fissile material. In that situation it should be possible for the NSF to dismantle the last nuclear warheads.

Nuclear Weapon Scientists and Research

Nuclear weapons cannot disappear without leaving any trace. One of these traces would be the remaining number of nuclear weapon specialists. This problem is already here; some countries which are seeking to develop nuclear weapons may attempt to recruit nuclear scientists from the former Soviet Union. The best solution is to avoid this potential brain drain by ensuring full employment for these specialists in international facilities under international control.

The total elimination of all nuclear warheads could not be followed by the immediate elimination of highly enriched uranium, since a number of civil technologies use this fissile material--for example, fuel for nuclear submarine reactors or fuel for power modules of deep-space missions. All such activities should be under strict international control. There could, for example, be an International Fissile Material Centre (IFMC), which would be responsible for the production of uranium fuel and for the construction of certain nuclear explosives.

The IFMC should probably be permitted to conduct, for peaceful purposes, nuclear explosions exceeding the yield level which has been suggested for a comprehensive test ban--that is, 100 kg of TNT. One activity which exceeds this threshold is inertial confinement fusion (ICF) in which micro-explosions yield up to 300 kg of TNT, and could be contained in above-ground reactor vessels. [5] ICF could provide an experimental base for extensive studies of material effects and could be a key factor in maintaining a team of experts in fusion physics and diagnostics. Moreover, ICF micro-explosions might also act as a useful research tool in the study of X-Ray laser physics (XRL).

The practical cut-off for explosions that can be contained in seismically quiet vessels is equivalent to some 300 tons of TNT, and indeed a design for a so-called High Energy Density Facility (HEDF) has been under study since 1981 by scientists at the National Livermore Laboratory in the USA. This facility is supposed to be located at the Nevada Test Site, and would consist of a seismically quiet underground chamber able to contain nuclear detonations up to 0.3 kilotons. It would be reusable, operating with about one explosion a week. [6]

ICF studies on the design of imploding deuterium-tritium 'pellets' and fusion ignition in these implosions may result in the design and construction of more powerful thermonuclear explosives which would not contain fission products and could be used for non-military purposes without the danger of radioactive pollution.

XRL studies together with gamma-ray laser (GRL) studies can provide a unique technique for producing genuine holograms of single atoms and molecules. At the moment it is not known what level of explosive yield is needed in order to get a genuine understanding of the laser generation process: it could be around 1 kiloton.

There are a number of proposals for peaceful nuclear explosions, in addition to the XRL and GRL studies. There is the idea of creating large cavities for the safe containment of sewage and ecologically dangerous wastes. [7] A number of studies suggest that within 40-50 years practically all important petroleum sources will have been exhausted. Underground nuclear explosions could be a method of improving the productivity of old oil wells.

The conclusion here is that low-yield tests have a number of important non-military scientific applications, and that peaceful underground nuclear explosions may also be useful in some applications. Here a proposal made by one of the authors (VG) is relevant [3]:

> As for underground tests, if there is no way the United States can renounce them, let us reach agreement on conducting all such tests jointly, gradually reducing their frequency and the upper limit for the permitted yield of the explosion. Where? In Nevada, for example, since the authorities of that state gave

their consent to the functioning of a nuclear test site there. I believe that in this way we could really help to strengthen mutual trust, bring substantially nearer the complete cessation of nuclear tests, strengthen the Non-Proliferation Treaty, and make potential aggressors listen to reason: in other words, create the necessary preconditions for transition to a nuclear-free world.

A zero-nuclear-weapon level in a NWFW is not, *per se*, a self-stabilizing system, since any weapons-related fluctuations can introduce serious political and military disturbances. General physical laws suggest that, for stability, a system needs strong negative feed-back. After the need for a UN Nuclear Security Force has disappeared, the IFMC could provide negative feed-back of this kind. Its international team of scientists could, if necessary, be in a position, at short notice, to produce nuclear weapons again--so that there would exist not real but 'virtual' nuclear weapons which could be developed if the need arose.

One possible need is for the protection of humankind from the catastrophic collision of a huge meteorite, or comet nucleus, with Earth. The probability of such a collision for a Tunguska-type body (mass of the order of 10^5 - 10^6 tonnes, size of the order of a few hundred metres) is considered a low one, but it still has a finite value. Quite recently (March 1989) an asteroid *1989 fc* was discovered to have passed within one million kilometres from the earth. If it had collided with our planet, the effect would have been equivalent to a 5 megaton nuclear explosion.

The only realistic way of protecting humankind from such a catastrophe is to launch a deep-space mission with an on-board high-yield thermonuclear device against the incoming body. It would be most effective if it penetrated to the centre of that body, either to disintegrate it into smaller and less dangerous fragments or to change its trajectory. If a special International Space Observation Service were organized for the detection of suspicious objects in deep space, then bodies such as the *1989 fc* asteroid could be detected at distances which represented 5-6 months travel to the earth (according to the current state-of-the-art in astronomy).

Spacecraft for this purpose could be designed and tested by the international team well in advance. The IFMC could be responsible for designing a very-high-yield thermonuclear explosive device which could be assembled and launched in a few weeks so that the incoming body could be intercepted far enough away. This International Asteroid Protection Service should therefore have ready 'virtual' nuclear explosives within a zero-nuclear-weapon environment.

References

1.   Theodore Taylor, "The Global Abolition of Nuclear Weapons" and Stanislav Rodionov "Verification of Compliance and Deterrents to Violations" in *Towards a Secure World in the 21st Century: Annals of Pugwash 1990* eds. J. Rotblat and F. Blackaby, Taylor & Francis, 1991.

2.   Steve Fetter and Frank von Hippel, "The Hazard from Plutonium Dispersal by Nuclear-Warhead Accidents", *Science & Global Security*, Vol.2, no.1, Gordon & Breach, 1990

3.   Joseph Rotblat and Vitalii Goldanskii, "The Elimination of Nuclear Arsenals: Is it Desirable? Is it Feasible? in *Verification: Monitoring Compliance* eds. F. Calogero, M.L. Goldberger, and S. Kapitza, Westview Press, 1991. Vitalii Goldanskii, "UN Nuclear Forces? A Soviet Scientist's Proposals", *Izvestia*, no.311, 9 November 1990.

4.   Theodore Taylor, "Can Nuclear weapons Be Developed Without Full Testing?" in *Verification of Arms Reductions*, eds. J. Altman and J. Rotblat, Springer-Verlag, 1989.

5.   Dan L. Fenstermacher "The Effect of Nuclear Test-Ban Regimes on Third-Generation-Weapon Innovation" *Science & Global Security*, vol.1, nos.3-4, Gordon & Breach, 1990.

6.   Ray E. Kidder, "Military Significant Nuclear Explosive Yields" *FAS Public Interest Report*, vol.38, no.7, September 1985.

7.   A.P. Vasiliev, N.K. Prikhodko and V.A. Simonenko, "Underground Nuclear Explosions for Improvement of Ecological Situations" (in Russian) *Priroda*, no.2, February 1991.

13

An Asymptotic Approach to a NWFW

Francesco Calogero

In this chapter the idea to reach a nuclear-weapon-free world via the establishment, as an intermediary step, of a United Nations nuclear-weapon capability, is criticized, and a more direct route to achieve this most desirable goal is suggested: via the universal recognition of the uselessness and illegitimacy of nuclear weapons, of all other instruments of mass destruction, and indeed of war and violence as means to settle conflicts. The very notion of a NWFW is also scrutinized, and it is emphasized that in this respect the question of the *time* required to use nuclear weapons eventually is no less important than the actual *number* of nuclear weapons in existence. This distinction has important implications as to the best route to be followed to arrive at a NWFW, including the first steps to be undertaken now.

The idea of *deterrence*, in its quintessential form (which is the only one that ever made any sense), is that nuclear weapons are needed to deter others from using them, by the threat of a retaliatory strike which would inflict unacceptable damage. This idea, in the context of the Cold War confrontation among, on one side, the United States of America and their 'Western' allies, and on the other, the Soviet Union and their 'Eastern' allies, had the potential advantage of implying the notion of 'sufficiency' of nuclear arsenals, and of downplaying the importance of the sophistication ('modernization') of nuclear weapons and of the capability to use them quickly. Indeed, just for these reasons, the 'pure' notion of deterrence was criticized or twisted by those who advocated the continual, unending, quantitative and qualitative expansion of nuclear-weapon capabilities, as well as the need to keep these arsenals on hair-trigger alert, with all the expensive paraphernalia that went with it.

But the notion of 'deterrence' does have some fundamental flaws, even in its more straightforward connotation, since it rests on 'motivational' arguments, which are always of questionable validity; and, most importantly, because it has a dangerous element and an ethically dubious connotation, as it requires that entire populations be held hostage to real prospects of tremendous, catastrophic devastation.

The eventual establishment of a NWFW will only be possible when reliance on 'nuclear deterrence' is replaced by the recognition that nuclear weapons have no use whatsoever. This transition will be easier if it is not blurred by the maintenance of a limited nuclear-weapon capability, hypothetically assigned, just for deterrence purposes (against cheating or rejectionism), to the United Nations.

In order for deterrence to have any chance to 'work', the notion that nuclear weapons will in fact be eventually used (in retaliation--with devastating consequences) must retain credibility. It is hard to envisage how this could be realized in the case of a United Nations nuclear-weapon capability. In this connection, the fundamental questions of where the UN nuclear arsenal should be deployed and who would actually retain the (negative *and* positive) control on its actual use, would have to be squarely faced. The model, presented elsewhere in this book, of how this could be practically achieved, by establishing an *ad hoc* UN Agency, does not appear very convincing. It seems to me to lack practicality, and therefore to be unlikely to be accepted and implemented; and even if it were accepted and implemented, to be unlikely to serve any useful purpose, i.e. neither to reassure potential victims of nuclear aggression, nor to discourage potential perpetrators of such aggression. And it entails the same kind of dangers, and ethical dubiousness, as indicated above.

Moreover, for deterrence to be robust, and in particular not prone to pressures for pre-emption and/or for reliance on hair-trigger time-urgent responses, it might have to rely on relatively large arsenals; which is hardly compatible with the notion of a NWFW.

The prospect that nuclear weapons be eventually recognized as totally useless is still considered Utopian by most experts. In fact, this notion of uselessness already prevails among decision-makers.

As pointed out in other chapters of this book, the USA, while possessing an enormous and diversified arsenal of both strategic and tactical nuclear weapons, did not use them in Vietnam, even in the face of defeat. Ditto for the USSR in Afghanistan. Possession of nuclear weapons by the United Kingdom did not deter Argentina from occupying the Falklands; nor were nuclear weapons of any use or relevance in the resulting war (except, perhaps, as operational impediments to those who had the burden to possess them). In the heated arguments among various European states that accompany the process of European integration, the fact that some of them possess nuclear weapons and others do not, plays absolutely no role (it is rather the state of their respective economies that carries weight).

It is of course easy to envisage international scenarios in which possession of nuclear weapons would play a crucial role; it is much more difficult to provide real, historical examples, after Hiroshima and Nagasaki (even in that context it would be hard to argue that the catastrophic use of nuclear weapons was in fact instrumental in changing the final outcome). Those who assert that nuclear weapons are indeed, already now, generally considered unusable by statesmen and decision-makers (rather than by armchair strategists and speech-writers)--namely, that these weapons are already now useless, *de facto* if not *de scriptis*-- are like naive children who point out that the king wears no clothes, when the king is indeed naked. Still not many people recognize this truth; but our number is destined to grow, especially as long as no novel justification for the retention of nuclear weapons is concocted (such as the need to provide for a UN nuclear deterrent), and their evident unusability, hence uselessness, is made more and more explicit.

Of course, this observation does not suffice to understand present realities. The decision-makers who are in control of nuclear weapons still cling to them, and indeed tend to behave as if their possession were essential, although it is known that these same decision-makers are generally quite reluctant to pay much attention to the operational underpinnings of any eventual employment of such weapons, thereby demonstrating their psychological reluctance to face any prospect of actual use. Recently, the shifting stands with respect to the control of nuclear weapons taken by the leaders of the republics which have emerged from the dissolution of the Soviet Union, have signalled a rather schizophrenic message, including a stated willingness to do away altogether with them, and yet an intense interest in maintaining control over them (an attitude which does however have some justification, since such control may amount to a very valuable bargaining chip, not to be given away lightly).

A clearer determination to forsake nuclear weapons is of course displayed by the leaders and public opinions of the many nations who have joined the Non-Proliferation Treaty with the status of non-nuclear-weapon states. Some of these countries have undoubtedly the technological wherewithal to manufacture such instruments; some (for instance, Sweden) had even initiated programmes to this end, and were quite close to the goal, before taking the political decision to abandon this option (see Chapter 5).

The possibility that some of the present five official nuclear-weapon countries renounce the military nuclear option before the end of the century should not be ruled out. In Great Britain, this possibility has been for a long time a much debated political issue, and has been at one time adopted as part of the political platform by the Labour Party. In France, the apparent unanimity on the retention of an autonomous nuclear-weapon capability reflects the lack of real debate on this issue, and therefore keeps open the possibility of a sudden reversal (a phenomenon not uncommon in French politics), of which the recent shift of policy concerning nuclear-weapon testing might be the first sign. And of course the future of the Soviet nuclear-weapon complex is now in doubt; while the possibility that the collapse of the Communist ideology and regimes will eventually infect China may eventually affect the determination of this country to cling to its nuclear deterrent.

Renunciation of nuclear weapons by China would go a long way towards the establishment of a nuclear-weapon-free zone covering all South and East Asia, and including in particular both

India and Pakistan, as well as Taiwan, the Korean peninsula and of course Japan.

The implementation of these important moves towards the establishment of a NWFW is not likely to be improved by the prospect of setting up a UN nuclear-weapon capability. Such a need is, instead, likely to be adopted as a convenient platform by those who oppose abandoning nuclear armaments, but might find it more convenient to mask their opposition under a more appealing guise than old-fashioned *realpolitik*, or myopic nationalism, or protection of vested interests.

The main reason why the idea of establishing a nuclear-weapon UN capability is put forward in good faith, is to counter a common objection against the prospect of a NWFW, namely the fear that, in such an environment, a country or some non-governmental group might cheat and, having acquired clandestinely a nuclear-weapon capability, become capable to dictate their own terms and indeed, in some sense, to 'dominate the world'.

The main approach against the risk of cheating in a NWFW is prevention--namely, making the clandestine acquisition of nuclear weapons very difficult, perhaps impossible. How this can be achieved is outlined below.

A different question is how best to respond in case someone does cheat or reject the NWFW regime. To address this contingency, the idea of a nuclear-weapon capability possessed by the UN does not appear to provide an effective approach.

This idea is based on the concept of deterrence, and on a narrow version of this notion, in which the threat of using nuclear weapons is considered essential to eliminate the threat of such use by others. In fact, possession of a nuclear-weapon capability is neither sufficient nor necessary to deter others from using, or threatening to use, nuclear weapons.

It is first of all obvious that nuclear deterrence is not likely to work against non-governmental groups; nor against governments who do not really care about the fate of their own populations (the case of the Saddam Hussein regime in Iraq is a rather good approximation of such a situation).

Moreover, a nuclear-weapon retaliatory capability must be credible to provide an effective deterrent, and it may only be applicable to situations in which there is some balance of forces and of risks. It is for instance unlikely that a country like the USA would ever consider a UN nuclear-weapon capability as more adequate than its own nuclear deterrent, to provide security against the possible emergence of a nuclear-weapon threat.

Indeed, the most serious objection against the idea that a UN nuclear-weapon capability is a necessary intermediate step on the road towards a NWFW, is the recognition of the impracticality of this arrangement. Hence, to focus on this intermediate step as an essential one to arrive at a NWFW entails the risk of causing a major--and, in my opinion, unnecessary--impediment to progress towards this goal.

Finally, and most importantly: a nuclear-weapon capability is by no means necessary to deter the use of nuclear weapons, or the threat of such use. If deterrence is considered as the only reliable approach against cheating, then it must be pointed out that, under the circumstances which would be likely to prevail in this unlikely eventuality, it would indeed be possible to inflict unacceptable damage also by other, non-nuclear, means. So where is the absolute need to retain a 'benign' nuclear-weapon capability? Moreover, the option also to acquire, or re-acquire, a nuclear-weapon capability, could always be exercised, if need be, as soon as a clandestinely developed nuclear threat surfaced. Hence such a threat could at most provide a temporary leverage. Of course, every effort should be made to avoid such an eventuality; yet it must be recognized that it would not be much more catastrophic in a NWFW context, than if it were to emerge under the present circumstances, namely, if nuclear weapons were to fall now into irresponsible hands.

The best approach against the risk of cheating is prevention--namely, to make such cheating unlikely to succeed. There can be little doubt that this is possible; the acquisition of a nuclear-weapon capability is a major enterprise, not easy to hide (in spite of what the recent Iraqi example might seem to imply). But, in order to achieve this goal, substantial changes will have to be realized (as the Iraqi case suggests). Since in any case the attainment of a NWFW must be seen as a long-term prospect--many years will be required to eliminate the enormous nuclear arsenals now in existence--the substantial changes required will have a chance to be realized; and a recognition of their need should focus efforts on their implementation.

Two elements will be essential to prevent cheating: (a) a strong commitment by all industrialized countries to monitor relevant technologies and to intervene with decision against anybody who misbehaves in this respect, by raising the stakes in terms of individual and corporate punishment under criminal law and by stiff economic sanctions, not only for malevolent behaviour (be it motivated by economic considerations or otherwise), but as well just for laxity; (b) movement towards the prevalence of more open societies, and the widespread promotion of effective opportunities for societal verification (in addition to the standard international verification procedures). No more needs to be written here on this last topic, since it is excellently dealt with in Chapter 6 of this volume.

Closely associated with the question of cheating--and considered by some no less serious a problem--is the risk of 'breakout'. This refers to the eventuality that, in a NWFW, a country suddenly announces its intention to acquire (or re-acquire) nuclear weapons, and proceeds to do so speedily (see also Chapter 5). This risk is associated with the impossibility to 'disinvent' nuclear weapons, which some see as proof of the infeasibility of a NWFW (by which they mean precisely this instability against breakout).

The main objections against this objection to the viability of a NWFW are analogous to those outlined above in the context of a discussion of the risk of cheating. It is not something that is likely to occur quite out of the blue; and it would not quite signify the end of the world. It would, of course, eventually restart a nuclear arms race, namely, a return to a situation analogous to the present one, or rather to the situation we hope to achieve in the foreseeable future, after the drastic cuts of nuclear weaponry that are now envisaged.

But the main argument to allay the concerns about cheating and breakout must be the fundamental notion that a NWFW will be realizable only after the irrelevance of nuclear weapons to the resolution of conflicts will be universally recognized by all major international actors (with the minor ones held in check, if need be, by conventional deterrence). As we have emphasized above, this situation is already now largely realized.

The discussion of the danger of breakout has the merit to focus attention on the *time* factor. It is indeed true that nuclear weapons cannot be disinvented, namely that the possibility that they be reintroduced will always remain, even after their total elimination. But an important question is the time delay that would be required for their reintroduction, as well as for their eventual use.

This is relevant to the very definition of a NWFW. The more current definition focuses on the *number* of available nuclear weapons, and it points to a situation where this number equals *zero*. Another, no less useful, definition focuses on the minimal *time* which would be required for the use of nuclear weapons, and points to an asymptotic situation in which this time is *extremely large*. An advantage of this second definition is to clarify that a NWFW cannot be considered a static achievement, but rather an asymptotic goal. But of course the real essence of a NWFW is more importantly determined by unquantifiable political circumstances, than by any single figure, be it the number of nuclear weapons available, or the minimal time required for their use.

Concentration on the time factor is also helpful in order to speculate about the route to be followed to reach a NWFW. Of course, the traditional definition in terms of numbers of nuclear weapons points to numerical reductions, all the way down to zero; certainly a most important goal. But it is also of utmost importance to minimize the likelihood that nuclear weapons be used--as long as they are around. To this end the time delay involved in any decision to employ them should be increased. To repeat: since even under the most optimistic assumptions the actual elimination of nuclear weapons will take many years, it is important in the meantime to make sure that any prospect of their use becomes less and less likely--and perhaps the most important technical measure in this respect is to modify deployment patterns and operational procedures so as to expand the time delay intrinsic in any eventual use of nuclear weapons.

A decision in principle to eliminate 'tactical' nuclear weapons has been already taken; but since it will take several years to be actually realized, its implementation should begin by placing--as quickly as possible--all these weapons in safe storage, well separated from their means of delivery, and well guarded against any potential diversion. As for 'strategic' nuclear weapons, the route to go--along with their reduction--is not only to take them off any 'alert' status, but indeed to 'download', as quickly and as universally as possible, the nuclear warheads from their delivery vehicles, and transfer them as well to safe storage (once this has been done for bombers and ICBMs, in a manner easily monitored by national technical means and perhaps also by cooperative verification, it will be justified and expedient to 'download' as well all SLBMs, and keep all strategic submarines in port). In this manner, it should be possible to increase the time interval involved in any nuclear engagement from a few minutes to many hours, to days, to weeks; with the transition to a NWFW eventually involving the expansion of these times to months and years.

In the immediate future, it will also be important to shift strategic thinking--and accordingly employment doctrines, operational procedures, targeting plans--towards de-emphasizing the relevance of nuclear weapons, indeed towards excluding their use except as weapons of last resort, in a retaliatory mode intended exclusively to deter the use of nuclear weapons by others. This transition will entail not only universal acceptance of 'no-first-use' policies, but also the choice of 'no-second-use-unless' doctrines, which emphasize in all circumstances the advisability to wait and see, before authorizing any use of nuclear weapons.

This will eventually be followed by the delegitimization of nuclear weapons, in analogy--and, of course, in addition--to chemical weapons and all other means of mass murder.

Of course, the movement towards a NWFW entails a much tougher nuclear non-proliferation policy than has been practised until now. The moral strength and political will to enforce such a stand will be justified precisely by the prospect of moving towards a NWFW.

A NWFW is less far away than it is generally believed; indeed it is already with us, to the extent that the possession of nuclear weapons does not seem now to play any significant role in promoting national interests. But an effective implementation of this goal--which of course implies the actual elimination of all nuclear weapons--will require some time, and it must be coupled with an effective recognition that *the resolution of international conflicts can only be achieved by non-military means.* An important step to achieve this goal will presumably be an enhanced role of the United Nations, to act as mediators, actually to keep the peace, and to promote the eventual prevalence of the rule of law in international relations. But there is no need, in this perspective, to envisage a nuclear armament of the United Nations.

The elimination of nuclear weapons will be achieved by de-emphasizing their relevance, thereby coming eventually to a situation in which nobody really cares much about them, because they indeed play no significant role. To this end, arguments in favour of attributing a nuclear-weapon capability to the United Nations may in fact be counter-productive.

Concurrently, a progressive demilitarization of international relations will have to be achieved--following the pattern set by the technologically and economically more advanced countries of the world, who also tend to be the most democratic and open societies, and who have essentially already learned to resolve their contrasts by non-military means. The prospect of extending this lesson to the entire world is not immediate, but neither is it Utopian, nor does it necessarily require such a drastic change in international affairs as the establishment of world government. It may require the emergence of more democratic and open societies, at least in all major countries; a goal which is far from being established, but towards whose achievement progress--perhaps through several zigzags--is not beyond hope.

Towards this progress should be focused our individual commitments.

The thrust of this chapter has been towards emphasizing that the transition to a NWFW should be recognized as being already in progress and indeed partly achieved, and that this trend, away from *any* conception of nuclear weapons as usable instruments, should be energetically pursued and reinforced. While this points to a realization of a NWFW 'not with a bang but a whimper', it does by no means underplay the need to study, plan and advocate progress towards this most important--if asymptotic--goal. Indeed, it suggests what the best avenue towards its attainment could and should be. It is a route which can and must be supported, at least in its immediate phase, even by those who are not yet enthusiastically convinced of the eventual feasibility of a NWFW, but who nevertheless agree on the desirability that any use of nuclear weapons becomes less and less conceivable.

PART E

Intermediate Steps

14

Approaches Towards a Nuclear-Weapon-Free World

*Bhalchandra Udgaonkar, Raja Mohan,
and Maj Britt Theorin*

Introduction

Chapter 1 sets out the history of the attitudes of the nuclear-weapon powers to the idea of a NWFW. With the exception of one brief interlude, at Reykjavik, the nuclear-weapon powers have continued to insist on the indefinite maintenance of nuclear stockpiles as a deterrent. On the other hand, the non-nuclear-weapon powers have always considered that a NWFW should be a major objective of international policy.

India has tried to put a NWFW on the global agenda time and again, [1] e.g. the Delhi Declaration of Mikhail Gorbachev and Rajiv Gandhi (November 1986) on the Principles of a Nuclear-Weapon-Free and Non-Violent World [2]; the Action Plan submitted by India to the Third Special Session on Disarmament of the UN General Assembly in May 1988; [3] the International Conference *Towards a Nuclear-Weapon-Free and Non-Violent World* at New Delhi on the occasion of the centenary of the birth of Jawaharlal Nehru (November 1988). There has also been, since 1984, the Six-nation Five-continent initiative [4].

There have been some major movements in recent years towards a reduction of the nuclear stockpiles of the USA and (what was) the USSR, which could take us to a NWFW, *if they are given a larger visionary purpose.* Soon after the unsuccessful August 1991 coup in Moscow came the initiative on nuclear arms announced by President Bush on September 27th 1991, and the positive response to it of President Gorbachev a week later. These involved radical proposals for the virtual disbanding of the tactical nuclear arsenals, and pulling a number of strategic systems out of the alert status. In the summer of 1992, Presidents Bush and Yeltsin agreed on further reductions in the strategic arsenals, going beyond the earlier START agreement. These various cuts will eventually reduce the nuclear arsenals of USA and Russia to about one tenth of their peak levels. Such cuts were unimaginable even in the late 1980s. One only hopes that the momentum will be maintained so as to take the world close to zero in the near future.

Need to Supplement Recent Positive Developments

The above-mentioned developments are most welcome. Withdrawal of the tactical nuclear weapons from Europe will make that continent a far safer place than it has been for decades. The proposed withdrawal of tactical nuclear weapons from the navies of the USA and Russia has addressed a major concern in many parts of the world on the spatial proliferation of these weapons. However, even if one conceives of an approach to a NWFW narrowly in terms of a warhead-count, this does not constitute, by itself, a significant movement towards a nuclear-weapon-free world. The actions under these initiatives are not conceived within the framework of a NWFW; in fact, there is no mention of an objective--even a distant one--of a NWFW, as a part of the goal in the post-Cold-War 'new world of peace and security' that was mentioned by President Bush.

Taking an optimistic view, one could say that the arms reductions represent progress, even if a goal of zero has not been accepted. The first steps to such a goal can be hesitant, and both the abolitionists and the arms control advocates could march together for a considerable distance, with the former hoping that the latter will some day accept the goal of NWFW. To maintain a balanced perspective, however, it is good to keep the limitations of these developments in view:

1. Some (an unspecified number) of the nuclear warheads will not be destroyed, but only withdrawn, and so will be available for future use.

2. Although at the time of writing a moratorium on testing was in force in France, Russia and the United States, there were still no formal negotiations on a Comprehensive Test Ban.

3. In July 1992, the Bush Administration announced a major unilateral initiative ending the production of highly enriched uranium and plutonium. This again is welcome, especially in view of earlier reluctance to take this step. However, such a step cannot be considered in isolation. One has also to consider the existing stockpiles, augmented by the fissile material released from the eliminated warheads.

4. The weapons-usable nuclear material will continue to remain with the respective countries. There is no attempt yet to bring it under any form of international control.

5. The strategic concept spelt out by President Bush continues to depend on the maintenance of "a credible nuclear deterrent"; and the retention of "the national capacity to rebuild our forces should that be necessary". This means that the commitment to nuclear weapons as instruments of policy remains unshaken. Further, while maintaining the nuclear arsenals of the nuclear-weapon powers, there is a declared intention to intensify the efforts to curb nuclear and missile proliferation--i.e. to maintain and enhance the present asymmetry between the nuclear haves and have-nots.

6. While an advantage of unilateral measures is that they are rapid, the disadvantage is that the weapons can be brought back again. They have therefore to be followed by international treaties, verified and controlled by the international community. Verification so much emphasized in the past (to the extent of becoming an obstacle to progress) has become de-emphasized in recent developments. Verification and transparency in the implementation of announced measures cannot be dispensed with.

7. The accelerated reduction of nuclear warheads is conceived as a bilateral matter between the USA and Russia, with no role for multilateral agencies. The goal, though limited, should have been the destruction of the weapons *under international control*, so as to build up world-wide confidence in a process which is of more than bilateral interest.

The drastic reductions proposed recently by the USA and Russia will start being real steps towards a NWFW if the abolitionists and the reductionists can find a way to remove progressively the above deficiencies from the point of view of a NWFW. Even after the presently proposed reductions there will still be several thousand warheads in the arsenals of the world. So the abolitionists and the reductionists could work together for some time, to get the arsenal of 3000-3500 strategic warheads each, which will still remain after the recent agreements, reduced to 1000 each or a few hundreds each. The paths would, however, diverge unless a clear-cut objective of a NWFW gets accepted by all in the meantime, and while doing so the doctrine of nuclear deterrence is given up. How soon, will depend on the level of the minimum deterrent: 1000 as frequently mentioned, or somewhere in the range of 1, 10, or 100--closer to one than to a hundred--as mentioned by Herbert York [5] recently.

Obstacles to a NWFW

It has been clear for some time that the main obstacles to a NWFW are political; they arise from doctrines and ideologies, rather than from technical considerations. The manner in which recent drastic reductions have been made enhances this feeling.

A key impediment now is the new sense of complacency that has overtaken strategic thinking in Washington. *"The day is over, for as far ahead as we can see"*, a senior official of the Bush Administration was telling the Press on 15 July 1992 in Washington, for the *"big, megaton arms control agreement"*. *"Politically dazzling"* efforts, he said, will no longer be the norm. [6] The focus, instead, would be on completing the nuclear cuts currently on the anvil.

Secondly, the Soviet military threat is being replaced by an exaggerated notion of a threat from the developing world. Senior American officials have repeatedly suggested that even though the Soviet threat has disappeared, the danger of the developing countries acquiring mass destruction weapons and the means to deliver them is real. Given this threat, the North needs both nuclear weapons as well as a defence against them. The new acronym is GPALS--Global Protection Against Limited Strikes. The

US Congress has approved a limited, experimental development of a land-based ABM system. There are proposals for US-Russian cooperation--though as yet this seems limited to early-warning systems. But it does seem that the idea of combining nuclear forces with missile defence is beginning to take hold in the North.

However, any efforts in these directions by the South are considered reprehensible. President Bush has declared that he will seek international cooperation to discourage the production of fissile material in volatile regions such as the Middle East, the Persian Gulf, South Asia and the Korean Peninsula. The focus is once again on Non-Proliferation, rather than taking advantage of the current international situation to construct a more rational nuclear arms control regime.

The problem of proliferation of mass destruction weapons and their delivery systems is a real one, but there is great danger in picking only on horizontal proliferation and elevating it to the highest level in the international agenda, and whipping up public fears about it. This has helped push the agenda of a NWFW to the background and has introduced a needless North-South divide. The last two years have seen a dramatic extension of the (horizontal) non-proliferation agenda in the form of expanded international controls on transfers of technology, and denial of rights that have been conceded to the developing countries in the NPT.

In this context, it is important to emphasize the difference between real steps towards a NWFW, and the pseudo-steps (Non-Proliferation Treaty, Nuclear-Weapon-Free Zones, penalties if they persist with acquisition of certain technologies, etc.) which are being forced on the nuclear have-nots by the nuclear haves, using such means of pressure as their control of international financial institutions and of flows of development assistance.

This is not the place to discuss NPT or NWFZs. [7] Suffice it to emphasize that the divergence of opinion between the nuclear and the non-nuclear states, with regard to the value and effectiveness of the NPT, and the failures of successive NPT Review Conferences, including the one in 1990, should not be lost sight of. The perception of some nuclear have-nots is that the nuclear-weapon states consider the NPT merely as a means of keeping others out of the nuclear club. The non-nuclear states initially considered the NPT as a step towards a NWFW. Since this has

not materialized over 25 years, NPT has to be replaced by
something better. That something has now to be a time-bound
programme of action towards a NWFW to which all nations are
committed, with strict international verification procedures which
apply to all of them.

The feeling that many have in the South is that the NPT and
NWFZs are really meant to maintain the hegemony of nuclear-
weapon powers--many of which were colonial powers until a few
decades ago--over both nuclear weapons and nuclear energy. It
would be appropriate at this point to dwell on the different
perceptions in the North and the South with regard to the nuclear
menace and related security, and also with regard to security *vis-à-
vis* each other.

As perceived by the South, nuclear-weapon states of the
North treat denuclearization as merely a problem of the security
of the North, a proliferation problem, a law and order problem,
with the recalcitrant states of the South to be brought under NPT
and/or NWFZs by various threats and pressures. There is also a
persistent tendency in the countries of the North to consider
certain countries as responsible in behaviour (even though many
of them have been ruthless colonial powers not so long ago, or
have used their military power even recently in a blatant manner,
or cynically supplied arms worth billions of dollars to countries in
sensitive zones) and to consider the rest as irresponsible.
Acquisition of a nuclear power station or even a nuclear research
reactor is suspect. The same is true with a few grammes of
plutonium, while tonnes of plutonium or enriched uranium
floating around is considered safe with a country of the North,
even though fissile material which is enough to make many atomic
weapons is unaccounted for. Even peaceful nuclear technologies,
under international safeguards, are denied to certain countries like
Iran, while their development, including the setting up of a fuel
reprocessing plant, is respectable for a NPT signatory country of
the North.

Such attitudes in the North, and the setting up of the Nuclear
Suppliers' Club and the Missile Technology Control Regime, as
well as other restrictions on transfer of technology create a feeling
in the South that the Northern white nations are ganging up to
deny any access to high technologies to them. And technology is
a well-recognized instrument of domination.

Contrary to the accepted wisdom in the USA and its satellites, the greater threat to the security of the world is not from an odd 'rogue' country making a few crude bombs, but from the hegemonistic designs of the nuclear powers and their allies, which continue to hold on to their huge stockpiles and doctrines. Those in the North who champion non-proliferation need to be aware of the deep, and often irrational, anti-West sentiments that this arouses, and the forces of immoderation it feeds in the South.

Confidence in motivations is very important in the context of any steps proposed in the domain of denuclearization, since the whole NWFW regime, including the approach to it, will depend on mutual confidence. *Nuclear-weapon states have a greater responsibility in this regard.* The concepts of confidence building and common security, so assiduously developed in the East-West context, need now to be extended globally, in particular to North-South relations.

Any real steps towards a NWFW have to be consistent with the ultimate (not-too-distant) objective and its commitments, including an equitable and just world order, without which NWFW cannot be stable. [2] They should be part of an overall effort to build up genuinely global common security, [8] and not security as perceived by the big powers and their satellites which are in command of nuclear weapons. They must not perpetuate the present skewness between nuclear haves and have-nots. Non-nuclear states do not wish to remain permanent nuclear hostages whose fate is to be decided without their participation in the arrangements that may be worked out.

The seriousness of the problem is highlighted by the recent events in the former USSR. *"The issue of ownership of nuclear weapons in Ukraine, Belarus and Kazakhstan is still unresolved, and the positions taken by the new states at a given time can be readily reversed".* [9] The danger of metastasis of nuclear weapons, expertise, technology and materials has not yet passed. The collapse of the mighty USSR could not have been foreseen a couple of years ago. Different scenarios, posing problems about the control of nuclear weapons, for example through their possession by organized groups of terrorists, could emerge in coming years in China or even in the USA. Complacency in this domain will be extremely hazardous. The problems of terrorism and those arising out of the break-up of the Soviet Union cannot be met if nuclear weapons continue to be legitimate. The only sane solution is a rapid movement towards a NWFW. Common sense and strategic sense are converging.

Doctrines and Attitudes

Doctrines and attitudes play an important role in confidence building, and thus affect the prospects of a NWFW.

The doctrine of deterrence (minimum, flexible etc.) tenaciously held by NATO and many of the nuclear-weapon powers, is the greatest hurdle to a NWFW, or even to horizontal non-proliferation in a narrow sense. This was emphasized in the Pugwash Statement on the eve of the Fourth NPT Review Conference: [10]

> *Probably the most unfavourable factor of all is the continued adherence of nuclear-weapon states to explicit or implicit doctrines that insist on the need for maintaining national nuclear forces as deterrents against nuclear or even conventional attack. It needs to be recognized that one of the gravest liabilities of nuclear deterrence strategy, overt or covert, is its fundamental incompatibility with non-proliferation goals, in as much as there is no logical basis for denying the 'right' to a nuclear deterrent to some States while according it to others.*

It is clear that the nuclear option has to be closed by prohibiting the use of nuclear weapons in any circumstance.

The attitude adopted by the nuclear-weapon powers towards the rest has been well described by B. Sanders [11] as a taboo: "What you are doing is bad. I do it, and I cannot stop doing it. But I shall do what I can to stop you".

The goal of preventing nuclear weapons from falling into irresponsible hands is indeed a pressing one. But the attempt to do this without a fundamental rethinking about the nuclear menace (NWFW), and a measure of equity and non-discrimination in the creation of an effective and verifiable wedge between civil and military uses of nuclear power, will not have much international credibility.

Comprehensive Test Ban Treaty

The case for ending nuclear testing rests on the need to put an end to the mad security system, built on nuclear deterrence, whose 'stability' requires the development of more and more effective weapons. The importance of a comprehensive test ban treaty (CTBT) has long been acknowledged by the international community. Year after year, the General Assembly of the United Nations has underscored the urgent need for it.

The Conference held in January 1992 to amend the Partial Test Ban Treaty (PTBT) into a CTBT, turned out to be infructuous, because of the vehement opposition of the USA and its nuclear-weapon allies.

A step-by-step approach towards a CTBT is inconsistent with the objective of a NWFW. It implies a continued legitimacy of development, possession and use of nuclear weapons. This legitimacy must be put to an end.

A CTBT will be a major step towards a NWFW. It has a symbolic significance in view of the persistent opposition to it, over a long period, of some nuclear powers. But one need not overrate its significance from the point of view of its contribution in real terms to the reduction of the risk of a nuclear holocaust, or in the control of horizontal or vertical proliferation. *A CTBT has to be followed up by several other steps in a time-bound programme of action.*

Need for a Holistic Approach Based on New Thinking

In his address at the Pugwash Conference in Beijing in September 1991, Robert McNamara called for a *totally new vision of relationships among nations.* [12]

New thinking does not come easily, as seen from the progress, or the lack of it, towards a NWFW in the 37 years since the Russell-Einstein Manifesto. Even before it, Jawaharlal Nehru had observed, soon after the Bikini test of a hydrogen bomb in 1952, *"though the atom bomb has come to blast the world, no bomb has yet touched the minds of our statesmen and men of authority who cannot yet get out of their old ruts and still want to preserve the old world".*

The old ruts are the narrow national interests, remnants of

colonialism and racialism, hegemonistic thinking, and ethnocentric glasses which one is accustomed to wear. Also, the anachronistic concepts of nuclear deterrence, balance of power, dominance of power blocs, spheres of influence, and of special rights and privileges of a select group of nations. The deification of market-forces and a growth-mania in a world of limited resources and on the brink of ecological disaster are also part of the mind-set to be changed.

The Dagomys Declaration [13] of Pugwash calls upon scientists *"to expand our concerns to a broader set of inter-related dangers: destruction of the environment on a global scale and denial of basic needs for a growing majority of mankind"*.

The new vision must start with the *NWFW as imperative* (going beyond the debate of desirability and feasibility). Acceptance of the unambiguous objective of a NWFW is important for creating the psychological climate in which other actions will become possible. This will imply giving up the doctrine of deterrence (minimum, flexible, discriminate etc.) tenaciously held by NATO and many of the nuclear-weapon powers. It will make it possible for nations to agree that the use of nuclear weapons is a crime against humanity and to sign a convention against the first use or threat to use of nuclear weapons--in other words, to delegitimize nuclear weapons.

But a world without nuclear weapons will not necessarily be more safe than the world of 1939, unless we have a sea-change in attitudes and adequate instruments for curbing the hegemonistic tendencies of some big powers and for conflict resolution and peace-keeping.

The new vision must approach security from the point of view of the East and the West, and the North and the South, taking account of the images [14] of what threatens each, in the short-term and in the long-term. Common security should be the key concept.

It will help if the nuclear-weapon states, or at least the concerned scientists in them, tried to look at issues like NPT from the point of view of the non-nuclear-weapon states, the threshold states in particular. Would they make all the specious arguments in favour of the NPT or NWFZs if they were in the position of the citizens of the developing world, which have been under long periods of domination of Western powers? Would they then advise the threshold countries not to cross the threshold, unless they see a rapid movement towards a NWFW and a new just world order emerging--an environment in which they feel secure about their autonomous development? Would they still insist on non-nuclear security for non-nuclear states, while nuclear states continue to 'enjoy' nuclear security? Would they agree to the prospects of all sorts of intrusive inspections, by a machinery dominated by the big powers?

The new vision must give up obsession with weapons and militarist thinking. Both military and non-military threats have to be taken into account. The Pugwash concern about the non-military dimensions of threats to global security should be considered as part of the efforts towards a NWFW.

Security has to be considered along with peace and justice. The final document from the UN conference on relations between Disarmament and Development in 1987 states:

> *Security consists of not only military, but also political, economic, social, humanitarian and human rights and ecological aspects .... A process of disarmament that provides for undiminished security at progressively lower levels of armaments could allow additional resources to be devoted to addressing non-military challenges to security, and thus result in enhanced overall security.*

At a time when concern about democracy and human rights within nations is growing, these concerns should manifest themselves also outside national boundaries in inter-state relationships. The new vision must include a democratic world order, including more democratic mechanisms of ruling the world and sharing its resources. The steps towards a NWFW must include genuine efforts towards the establishment of such an order. The stalled North-South dialogue must be given a new life. The perception of the North-South problematic as a zero-sum game must be transformed into one of a quest for joint prosperity. Peace and justice have so far not been on centre-stage in the discussion of future international relations. They have been marginalized or deported to the development debate, as if they could be dealt with in isolation from other aspects of security, disarmament and sustainability.

The new vision will involve a greatly enhanced role for the

United Nations and its agencies. The decision-making at the UN has to be participative in form and substance, so that the moral authority of the UN, which is the ultimate sanction on which it has to rely, is not undermined by actions that smack of arrogance of power. A close look at the Charter and functioning of the UN and its agencies is necessary to make them more effective for peace-keeping, conflict resolution, and the other tasks which will fall on them. It will be necessary to have a standing international peace force capable of acting fast in the face of a threat of aggression, and an expanded system of world courts and institutions for mediation and arbitration, as an alternative to the battlefields as a way of solving disputes. In working out such mechanisms valuable lessons from the Gulf War will have to be used, so as to avoid the possibility of one or a few powers using the Security Council to legitimize their actions.

There is a considerable concern for stability. However, what is stability in an unjust world? While transforming it into a more just world, there will be instability, there will be jolts to vested interests. Nuclear weapons must not be allowed to be perceived as a means of slowing down this process. This fear must be removed by the nuclear-weapon powers by agreeing to a NWFW.

Rotblat [15] has observed that human loyalties have gradually enlarged over the millennia, from family and clan to the level of a nation, and now they have to embrace the whole world, the whole of humanity. The difficult question is how to operationalize these larger loyalties, and do so fast enough. The loyalty to humanity must start from the more fortunate affluent countries, which are at least partly responsible for keeping the rest of the world underdeveloped and poor, and who continue to try to maintain their hegemonistic control over it. The democratic temper and human rights have to grow within nations and internationally so as to promote the larger loyalties. The creation of a global democratic cooperative order, and a new dynamic multilateralism [16] will have to be an essential part of the operationalization. Today even in a large country like India, distinguished intellectuals find it necessary to organize a National Seminar and Convention in Defence of Sovereignty.

That asymmetry between North and South is a part of history, and is bound to remain so; it is a pernicious attitude and doctrine, going against the present worldwide trends of democratization and concern for human rights everywhere, and also against the call for wider loyalties.

Larger loyalties will be promoted by undertaking large global projects, selected and executed jointly by the countries of the East and the West, the North and the South, so as to build up mutual understanding and confidence in the commonality of interests on the ground. They will be undermined by the arm-twisting characteristic of today--showing up through such matters as IMF conditionalities, or countries being listed under the Special 301 provision of the USA's Omnibus Trade and Competitiveness Act which essentially threatens retaliatory action against a country's exports if it does not meet complaints about the lack of protection of intellectual property rights.

On the whole, steps towards a comprehensive collective security, perceived as such by all countries--rich and poor, developed and developing, nuclear haves and have-nots--should go hand-in-hand with an accelerated arms reduction programme. Durable peace and global common security demand a just world order. A NWFW will be fragile without serious steps towards such a world order. The value system of such a world order and its urgency, along with that of a NWFW, must be visible from the step-by-step timetable.

It is of course unrealistic to consider these as preconditions for a NWFW. They are only mentioned here as long-term agenda items, not to be lost sight of when working towards a NWFW and for its preservation.

The Agenda for a NWFW:
Importance of a Time-Bound Programme

It has already been mentioned that those who are for a NWFW and those who wish to retain a minimum deterrence can work together for a considerable distance along the path. Further, many actions on reduction of nuclear arsenals already agreed to by the USA and Russia are in the course of implementation. It will therefore be useful to list the major tasks to be accomplished on the way to a NWFW, so as not to lose sight of what still remains to be done. This may also induce the reductionists to get some of their doubts examined and clarified, and to take some additional steps without necessarily committing themselves to a NWFW.

A programme for a NWFW, to be credible, cannot be too long drawn-out. A period of about 15-20 years is perhaps the maximum to which it could be stretched. This period may be divided into three stages: a preparatory stage of about five years for the implementation of agreements already signed or unilateral actions already announced, and for new declarations, conventions and initiation of negotiations towards new agreements; and two successive implementation stages of about five years each. Time targets will have to be defined/redefined for each step in the first, second and the third stage. The detailed phasing will require international negotiations, since decisions with regard to it have a large political component. It should, however, be emphasized that the main hurdles are psychological and political, and not technical.

(a) *Nuclear Disarmament*

*   The immediate need is to ensure that the very large reductions in US and Russian nuclear warheads, which have already been agreed, proceed without impediment. This should include not only straight reductions in numbers. Multiple-warhead land-based missiles and silo-busting submarine-launched missiles should be eliminated at an early stage. The combat-readiness of the nuclear weapons that remain should be reduced. All nuclear-weapon systems should be withdrawn to the territory or territorial waters of the nuclear-weapon powers themselves.

*   The production of nuclear warheads, the production of new delivery systems, and the military production of weapons-usable material should be stopped.

*   There should be a much greater involvement of an international authority: all stockpiles of warheads and weapons-usable material should be notified to this authority; nuclear warheads should be registered and tagged; and the authority should supervise the process of dismantling.

*   Plans should be prepared for further reductions in warhead numbers, to 1000, 500, 100 ..; other nuclear-weapon states should be brought into the negotiations.

* There should be a comprehensive test ban.

* There should be a solemn declaration by all nations that (a) the use of nuclear weapons is a violation of the Charter of the United Nations, a crime against humanity; (b) the use of nuclear weapons is prohibited, pending nuclear disarmament under strict and effective international control; and (c) that they will work towards a NWFW by the year 2010.

* All non-nuclear-weapon states should agree not to acquire nuclear weapons.

(b) Other Disarmament Proposals

The move towards a NWFW will be greatly helped if at the same time there is progress in general and conventional, and not just nuclear, disarmament.

* A moratorium, followed by a ban, on the development, testing, and deployment of all space weapons.

* Removal of all military forces and bases from foreign territories and also the open seas, and their replacement by a UN peace-keeping force where necessary.

* Multilateral negotiations reducing levels of conventional arms and armed forces world-wide.

* Agreement on international mechanisms for monitoring the world arms trade, focusing on both supplier and recipient countries.

* Banning technological missions designed to develop new weapon systems; improvement of arrangements for conversion of military R&D to peaceful purposes; the provision of guidelines for the conduct of research where there are potential military applications, with monitoring and assessment of such research.

* Creation of an integrated multilateral verification system or systems under the auspices of the UN, so as to ensure security during the processes of disarmament; the verification procedures would have to apply equally to all countries, nuclear and non-nuclear.

(c) Collateral Measures

There are, in addition, a number of non-military measures which would make progress towards a NWFW easier:

*   There would have to be a more powerful global security system in place, to deal with military and non-military threats to security and thereby ensure the effective implementation of the provisions of the United Nations Charter. This should include steps to democratize the UN system.

*   There should be an agreement on the implications of a more open world--for such a world is necessary for the stability of a NWFW. This would probably mean the abandonment of national secrecy in all matters pertaining to the nuclear industry and related industries.

*   There should be an intensification of the North-South dialogue, and further confidence-building measures to give substance to the concept of common global security.

Concluding Remarks

The agenda is large. It calls for an advance in parallel and simultaneously on a number of fronts. The tasks are many and complex, calling for a holistic bold new thinking. A piecemeal, fragmented approach will not take us very far. A statesmanship of the highest order is called for, imbued with a grand vision about the future of humanity--about the kind of world one wants to create. It is a challenge to the best brains around the world.

Daniel Ellsberg [5] makes a case for a focused effort of the highest urgency, reminiscent of the Manhattan Project of 50 years ago, with the difference that this Manhattan Project II must be overt and international, with participation by the developing countries.

Elements of the agenda exist in the INF and START treaties; the more recent unilateral announcements of Bush and Gorbachev, and the agreements of Bush and Yeltsin; in the Convention on Chemical Weapons; various resolutions of the UN General Assembly; recommendations of the Non-Aligned Movement [17] and Parliamentarians Global Action [18]; and a series of governmental and inter-governmental documents since World War II, e.g. the so-called McCloy-Zorin Principles of a comprehensive disarmament treaty, agreed to by the USA and the USSR in 1961 (see Chapter 1). These could serve as the starting point of fresh negotiations, involving all nations. However, *one has to move fast*, in putting them together, discarding and supplementing, amplifying and modifying, so as to evolve a holistic approach equal to the challenge. The grand historic opportunity to move the world firmly away from the nuclear abyss must not be missed.

The Bush initiative of September 1991 underlines the possibility of contracting the time-scale needed for different steps if a political decision is made. *Drastic reductions are needed not only in the number of nuclear warheads, but also in militarized thinking and the hegemonistic proclivities of a few powers.*

One does not have to wait until all the detailed elements of the path are worked out, especially as there is still a considerable gap between the thinking and perceptions of those who stand for a NWFW, and those who do not want to go beyond a 'minimum deterrence' level. This level would still be considerably below the reduced levels of arsenals currently agreed upon and so the abolitionists and reductionists could travel together for a considerable distance. This period of working together could be used by the abolitionists and the reductionists to explore further the conditions that could make a NWFW acceptable to all.

Both abolitionists and reductionists could work together on most items on this agenda. In the nuclear-weapon field, there is a great deal of work to be done on the nature of the international authority which should supervise the present processes of disarmament and dismantlement. Both groups could intensify the campaign for a Comprehensive Test Ban, and they could prepare the ground for other nuclear-weapon powers to join the process of disarmament. Abolitionists and reductionists could join in pressing for the next steps in conventional disarmament, and in helping to bring about a better and more democratic international structure for United Nations action on world conflict resolution.

These are examples of items of an interim agenda on which the abolitionists and those who stand for minimum deterrence could agree to work together.

An agreement on the objective of a NWFW, with a definite time-bound programme would itself create the climate of trust in which political solutions to the remaining problems will become possible.

The time-scale can be periodically reviewed in terms of the progress achieved and its implication for the steps to follow, as also the resolution of the presently unresolved problems by the abolitionists and the reductionists working together in Manhattan Project II.

A major problem that would still divide the abolitionists and the reductionists would be the question of delegitimization of nuclear weapons. The demand for accepting that the use of nuclear weapons or any weapons of mass destruction is a crime against humanity has been around for a long time. [19] Is their use consistent with the Charter of the United Nations, and various international conventions that already exist? It would be useful to seek the legal opinion of the International Court of Justice on the legitimacy of nuclear weapons, so as to influence the public opinion in the West.

A NWFW will be possible only if the rich industrial nations move away from the greedy growth-mania of today to a path of sustainable development for all. A stable and lasting peace can only be built on real sincere disarmament and a just international economic and political order. The struggle for such a new world order is to be recognized as part of the efforts to approach a NWFW.

References

1.   For the Indian initiatives until a few years ago, see *Disarmament: India's Initiatives*, Ministry of External Affairs, Government of India, New Delhi, 1988.

2.   Delhi Declaration on Principles for a Nuclear-Weapon Free and Non-Violent World, issued by Rajiv Ghandhi and Mikhail Gorbachev, 27 November 1986, reporduced in ref.1, pp.81-86.

3. Action Plan for Ushering in a Nuclear-Weapon Free and Non-Violent World Order, submitted by India to the Third Special Session on Disarmament of UN General Assembly, May 1988, ref.1, pp.44-53.

4. Ref.1, Annexure 3, pp.87-135.

5. Herbert York, quoted by Daniel Ellsberg, "Manhattan Project II", *Bulletin of the Atomic Scientists*, May 1992, pp.42-44.

6. Cited in Jacquelin S. Perth, "Nuclear Testing Ban Won't Aid Arms Control", USIS Wireless File, New Delhi, July 16 1992.

7. These have been discussed in detail in B.M. Udgaonkar, "Beyond Non-Proliferation", in *Nuclear Non-Proliferation and the Non-Proliferation Treaty*, eds. M.P. Fry, N.P. Keatinge, and J. Rotblat, Springer-Verlag, 1990.

8. "Common Security", Report of the Palme Commission, 1982; see also, *Global Problems and Common Security: Annals of Pugwash 1988* eds. J. Rotblat & V.I. Goldanskii, Springer-Verlag, 1989.

9. Report on the 1st Pugwash Workshop on "The Future of the Soviet Nuclear Weapon Complex", Moscow, Russia, 6-7 March 1992.

10. Pugwash Statement on the Fourth NPT Review Conference, *Pugwash Newsletter*, vol.26, 1989, pp.181-182.

11. B. Sanders, "The Treaty on the Non-Proliferation of Nuclear Weapons and the Relations between the Superpowers", in *Nuclear Non-Proliferation and the Non-Proliferation Treaty*, ref.7, pp.80-90.

12. Robert S. McNamara, "Security in the Post-Cold War World", *Striving for Peace, Security and Development: Annals of Pugwash 1991*, ed. J. Rotblat, World Scientific Publishing, 1993.

13. Dagomys Declaration of the Pugwash Council: "Ensuring the Survival of Civilization" *Global Problems and Common Security*, ref.8, p.259.

14. Klaus Gottstein, "Obstacles to Confidence-Building: How can they be Overcome?", *Global Problems and Common Security*, ref.8, p.143.

15. J. Rotblat and V.I. Goldanskii, "The Elimination of Nuclear Arsenals: Is it Desirable? Is it Feasible?" in *Verification: Monitoring Disarmament*, eds. F. Calogero, M.L. Goldberger, S.P. Kapitza, Westview Press 1991, p.220.

16. M. Dubey, "A New Dynamic Multilateralism", paper presented to the 1st International Pugwash Workshop on Non-Military Dimensions of Global Security, Suraj Kund, India, 21-24 November 1989.

17. "NAM and Disarmament" in *Surviving the Second Millennium: Disarmament and Information*, Research monograph for UNESCO, NAMEDIA Foundation, New Delhi, 1987.

18. e.g. "Global Security: Parliamentarians Global Action", presented to the conference "Towards a Nuclear-Weapon Free and Non-Violent World", New Delhi, 14-16 November 1988.

19. e.g. Resolution 33/71 B, presented by India and adopted by the 33rd Session of the UN General Assembly.

Index